Justified in Christ

Justified in Christ

The Doctrines of Peter Martyr Vermigli
and John Henry Newman and Their
Ecumenical Implications

Chris Castaldo

☙PICKWICK *Publications* • Eugene, Oregon

JUSTIFIED IN CHRIST
The Doctrines of Peter Martyr Vermigli and John Henry Newman and Their Ecumenical Implications

Copyright © 2017 Chris Castaldo. All rights reserved. Except for brief quotations in critical publications or reviews, no part of this book may be reproduced in any manner without prior written permission from the publisher. Write: Permissions, Wipf and Stock Publishers, 199 W. 8th Ave., Suite 3, Eugene, OR 97401.

Pickwick Publications
An Imprint of Wipf and Stock Publishers
199 W. 8th Ave., Suite 3
Eugene, OR 97401

www.wipfandstock.com

PAPERBACK ISBN: 978-1-5326-0123-1
HARDCOVER ISBN: 978-1-5326-0125-5
EBOOK ISBN: 978-1-5326-0124-8

Cataloguing-in-Publication data:

Names: Castaldo, Chris, 1971–.

Title: Justified in Christ : the doctrines of Peter Martyr Vermigli and John Henry Newman and their ecumenical implications / Chris Castaldo.

Description: Eugene, OR: Pickwick Publications, 2017 | Includes bibliographical references.

Identifiers: ISBN 978-1-5326-0123-1 (paperback) | ISBN 978-1-5326-0125-5 (hardcover) | ISBN 978-1-5326-0124-8 (ebook)

Subjects: LCSH: Vermigli, Pietro Martire, 1499–1562 | Newman, John Henry, 1801–1890 | Justification (Christian theology)—History of doctrines | Christian union

Classification: BT764.3 C35 2017 (print) | BT764.3 (ebook)

Manufactured in the U.S.A.   01/06/17

To my wife, Angela, whose countless acts of love and support have moved far beyond the forensic into the tangible loveliness of Christ.

Since no one has fulfilled or can fulfill [the command to love God with heart, soul, and strength], it follows that we should fly to Christ through whom we may be justified by faith. After being justified, we may in some way begin to do what is commanded, albeit imperfectly.

—Peter Martyr Vermigli

Justification comes through the Sacraments; is received by faith; consists in God's inward presence; and lives in obedience.

—John Henry Newman

Contents

Acknowledgements | xi
Abbreviations | xii
Introduction | xiii

Chapter 1: Background to Peter Martyr's Doctrine of Justification | 1
    A. The Study of Peter Martyr Vermigli · 1
    B. The "Quite Learned" Man from Italy · 5
    C. The Italian Renewal Movement—*Evangélisme* · 8
    D. Religious Discourse in Italy: 1490–1530 · 11
    E. Italian *Evangélisme* and the Doctrine of Justification · 15
    F. Vermigli's Doctrine of Justification · 20
    G. Peter Martyr at Oxford · 25
    H. Peter Martyr's *Locus* on Justification · 30
    I. Conclusion · 33

Chapter 2: Peter Martyr Vermigli's Doctrine of Justification | 35
    A. Theological Contours of Vermigli's Doctrine of Justification · 35
    B. Regeneration and Pneumatic Renewal · 38
    C. The Forensic Framework of Justification · 45
    D. Faith Alone · 49
    E. Justification's Formal Cause and the *Duplex Iustitia* · 58
    F. Conclusion · 67

Chapter 3: Newman's Historical Background | 70
    A. The Study of John Henry Newman · 70
    B. The World of John Henry Newman · 74
    C. Newman the Calvinist · 79
    D. Newman Questions His Evangelical Assumptions · 82
    E. "Shreds and Tatters" of Evangelicalism · 85

F. The Making of Newman's *Via Media* · 87

G. The Oxford or Tractarian Movement · 91

H. The *Lectures on the Doctrine of Justification* · 98

I. Conclusion · 104

Chapter 4: John Henry Newman's Doctrine of Justification | 106

A. Theological Contours of Newman's Doctrine of Justification · 106

B. Incarnation · 111

C. The Sacramental Framework of Justification · 114

D. Justifying Presence · 117

E. The Christocentric Focus of Justification · 119

F. Pneumatic, Resurrected Life · 123

G. The Formal Cause of Justification · 126

H. Conclusion · 134

Chapter 5: A Comparison of Newman and Vermigli on the Doctrine of Justification | 136

I. Common Concerns

  A. Newman and Vermigli in Conversation · 136

  B. Works Righteousness · 138

  C. Cheap Grace · 140

  D. Holding Forensic and Actual Righteousness Close Together · 141

  E. Common Concerns: Distinguishing Forensic and Actual Righteousness · 143

II. Common Commitments

  F. An Augustinian Harmatology · 144

  G. Union with Christ · 145

  H. The Need for Forensic Imputation · 147

  I. The Gift of the Holy Spirit and Manifestation of "Works" · 149

  J. Common Commitments: *Duplex Iustitia* · 151

III. Different Commitments

  K. Sacramental Framework of Justification · 153

  L. Faith Alone · 154

IV. Different Conclusions

  M. Formal Cause · 157

  N. *Habitus* · 161

  O. Perseverance · 163

  P. Merit · 164

  Q. Conclusion · 166

Chapter 6: Justification in Contemporary Roman Catholic
and Reformed Theology | 168
- A. Justification in Contemporary Ecumenical Focus · 168
- B. Human Powerlessness and Divine Initiative · 171
- C. Justification's Formal Cause · 174
- D. Concupiscence or Sin · 179
- E. Faith Alone and Works · 181
- F. Assurance of Faith · 184
- G. The Role of Merit · 185
- H. Conclusion · 187

Bibliography | 193

Acknowledgements

THE COMPLETION OF THIS work would not have happened without encouragement from several friends and colleagues, namely Dr. Michael McDuffee, Dr. Timothy George, Msgr. Dr. John Cihak, Dr. Jerry Root, and Dr. Lon Allison.

I am indebted to the staff at Buswell Library in Wheaton, particularly Gregory Morrison for helping me obtain several monographs. I am grateful to Gianni Saillen for providing me access to the *Villa I Tatti* in Florence to enjoy its collection of Vermigliana. Likewise, I am thankful to Dr. Damon McGraw and Dr. Kevin Mongrain of the National Institute for Newman Studies for graciously providing full access to the Newman Knowledge Kiosk.

I am especially grateful to Dr. Frank James III, who offered me valuable input at the outset of my research and who has been available to answer questions along the way. Similarly, I am indebted to Dr. John Patrick Donnelly, SJ, for reading nearly every chapter of this research and offering incisive feedback. I am also thankful to Dr. Thomas Sheridan, SJ, who took time to discuss Newman's doctrine of justification and offered valuable insight into its significance for Christian life and ministry. And thanks to Kirk Vukonich and Susanne Calhoun for graciously reading and copy editing portions of the thesis.

I cannot adequately express gratitude for my supervisor, Professor Anthony Lane, whose patience, encouragement, and example of academic rigor are gifts for which I will always be grateful.

Finally, I thank my dear wife, Angela, whose unfailing love and support has enabled me to take up and read, and our children, Luke, Philip, Simeon, Aliza, and David Malachi for your enduring love.

Abbreviations

Apo	John Henry Newman. *Apologia pro vita sua: being a history of his religious opinions*. London: Longmans, 1882.
AW	John Henry Newman. *Autobiographical Writings*. Edited by Henry Tristram. London Sheed and Ward, 1956.
CCC	*Catechism of the Catholic Church*. 2nd ed. Citta del vatticano: Libreria Editrice Vaticana, 1997.
ID	Alister E. McGrath. *Iustitia Dei: A History of the Christian Doctrine of Justification*. 3rd ed. Cambridge: Cambridge University Press, 2005.
Jfc	John Henry Newman. *Lectures on the Doctrine of Justification*. 3rd ed. London: Rivington, 1874.
PMI	Philip McNair. *Peter Martyr in Italy: An Anatomy of Apostasy*. Oxford: Clarendon, 1967.
PMR	Peter Martyr Vermigli. *The Peter Martyr Reader*. Edited by John Patrick Donnelly, Frank A. James III, and Joseph C. McLelland. Kirksville: Truman State University Press, 1999.
PPS	John Henry Newman. *Parochial and Plain Sermons*. San Francisco: Ignatius, 1997.
Romanos	Pietro Martire Vermigli. *In epistolam S. Pauli apostoli ad Romanos D. Petri Martyris Vermilii Florentini, professoris divinarum literarum in schola Tigurina, commentarii doctissimi, cum tractatione perutili rerum & locorum, qui ad eam epistolam pertinent*. Basel: Apud Petrum Perna, 1560.
JD	The Lutheran World Federation and the Roman Catholic Church. *Joint Declaration on the Doctrine of Justification*. Grand Rapids: Eerdmans, 2000.

Introduction

UNDERSTANDING THE PRECISE RELATIONSHIP between justification and sanctification continues to be a *crux theologorum* (cross of theologians), a challenge that we have inherited from the texts with which we build our faith. Paul the Apostle, for instance, asserts, "For by works of the law no human being will be justified in his sight, since through the law comes knowledge of sin" (Rom 3:20). But then, in the same biblical canon, we read James's words, "You see that a person is justified by works and not by faith alone" (Jas 2:24).

After sixteen centuries, the need to reconcile these statements in a doctrine of justification rose to the fore in the Protestant Reformations.[1] Whether one considers Luther's *anfechtungen*, Contarini's illumination on Holy Saturday in 1511, Peter Martyr's "greater light of divine truth," or Calvin's "chief hinge," the doctrine of justification emerged as an instigating force of the Reformation. Such figures wrestled with Pauline texts, compared them with the teaching of James, and asked the perennial question, "What must I do to be saved?" (Acts 16:30).

Concerning the word "Protestant," Diarmaid MacCulloch rightfully cautions us against employing it as a simple designation for "sympathizers with reform in the first half of the sixteenth century, since inclinations toward renewal were shared by Roman Catholics."[2] Moreover, it is valuable to remember that Protestants initially understood themselves to be working

---

1. Carter Lindberg, for example, provides reasons for the plurality of Reformation movements in his classic text *The European Reformations*, 2nd ed., 11–22. For a full treatment of the Reformation debates on justification and the Catholic response, see Alister E. McGrath's magisterial work, *Iustitia Dei: A History of the Christian Doctrine of Justification*, 3rd ed., 208–357. Berndt Hamm evaluates a variety of positions on the doctrine of justification among the first and second generations of Reformers in his chapter "What was the Reformation Doctrine of Justification?" in *The Reformation of Faith in the Context of Late Medieval Theology and Piety*, 179–216.

2. MacCulloch prefers the word "evangelical" as a more indicative description of the movement's beliefs and also the nomenclature of the period. MacCulloch, *The Reformation: A History*, xviii.

for reform *within* the Roman Catholic Church.³ Our first chapter, which examines the movement of evangelical renewal on the Italian peninsula, will illustrate this phenomenon.⁴

The second historiographical caution is to distinguish the writings of individual reformers (particularly those of the first and second generations) from the development of confessional documents, which reflect the consensus view of the Reformed churches later in the century. David Fink addresses this distinction by proposing that we understand the sixteenth-century *Konfessionsbildung* process as having occurred in two distinct waves,⁵ first from 1528 to 1537,⁶ and then between 1559 and 1577.⁷ While Fink is careful to affirm that the second wave is in basic continuity with the first, he argues convincingly that it is in the latter period that a clear consensus on the doctrine of justification emerged in terms of a formulaic explanation of forensic imputation.⁸

Even though confessional statements took time to develop, there appears to have been basic conceptual agreement on the doctrine of justification among the earliest generations of Reformers. According to Alister McGrath, the leading characteristics of the Protestant outlook on justification were threefold: Firstly, justification involves a "forensic declaration that the Christian is righteous," that is, a change in one's legal status before God (as opposed to a process of internal renewal by which one is made righteous). Secondly, there is a "deliberate and systematic distinction" between the forensic activity of justification and the internal process of sanctification

---

3. So David Steimetz asserts, "It is important to remember that the Reformation began as in intra-Catholic debate." Steimetz, "The Intellectual Appeal of the Reformation," 459–72 (459). McGrath explains that for early Reformed theologians, the driving concern was to renew life and morals of the church and of individual Christians. McGrath, *Iustitia Dei*, 248–58.

4. Martin Bucer's ongoing attempts at rapprochement into the early 1540s are a prime example from outside of Italy. Greschat, *Martin Bucer: A Reformer and His Times*, 168–205.

5. Fink. "Was There a Reformation Doctrine of Justification?" 205–35.

6. Ten Theses of Bern (1528), Tetrapolitan Confession (1530), First Confession of Basel (1534), First Helvetic Confession (1536), Lausanne Articles (1536), The Ten Articles (1536), and The Geneva Confession (1536).

7. French Confession (1559/71), Scots Confession (1560), Belgic Confession (1561), Heidelberg Catechism (1563), and the Second Helvetic Confession (1566).

8. Fink explains the time frame in which Reformed theology reached a "two-state model" on justification, that is, the notion that justification involves the iustitia Christi imputata in addition to the remission (or non-imputation) of sin. In addition to analyzing Reformed confessions, Fink also explains how Lutheran confessional statements unfold in a parallel chronology. Fink, "Was There a Reformation Doctrine?," 235.

or regeneration. Thirdly, "justifying righteousness or the formal cause of justification" is alien, external, and imputed.[9]

On the other side of the ecclesial divide, the Roman Catholic Church responded to Protestant arguments by convening the Council of Trent (1545–63), through which it defined its doctrine in its *Decree on Justification* (1547). Rejecting the Protestant view of "faith alone" grounded in the forensic imputation of Christ's righteousness, the Roman Church chose to emphasize the "process" of justification, whereby the gift of righteousness is internally "infused" through her sacraments. This process is, in turn, expressed in moral virtues and good works as the necessary condition for man's final absolution.[10] As for the contemporary significance of Trent's teaching, Avery Cardinal Dulles, SJ, explains that the "theology of justification in Roman Catholic teaching has undergone no dramatic changes since the Council of Trent."[11]

The fundamental difference between the Roman Catholic and Reformed Protestant doctrines of justification is the so-called "formal cause"[12]—a subject's intrinsic component, or that which makes it what it is.[13] Taking its cues from Aristotle's list of four "causes,"[14] the Council of Trent explicated justification's formal cause as follows:

> Finally, the one formal cause [*unica formalis causa*] is the justness of God: not that by which he himself is just, but that by which he makes us just and endowed with which we are renewed

---

9. McGrath, "Forerunners of the Reformation?" 219–42; McGrath, *Iustitia Dei*, 212–13. Hamm's conclusions support this taxonomy vis-à-vis the formal cause, imputation, and distinction of justification from sanctification. Hamm, *The Reformation of Faith*, 192, 194, 196. For the historical antecedents to these characteristics, see Lane, *Justification by Faith*, 138–40.

10. Chapter seven of the *Decree on Justification* explains "What the justification of the sinner is and what are its causes." Tanner, *Decrees of the Ecumenical Councils*, vol. 2, 673.

11. Dulles, "Justification in Contemporary Theology," 256. According to Lane, even if the *Joint Declaration on the Doctrine of Justification* (1999) is taken into account, the positive exposition of the Tridentine decree remains incompatible with a Protestant understanding, even though the gap is narrower than it was previously. Lane, *Justification by Faith*, 223.

12. Yarnold, "Duplex iustitia," 208; Lane, *Justification by Faith*, 72; Newman, *Lectures on the Doctrine of Justification*, 3rd ed., 343; Vermigli, *Predestination and Justification*, 159; Toon, *Evangelical Theology*, 145–46.

13. Lane, *Justification by Faith*, 70.

14. In seeking to explain the "why" of a thing, that is, its cause, Aristotle describes changes of movement in terms of material, formal, efficient, and final causes. Aristotle, *Physics* 2:3, 1:128–31.

in the spirit of our mind, and are not merely considered to be just but we are truly named and are just . . . [15]

The Protestant Reformers were also interested in defining justification's formal cause.[16] In his *locus* on justification, Peter Martyr Vermigli expresses general agreement with the overall causal framework of Trent in terms of the "final" cause (the glory of God), the "efficient" cause (divine mercy), and the "meritorious" cause (the death and resurrection of Christ).[17] Vermigli then explains that the point of contention is particularly the "formal cause."[18] Unlike Trent, which defines this cause in terms of the righteousness with which one is counted and made just, Peter Martyr, with Reformed Protestantism, limits the strict sense of justification to the forensic reckoning of righteousness.[19] He thus concludes: "Therefore, we say that justification cannot consist in that righteousness and renewal by which we are created anew by God. For it is imperfect because of our corruption, so that we are not able to stand before the judgment of Christ."[20] Peter Toon helpfully summarizes how fundamental this difference is among Catholics and Protestants:

> On the *formal cause* of justification, that by which God actually pronounces and accepts a sinner as righteous, there had never been agreement. The traditional Roman Catholic position was that at baptism God infuses into the soul his divine grace and that this grace purifies the soul. On seeing this infused righteousness in a human being God accepts him or justifies him. This new grace of the soul is thus the formal cause of justification and is at the same time the means of sanctification. With this view Protestant scholars had no sympathy. They argued that once God's grace enters the soul it becomes a human righteousness and no human righteousness is sufficient in quality to be the basis for justification and full acceptance with the eternal

---

15. Tanner, *Decrees*, 673. The causal scheme of Trent, which develops the final, efficient, meritorious, instrumental, and formal causes, varies somewhat from the Aristotelian taxonomy.

16. Muller, *Dictionary of Latin and Greek Theological Terms*, 61. For an explanation of how Calvin's causal scheme relates to Trent, see Lane, *Justification by Faith*, 68–72.

17. In this section, Vermigli does not mention Trent's "instrumental cause," namely, the sacrament of baptism. Vermigli, *Romanos*, 1252 [159].

18. Ibid.

19. Outside of his response to Trent's causal framework, in which he identifies justification's formal cause as the imputation of Christ's righteousness (ibid., 1251–52 [159]), Vermigli does not explicitly address the *causa forma*.

20. Vermigli, *Romanos*, 1251–52 [159].

God. So they pointed to the external righteousness of Christ the Mediator and argued that his righteousness was imputed or reckoned to the Christian as the formal cause of acceptance of justification. Within both of these camps, the Roman and the Protestant, there was a limited variety of teaching within the fixed limits of either the infused, inherent righteousness or the external righteousness of Christ, as the *formal cause*.[21]

The following analysis is in agreement with Toon that the formal cause is the basic line of demarcation between the Roman Catholic and Reformed Protestant doctrines of justification. This difference remains fundamental and seemingly irreconcilable. However, besides the formal cause, there is in fact a significant amount of agreement between the two traditions regarding justification.

To evaluate agreements and differences between the Roman Catholic and Reformed Protestant positions on the doctrine of justification, the following chapters will consider two figures in whose writings the issue featured prominently: the Protestant, Peter Martyr Vermigli (1499–1562) and the Catholic, John Henry Newman (1801–90). Despite a marked increase of Vermigli scholarship during recent decades and the massive amount of research on all things Newman, relatively little consideration has been given to these figures' treatment of the doctrine of justification. The following study seeks to fill this lacuna.

There are many reasons why Vermigli and Newman are suited for comparison. Having experienced opposite conversions from one side of the divide to the other, both had particular influences on Anglicanism and worked at the intersection of Roman Catholic and Protestant thought,[22] while writing significant volumes on justification in which a forensic declaration and the internal operation of the Holy Spirit feature prominently. We dedicate two chapters of this study to examining their respective positions (chapters 2 and 4), followed by a comparative chapter that explores their common concerns and commitments alongside differing commitments and conclusions (chapter 5).

Because Vermigli and Newman were separated by three centuries, two chapters also examine their individual historical contexts (chapters 1 and 3). Such analysis reveals that, despite the gulf in time, there are a number of significant similarities in the two men's personal and theological

---

21. Toon, *Evangelical Theology*, 145–46.

22. For instance, the chief works that we consider in this thesis—Vermigli's *locus* on justification from his Romans commentary and Newman's *Lectures on the Doctrine of Justification*—explicitly level their arguments across the Catholic/Protestant divide.

development. We observe, for example, that their years of study and ministry formation occurred in monastic settings. We note how both experienced religious conversion during periods of personal illness. We see them reacting with enthusiasm and spirited polemics to the traditions of their youth. The work of both men developed within dynamic religious movements (i.e., Italian *Evangélisme*, Reformed Protestantism, the Oxford Movement, and nineteenth-century Roman Catholicism) which were defined by collaborative efforts involving clergy, laity, literati, and secular rulers. Most significant of all, however, is Vermigli's and Newman's common reliance upon two-fold righteousness (*duplex iustitia*) in their reflection upon justification.

This is an appropriate point to say a word about the particular texts on which we will rely and how we will cite them. Peter Martyr's *locus* on justification was first published within his commentary on Romans in 1558. All references to this commentary will cite page numbers from his 1560 Latin version (which is available on the Digital Library of Classic Protestant Texts) followed in brackets by the equivalent page reference from Frank James's English translation: *Peter Martyr Vermigli, Predestination and Justification: Two Theological Loci*. With regard to John Henry Newman's *Lectures on the Doctrine of Justification*, we will concentrate on his third edition. Since this edition was published in 1874, when Newman had become a Catholic and, therefore, is his final and most definitive version, it will be featured first in the citations. To the right of these citations in the footnotes will be page numbers in brackets, indicating where the same reference appears in his first edition, which Newman published as an Anglican in 1838. The second edition was published just two years after the first, in 1840. Since the second edition is merely distinguished by formatting changes, it is unimportant for our purposes.

With the five-hundred-year anniversary of Luther's Ninety-Five Theses upon us, there is much to discuss among Roman Catholics and Protestants concerning the doctrine of justification. The following study hopes to enrich this conversation by clarifying where soteriological lines of continuity and difference fall, thus enabling each side to utilize theological options at their disposal, while also elucidating genuine differences that are fundamental to each tradition. Toward this end, the following study will pursue three objectives.

First, we will seek to understand the factors that influenced the development of Vermigli's and Newman's thought on the subject of justification. Such insight informs ecumenical dialogue by illustrating the various theological commitments and concerns that drive our theology. It also has the potential of illuminating how the doctrine of justification may lead one to cross the Catholic/Protestant divide in religious conversion.

Second, in the course of examining how the positions of Newman and Vermigli developed, we will address issues that are currently topics of debate in Vermigli and Newman scholarship. For example, contra Frank James, we argue that *duplex iustitia* (two-fold righteousness) continued to be the essence of Vermigli's doctrine into his mature period. We also propose a way to answer the thorny question of whether the Catholic Newman maintained *increata gratia* (uncreated grace) as the formal cause of justification.

Third, we wish to identify theological nomenclature for discussing justification at the Catholic/Protestant intersection, which recognizes our common concerns and commitments as well as our different commitments and conclusions. The perspective that this provides will help each tradition to approach discussion with a clearer understanding of where the lines of commonality and diversity fall and, thus, to more effectively differentiate negotiable from non-negotiable elements of the doctrine.

Chapter 1: Background to Peter Martyr's Doctrine of Justification

A. The Study of Peter Martyr Vermigli[1]

VERMIGLI'S FIRST BIOGRAPHY ORIGINATED as his eulogy. Josiah Simler (1530-76)—a disciple, colleague, and confidant of Vermigli—expanded his funeral oration for his mentor, which he had delivered on November 12, 1562, into the earliest and definitive biography of Peter Martyr's life.[2] A striking feature of Simler's *Oratio* is its tone. Earnest affection for Vermigli breathes from its pages, infusing the narrative with gravitas.

While sometimes described as "hagiography,"[3] Simler's *Oratio*, first published in 1563, is generally recognized as a carefully constructed historical record.[4] As such, it has been commonly employed as the starting point for subsequent biographies.[5] Part of its hagiographic feel is due to both its original purpose and the context in which it was written. As the fledgling Reformed movement of Simler's Zürich was plagued, in his description,

---

1. The Italian name, *Pietro Martire Vermigli*, was generally known as "Peter Martyr" outside of Italy (and equivalents in French and German), or simply "Martyr." It is not surprising that modern scholars vary between these options and his last name, "Vermigli." This study will use each of these appellations indiscriminatingly for the sake of variety.

2. Simler's *Oratio* was subsequently attached to the preface of Vermigli's *Commentary on Genesis* (1569) and also appeared in his *Loci communes* from 1582 onward. An English version of the *Loci communes*, published in 1583, included the first English translation of the *Oratio*. A contemporary, annotated translation of Simler's *Oratio* from the 1583 *Loci communes* is available in Vermigli, *Life, Letters, and Sermons*, trans. and ed. Donnelly, 9-62.

3. Baumann, "Josias Simler's Hagiography," 459.

4. Despite assigning the wrong year to Vermigli's birth, Simler's work has been embraced by scholars as a reliable account of Vermigli's life. McNair, *Peter Martyr in Italy*, xiv-xvii, 130; "Translator's Introduction," in Vermigli, *Life, Letters, and Sermons*, 2.

5. Most notably, Beza, *Icones, id est Verae imagines virorum doctrina simul et pietate illustrium*. Other major works indebted to Simler include Schlosser, *Leben des Theodor de Beza und des Peter Martyr Vermigli*; and Schmidt, *Peter Martyr Vermigli*.

with news of the "despoiling of churches . . . the sacking of cities, the terrible battles, the imprisonment and slaughter of good men,"[6] Simler applied the conviction and fidelity of Peter Martyr to the manifold challenges facing his Reformed brethren. According to Michael Baumann, Simler's goal for the *Oratio* was "not only preserving the remembrance of Peter Martyr, but at the same time posthumously incorporating him into the process of legitimizing the young Reformed church."[7] Inspiration, as much as instruction, was his goal.[8]

Simler was well suited to compose the *Oratio*. His relationship with Vermigli as a colleague at the academy in Zürich, and then as his successor in that institution, afforded him insight into the reformer's personal and professional life. He also had access to Vermigli's letters and commentaries, which he eventually helped to publish.[9] The closeness of Simler's association and the accuracy of his remembrances are affirmed by his sixteenth-century contemporaries. John Jewel, for instance, protégé of Vermigli at Oxford and Strasbourg (where Jewel lived in Martyr's house before taking the Bishopric of Salisbury), said of Simler's work, "I seemed to myself to behold the same old man with whom I had formerly lived upon such affectionate terms; and to behold him too, I know not why, more nearly and thoroughly, than when we were living together."[10] Likewise, modern historians support the reliability of Simler's account. Philip McNair marshals evidence to this effect on the basis of monastic records that he discovered in Ravenna in 1956.[11] John Patrick Donnelly, editor of Peter Martyr's *Life, Letters and Sermons* (which features a modern translation of the *Oratio*), also agrees with this assessment, pointing to the "excellence" of Simler's work.[12]

---

6. Simler, "Oratio," in Vermigli, *Life, Letters, and Sermons*, 10.

7. "Baumann, "Josias Simler's Hagiography," 459–65. For this reason, Fritz Büsser calls Simler a "pioneer in biography": in Büsser, "Vermigli in Zürich," in *Peter Martyr Vermigli: Humanism, Republicanism, Reformation*, ed. Campi, James, and Opitz, 204.

8. By the mid-sixteenth century, Protestant Martyrologies were being written. These were inspiring stories of faith, often against the backdrop of Catholicism. The most popular and enduring example was John Foxe's *Actes and Monuments*, written in 1563. See Brad S. Gregory, *Salvation at Stake*.

9. Simler, "Oratio," in Vermigli, *Life, Letters, and Sermons*, 10.

10. *The Works of John Jewel*, ed. Ayre, vol. 4, 126.

11. McNair, *PMI*, xxi-xxii. McNair explains his discovery in April of 1956 of a previously untapped series of monastic records, the Biblioteca Classense in Ravenna, which included a record of the yearly proceedings of Vermigli's order. Analyzing these against the backdrop of Simler's *Oratio*, McNair concludes: "For the most part they (the *Acta Capitularia*) confirm the statements of the *Oratio*, but they add a wealth of detail which would have taken a lifetime to assemble from subsidiary sources" (ibid., xxii).

12. "Translator's Introduction," in Vermigli, *Life, Letters, and Sermons*, 2.

Other accounts of Vermigli's life appeared between the years 1562 and 1809, particularly in the writings of John Sleidan,[13] Jon Strype,[14] and Anthony Wood.[15] The nineteenth century produced a modest number of studies.[16] Charles Schmidt's *Peter Martyr Vermigli: Leben und ausgewählte Schriften nach handschriftlichen und gleichzeitigen Quellen* is considered to have been the "fundamental and most solid authority for the life of Peter Martyr in exile" written in the nineteenth century.[17] Schmidt relied considerably upon Simler's *Oratio*, while also giving attention to German and Swiss Reformation sources. These documents, alongside writings by Celio Curione[18] and Girolamo Zanchi,[19] helped to develop the portrait of Vermigli. McNair describes Schmidt's work in the *Leben* as "sober, painstaking, usually well documented, thorough with Teutonic "Gründlichkeit" and a "balanced work of scholarship, despite its 'confessional tone.'" But the need for research continued.[20]

---

13. Sleidan, *The general history of the Reformation of the Church*, 443, 483–84, 590, 637.

14. Strype, *Annals of the Reformation*, vol. 1 pt. 1, 428–32.

15. Wood, *Athenae Oxonienses*, 2nd ed., vol. 1, 326–32.

16. The first monograph of the nineteenth century to focus on Vermigli came from Schlosser, *Leben des Theodor de Beza*. Nearly a half century later, this was followed by Gorham, *Gleanings of a Few Scattered Ears, During the Period of the Reformation in England and of the Times Succeeding A.D. 1533 to A.D. 1589*, which, as the title suggests, addresses elements of Vermigli's legacy and thought. The most rigorous and comprehensive work was by Schmidt, published in 1858. Schmidt's inclusion of Swiss and German Reformation sources, in addition to Simler's *Oratio*, raised the bar for Vermigli studies. Young, *The Life and Times of Aonio Paleario*, published two years after Schmidt's, provides a chapter on Peter Martyr. The forty pages of Durand, *Vie de Pierre Martyr Vermigli* outlines the major movements of Vermigli's life. Durand describes Vermigli in the opening words of the first chapter as "this miraculous Italian" (*Miraculum Italiane*) who followed a previous Reformer from Tuscany, namely Savonarola. This was not the first time the two men had been compared. Finally, there is the article at the end of the century by Paulus, "Die Stellung der protestantischen Professoren," 201–28.

17. McNair, *PMI*, xviii. Schmidt provides the first modern study, brief as it is, of Vermigli's Romans *locus* on justification. Schmidt, *Peter Martyr Vermigli*, 113–17.

18. A friend of Peter Martyr's in exile, Celio Curione (1503–69), translated writings of Juan de Valdés. Despite his apparent anti-trinitarian inclinations, Curione was invited by Heinrich Bullinger in 1542 to fill a principal post of a school in Lausanne.

19. Girolamo Zanchi (1516–90) first met Vermigli in the Italian city of Lucca in 1541. After fleeing Italy's Inquisition in October of 1551, he settled down in Strasbourg (where he married Curione's eldest daughter) to occupy the chair of Divinity in the College of St. Thomas. Zanchi, *De religione christiana fides*, 1–13.

20. McNair, *PMI*, viii.

At the beginning of the twentieth century, Vermigli remained in the shadows of obscurity apart from a few brief articles.[21] New light diminished the shadows with Mariano Di Gangi's Bachelor of Divinity thesis at Presbyterian College, Montreal in 1949, entitled "Pietro Martire Vermigli (1500-1562): An Italian Calvinist." Eight years later, in 1957, Joseph C. McLelland published *The Visible Words of God: An Exposition of the Sacramental Theology of Peter Martyr Vermigli A.D. 1500–1562*, the first full-length volume since Charles Schmidt's work in 1858.[22] In 1967, McNair published the next monograph dedicated exclusively to Vermigli, *Peter Martyr in Italy: Anatomy of Apostasy*.[23] In hindsight, this volume served as a veritable beacon, drawing scholars from various quarters to recognize the fertile opportunity in Vermigli study. Several doctoral theses were published in the 1970s.[24] Then, in 1980, Robert Kingdon produced a selection of Vermigli's political texts,[25] and in that same year McLelland published papers from the 1977 conference at McGill University addressing the "Cultural Impact of Italian

---

21. Notwithstanding J. W. Ashton's article, each of the following simply address Vermigli as a piece of the larger Reformation story: Gardy, in his "Les Livres de Pierre Martyr Vermigli," mentions the relocation of Vermigli's personal library to the Academy of Geneva; Paist catalogues the contributions of Vermigli at the Colloquy of Poissy in his "Peter Martyr and the Colloquy of Poissy"; Hugelshofer presents a portrait of Vermigli in his "Zum Porträt des Petrus Martyr Vermilius";. Ashton examines Vermigli's literary understanding in "Peter Martyr on the Function and Character of Literature."

22. It was originally McLelland's PhD thesis at New College University of Edinburgh, completed four years earlier under the supervision of T. F. Torrance. On its heels came two articles by Luigi Santini, "Appunti sulla ecclesiologia di P. M. Vermigli e la edificazione della Chiesa," and "La Tesi della fuga nella persecuzione nella teologia di P. M. Vermigli." During this time, the number of scholars doing Vermigli research grew. Gordon Huelin's doctoral thesis was produced in 1954 at the University of London, "Peter Martyr and the English Reformation," and within a decade Marvin W. Anderson had finished his unpublished thesis "Biblical Humanism and Roman Catholic Reform 1444-1563: A Study of Renaissance Philology and New Testament Criticism from Laurentius Valla to Pietro Martyre Vermigli."

23. McNair, *PMI*. Edoardo Labanchi published an Italian translation four years later: *Pietro Martire Vermigli in Italia*.

24. These included: Sturm, "Die Theologie Peter Martyr Vermiglis während seines ersten Aufenthalts in Strassburg 1542–1547," written at the University of Bonn under the supervision of Ernst Bizer; Donnelly, "Peter Martyr on Fallen Man: A Protestant Scholastic View," authored under the supervision of Robert M. Kingdon, later to be revised and published as *Calvinism and Scholasticism in Vermigli's Doctrine of Man and Grace* in 1976. Donnelly's work was substantially complete when Sturm's monograph was published, and, according to Donnelly, did not exercise any influence upon it (ibid., 5). Anderson produced, *Peter Martyr, a Reformer in Exile*, while Corda completed, *Veritas Sacramenti* at the University of Zürich under the supervision of Drs. Fritz Blanke and Fritz Büsser.

25. Kingdon, *The Political Thought of Peter Martyr Vermigli*.

Reformers."[26] Beyond these two works, the 1980s saw little productivity beyond an occasional article and chapter;[27] but in the 1990s, Vermigli research made profound gains. Di Gangi developed his previous work into a popular level biography of Vermigli in 1993.[28] Then there was the biggest development of all, the step that moved the "renaissance"[29] of Vermigli research into plain sight—the inauguration of *The Peter Martyr Library* in October of 1994.[30] The *Library* is an extensive work of English translation, annotation, and commentary by an international range of scholars. Since the 1990s, three particular scholars have championed the project: Donnelly,[31] McLelland,[32] and Frank A. James III.[33]

B. The "Quite Learned" Man from Italy

On October 28, 1542, Martin Bucer wrote a letter to John Calvin announcing, "A man has arrived from Italy who is quite learned in Latin, Greek, and Hebrew and well skilled in the Scriptures . . . his name is Peter Martyr."[34]

26. McLelland, *Peter Martyr Vermigli and Italian Reform*.

27. Anderson, "Rhetoric and Reality," 451–69; Courter Boughton, "Supralapsarianism and the Role of Metaphysics," 63–96; Dall'Asta, "Pietro Martire Vermigli (1499–1562)," 275–303; Muller, *Christ and the Decree*; Overell, "Peter Martyr in England 1547–1553," 87–104.

28. Di Gangi, *Peter Martyr Vermigli, 1499–1562: Renaissance Man, Reformation Master*.

29. Jason Zuidema uses the word "renaissance" in *Peter Martyr Vermigli (1499–1562)*, 17. Zuidema's section entitled "The Vermigli Research Renaissance" offers a cogent summary of this development.

30. *The Peter Martyr Library* is a collaborative effort on the part of Truman State University Press, Thomas Jefferson University Press, and Sixteenth Century Journal. Nine volumes have appeared so far.

31. Donnelly, *Calvinism and Scholasticism*; Donnelly, "Peter Martyr Vermigli's Political Ethics," 59–66. Donnelly also edited and translated three volumes in The *Peter Martyr Library*: *Dialogue on the Two Natures in Christ*; *Sacred Prayers*; and *Life, Letters, and Sermons*.

32. McLelland is the editor and translator of three volumes of *The Peter Martyr Library*: *Early Writings*; *Philosophical Works*; and *Commentary on Aristotle's Nicomachean Ethics*. He also served as co-editor with Donnelly and James of *The Peter Martyr Reader*.

33. James, *Peter Martyr Vermigli and Predestination*, based on his doctoral thesis, "*Praedestinatio Dei*: The Intellectual Origins of Peter Martyr Vermigli's Doctrine of Double Predestination," completed under the supervision of Alister E. McGrath, at St. Peter's College, Oxford in 1993. See bibliography for his many subsequent contributions.

34. "Advenit ex Italia vir quidam graece, hebraice et latine admodum doctus, et in scripturis feliciter versatus . . . Petro Martyri nomen est." Martin Bucer to John Calvin, 28 October 1542. Calvin, *Ioannis Calvini opera quae supersunt omnia*, vol. 11, sec. 430.

From the perspective of those who were north of the Alps, it may have appeared that Peter Martyr emerged *ex nihilo*. And before McNair's groundbreaking research, *Peter Martyr in Italy*, modern interpreters may have thought the same. The following sketch explores from whence Vermigli came, starting with his years in Italy (1499–1542). This background will illumine contributing factors to his doctrine of justification.

In 1514, at age fifteen, Peter Martyr entered the Augustinian order in the town of Fiesole, nearly eight kilometers from his native Florence.[35] After three years at the monastery, during which Martyr distinguished himself as a diligent student, he was judged worthy to begin studies under the order's most outstanding teachers. For this he was sent north to the monastery of San Giovanni di Verdara in Padua.[36]

Founded in 1222, the University of Padua reached the apex of its excellence and prestige in the first decade of the sixteenth century. It was at Padua where Peter Martyr encountered a serious-minded pursuit of doctrinal reform[37] and a rich tradition of Aristotle.[38] Without getting buried in hairsplitting partisanship, which occasionally erupted between Aristotelian schools,[39] Vermigli imbibed the Philosopher's logic and method from his professors, most of whom were Dominicans and Thomists.

Exceptionally focused, Vermigli supplemented his formal training in philosophy with a rigorous course of private study—a routine that was aided by his monastery's exquisite library.[40] After finding numerous errors in the Latin translations of Aristotle, he proceeded to study Greek by night in order to read the sources. The acquisition of this language opened the door for Martyr to engage Renaissance humanism with greater depth and immediacy. Under the tutelage of Professor Pietro Bembo, arguably the most distinguished humanist scholar to be associated with San Giovanni di Verdara, Vermigli acquired an insatiable appetite for the study of classical texts.[41] After eight years in Padua, Martyr underwent priestly ordination

---

35. According to Simler's *Oratio*, Martyr's mother had taught him Latin when he was a child. Simler, "Oratio," in Vermigli, *Life, Letters, and Sermons*, 11.

36. Sambin, "La formazione quattrocentesca della biblioteca di S. Giovanni di Verdara in Padova," 263–80.

37. Church, *The Italian Reformers*, 7.

38. For a taxonomy of the various Aristotelian "schools" of the day, see Donnelly, *Calvinism and Scholasticism*, 13–41; McNair, *PMI*, 86–115.

39. McNair, *PMI*, 86.

40. McNair says, "This library was one of the great formative influences on Martyr's early years." *PMI*, 93.

41. The "ambience of [Padua's] devout and learned humanism" is described by Fenlon in *Heresy and Obedience in Tridentine Italy*, 26.

and simultaneously received a doctorate in theology (1526).[42] If, in this period, he had been asked whether he was an Aristotelian or a humanist, Peter Martyr would likely have answered "yes."[43]

The seven years following Vermigli's departure from Padua opened new vocational horizons. He was elected to the office of public preacher, an illustrious position in his day. Martyr traveled through northern Italy lecturing on Scripture and philosophy (and Homer), and, whenever possible, he studied these subjects with careful attention.[44] In just a few years, while serving in Bologna, Vermigli also taught himself the Hebrew language—no small feat in those days—with the assistance of a certain Jewish doctor named Isaac.[45] So distinguished did Vermigli's ministry become, that his Augustinian order described him as *Predicatorem eximium* (an exceptional preacher).[46] But in the spring of 1530, Peter Martyr served as vicar to the prior at Bologna. And it was here, McNair suggests, that the activity of preaching and teaching started him on a trajectory that would eventually estrange Vermigli's mind from his scholastic training.

> From the Schoolmen he turned to the Fathers, from the Fathers to the Vulgate, and from the Vulgate to the Source itself—the lively Oracles of God in their original expression. At Padua he had learned Greek to read Aristotle: at Bologna he learned Hebrew to read Scripture.[47]

As his name grew famous in the largest Italian cities, Vermigli was promoted to an even higher position. By unanimous consent, he was made abbot of his order's monastery in Spoleto.[48] Effectively navigating the landmines of Spoleto's volatile politics, he managed to bring moral order out of chaos. It seemed that the vision and skill required to guide religious reform was part

---

42. Simler, "Oratio," in Vermigli, *Life, Letters, and Sermons*, 17.

43. James provides a helpful survey of how modern scholars position Vermigli on the historiographical map, particularly with regard to theological methodology. James posits three common profiles: "pioneer of Calvinist Thomism," "Protestant Humanist," and "intensified Augustinian." After examining each of these labels, James argues for the intensified Augustinian view. James, "*De Iustificatione*," 52–92.

44. According to Simler, such study would mostly happen in the houses of his Congregation at Padua, Ravenna, Bologna, and Vercelli. Simler, "Oratio," in Vermigli, *Life, Letters, and Sermons*, 17.

45. Simler, "Oratio," in Vermigli, *Life, Letters, and Sermons*, 17.

46. McNair, *PMI*, 118.

47. Ibid., 124–25.

48. Spoleto is roughly 200 kilometers south-east of Florence, a little more than half way to Rome.

of his spiritual character. Probably because of this distinction, Martyr was assigned a new post as abbot of San Pietro ad Aram in Naples.

Simler identifies Naples as the place where Vermigli's theological journey demonstrably turned a corner. During the three years of Peter Martyr's sojourn at San Pietro (1537–40), according to Simler, "the greater light of God's truth" began to shine upon him.[49] In McNair's analysis, this "greater light of God's truth" was basically "the doctrine of Justification by Faith alone in a crucified yet living Christ. The acceptance of this vital doctrine entailed so drastic a reorientation of heart and mind that it amounted to conversion"[50] Why was this the key doctrinal pivot for Vermigli? Understanding this requires some familiarity with the religious sociology of Italy during this period, particularly the nascent movement of *Evangélisme*.[51]

C. The Italian Renewal Movement—*Evangélisme*

The variegated shape of sixteenth-century Italian religious reform has resisted precise definition.[52] Eva-Marie Jung calls it "the last Catholic reform movement before the Council of Trent and the first ecumenical movement after the schism of the Reformation."[53] According to Elisabeth Gleason, the most helpful *terminus a quo* for assessing the movement is 1512; she

---

49. Simler, "Oratio," *Life, Letters, and Sermons*, 19. Simler also notes that it was during his three years in Naples that Martyr "fell into a serious and deadly sickness," although we have no indication whether this experience factored into his conversion (ibid., 22). This disease is thought to have been Malaria.

50. McNair, *PMI*, 179. James echoes this interpretation in his dissertation, in which he states, "There is little doubt that Simler understood this 'greater light of God's truth' to be the doctrine of justification by faith alone." James, "*De Iustificatione*," 1.

51. This study will use the term "*Evangélisme*" instead of the more common "Evangelism," to avoid confusion with the name used in current parlance to describe the activity of gospel proclamation. Eva-Maria Jung et al. employ "Evangelism" as a sociological designation, following the third volume of Perre Imbart de la Tour's study of the early Reformation in France: *Les Origines de la Réforme: L' Evangelisme*, vol. 3.

52. Significant works on this topic include: Bouwsma, *Venice and the Defense of Republican Liberty*; Cantimori, *Eretici italiani del Cinquecento*; Caponetto, trans. *The Protestant Reformation in Sixteenth-century Italy*; Church, *The Italian Reformers*; Fenlon, *Heresy and Obedience*; Gleason, "On the Nature of Sixteenth-century Italian Evangelism," 3–25; ibid., *Gasparo Contarini: Venice, Rome, and Reform*; Grendler, "Religious Restlessness in Sixteenth-century Italy," 25–38; Jung, "On the Nature of Evangelism in Sixteenth-century Italy," 511–27; Martin, "Salvation and Society in Sixteenth-century Venice," 205–33; Martin, *Venice's Hidden Enemies*; McNair, *PMI*; Nieto, *Juan de Valdés*; Jacobson Schutte, "Periodization of Sixteenth-century Italian Religious History," 269–84; Simoncelli, *Evangelismo italiano del cinquecento*.

53. Jung, "On the Nature of Evangelism," 512.

proposes the *terminus ad quem* should be extended to the 1560s, allowing for "echoes" into the seventeenth century.[54] Gleason has written a detailed historiographical survey of the movement, in which she warns interpreters not to lose sight of its vast scope.[55]

Among the first studies devoted to the movement in English was Jung's article, "On the Nature of Evangelism in Sixteenth-Century Italy."[56] In it, Jung famously defined the Italian reform movement's three characteristics as theologically undogmatic, aristocratic, and transitory.[57] In a similar vein, William Bouwsma argued for the movement's subjective impulse by highlighting its affinities with renaissance republicanism, an orientation that was especially vibrant in the territory of Venice. These political values are thought to have prepared the Italian soil from which *Evangélisme* eventually emerged.[58]

Such portraits have not gone unchallenged. The most ardent critique of Jung's and Bouwsma's historiography has been by McNair, who disagrees with their explanation of the movement's origin and nature. Regarding the former, he rejects the notion that *Evangélisme* was an indigenous, Catholic phenomenon in isolation from the Protestant north.[59] He cites evidence from "monastic records, humanist letters, Valdésian memoirs, and histories of Naples" to demonstrate the influence of Protestant literature that circulated among the friends of Vermigli.[60] A significant example from his arsenal is

---

54. Gleason, "On the Nature of Sixteenth-century Italian Evangelism," 25.

55. Ibid., 3–26. Gleason cautions that, on account of the dynamic nature of Italian *Evangelisme,* interpreters are especially prone to misconceptions. She explains how evaluations of the movement often depend on the writings of a relatively small number of well-known figures or on records from inquisitorial proceedings. Sometimes a narrow sampling of these sources has been the basis of judgment. The tenuous ground of these assessments is a methodological hazard to which scholars must be attentive. Gleason, *Gasparo Contarini,* 190–91. Four years after Gleason, the Italian scholar, Susanna Peyronel Rambaldi offered a literature survey in "Ancora sull'evangelismo italiano: Categoria o invenzione storiografica?," 935–67.

56. Jung, "On the Nature of Evangelism," 511–27.

57. Ibid., 520.

58. Bouwsma, *Venice and the Defense of Republican Liberty.*

59. For a counter-argument to McNair, see Fenlon, who argues for the indigenous origins of Italian *Evangelisme* in *Heresy and Obedience.* Fenlon points to Cardinals such as Pole, Contarini, Giberti, and Morone as examples of men who experienced renewal and worked out their doctrine of justification in the Roman communion of Italy. A credible case is also made by Nieto, who finds the roots of Valdés's thought in the mysticism of Spanish *alumbrados.* Nieto, *Juan de Valdés,* 314–22.

60. McNair, *PMI,* 142. McNair also questions the objectivity of Catholic historians who maintain this view, scholars such as Imbart de la Tour, Monsignor Jedin, and Dr. Jung. McNair argues that "Evangelism has been used [by them] as a Roman Catholic

a statement from Simler's *Oratio* that explains the three Neapolitan years in which Vermigli acquired and carefully studied Bucer's commentaries on the Gospels[61] and the annotations on the Psalms.[62] Martyr also read Zwingli's book, *On True and False Religion* and *On God's Providence*,[63] together with some works from Erasmus. According to Simler, "He [Vermigli] often frankly confessed that he made much progress from reading all of these."[64]

Following from this premise, McNair also questions the assumed nature of *Evangélisme*, particularly doubting that it can legitimately be regarded as undogmatic. In making his case, McNair correlates the theological concerns of the Valdésian circle of Naples (of which Peter Martyr was a part) with the contours of the Protestant Reformation. Common dogmatic concerns are evident in books and sermons that circulated through major Italian cities in the 1530s, particularly in Venice, Padua, Florence, Rome, and Naples.[65] Accordingly, McNair defines *Evangélisme* as a "positive reaction of certain spiritually-minded Catholics to the challenge of Protestantism, and, in particular, to the crucial doctrine of justification by faith."[66] While generally compelling, McNair's case is weakened by his failure to interact with Contarini's experience of spiritual illumination and embrace of justification by faith alone, as expressed in his letters.[67]

device for explaining away an embarrassing phase of Catholic Church history when what looks suspiciously like crypto-Lutheranism invaded the very College of Cardinals" (ibid., 6). The tools of historicism have also been used against McNair, suggesting that he too may have succumbed to prejudices, as evidenced by his reference to the Rome-imposed "Iron Curtain which had descended upon the Alps" (ibid., 1, 293). Anne J. Schutte questions whether these allusions betray a Cold War mentality in McNair's work. Schutte, "The *Lettere Volgari*," 643.

61. Bucer, *Enarrationes perpetua in sacra quatuor Evangelia*.

62. Bucer, *Sacrorum psalmorum libri quinque*. Bucer published this work under his pseudonym, Aretio Felini.

63. *De vera et falsa religione* (1525) and *De providentia Dei* (1530)—these are considered to be Zwingli's two most important works.

64. Simler, "Oratio," in Vermigli, *Life, Letters, and Sermons*, 20.

65. McNair, *PMI*, 6–15. See also Grendler, "Religious Restlessness in Sixteenth-century Italy," 26. By the early 1540s, *Evangélisme* "began to develop a significant popular following, especially in the cities and towns of northern Italy." Martin, "Salvation and Society," 208.

66. McNair, *PMI*, 8.

67. See Jedin, "Contarini und Camaldoli," 59–118. It was "on Holy Saturday of 1511," when Contarini "experienced a moment of illumination" that was likened to Luther's epiphany, in which "he was fully convinced that salvation could not be won by any human act but was God's free gift." Bouwsma, *Venice and the Defense of Republican Liberty*, 124. For a detailed examination of Contarini's experience, see Gleason, *Gasparo Contarini*, 11–18; Ross, "Gasparo Contarini and His Friends," 204–17. Alister McGrath agrees that Cardinal Contarini had embraced *sola fide* before Luther, even

While perspectives on Italian *Evangélisme* are many,[68] it is nevertheless possible to reliably discern the movement's basic orientation. The parameters of this study will not allow for a comprehensive treatment; but, in what follows, we will sketch out the basic agenda of *Evangélisme*. To that end, we will firstly consider religious discourse in Italy during the years immediately before and into the sixteenth century.

D. Religious Discourse in Italy: 1490–1530

"Criticism of ecclesiastical institutions and proposals for church reform," writes Gleason, "had been persistent themes of Italian religious thought during the first three decades of the sixteenth century."[69] This criticism was due to several factors, including an inadequate resolution of the Conciliar Movement in the Fifth Lateran Council (1512–17); the conspicuous immorality of Pope Alexander VI and his Borgia *famiglia* on whom he had lavished abundant privilege and wealth;[70] the Medici papacies which had made the city of Rome into a veritable haven of humanism;[71] ongoing conflict between the Holy Roman Emperor, Charles V and the pope(s);[72] the popularizing of humanist ideals by public intellectuals such as Erasmus (who visited Italy between 1506 and 1509);[73] and the distribution of Protestant

---

if he did not articulate it as such. McGrath, *ID*, 310–11. See also Firpo, "The Italian Reformation," trans. Tedeschi, 353–64.

68. Martin, "Salvation and Society," 209.

69. Gleason, *Gasparo Contarini*, 192.

70. In addition to making a mockery of Christian piety, most popes of this era lacked the spiritual fortitude to implement genuine renewal. These spiritually malnourished leaders included Pope Sixtus IV (1471–84), Innocent VIII (1484–92), Alexander VI (1492–1503), Pius III (1503), Julius II (1503–13), Leo X (1513–21), and Clement VII (1523–34). Adrian XI (1522–23) was a short-lived exception to this pattern. Their inability to instill confidence among the faithful inevitably catalyzed a movement of dissent.

71. Crews, *Twilight of the Renaissance*, 47.

72. Burke, *Culture and Society in Renaissance Italy*, 276. Political and military struggles plagued the peninsula from 1494 to 1559, in the so called the Great Italian Wars. During Charles V's reign, such conflict was most dramatically displayed in the sack of Rome in 1527. Machiavelli's invocation of a pragmatic prince and Savonarola's bonfire of the vanities were two early examples of how Italians responded to this unrest. The same trajectory of discontent can be traced in the salons of Naples where Vermigli et al. eventually crossed the Rubicon into Reformation theology.

73. Huizinga, *Erasmus and the Age of Reformation*, 62–68; Nieto, *Juan de Valdés*, 314–22.

tracts—multiplied numerously thanks to the new printing press technology—into Italy that questioned the accuracy of Catholic Church doctrine.[74]

On account of these factors, there was widespread recognition of the need for reform.[75] In the opening address at the Fifth Lateran Council in 1512, for example, the Augustinian Cardinal Egidio da Viterbo (1469–1532) declared: "Men must be changed by religion, not religion by men."[76] This "religious uneasiness," common to the whole of Europe at the start of the sixteenth century, sent thoughtful Christians to re-examine the roots of their faith.[77] This examination produced a wide range of initiatives aimed at producing spiritual renewal, the form of which differed according to the various geographical, political, cultural, and economic realities peculiar to each distinct region of the peninsula. At this time, the notion of a unified Italian nation was at best a theoretical abstraction in the poetry of Dante and Machiavelli. In reality, Italian states were divided from each other and often at war among themselves.[78]

In this context, it is not surprising that *Evangélisme* itself developed amidst numerous other movements, ensuring its complexity. As mentioned, its origins are significantly indebted to the humanist project of Erasmus, with *Inquisitio de fide* and *Enchiridion Militis Christiani* producing an intellectual climate that encouraged discovery. The *ad fontes* orientation of

---

74. "Erasmus belonged to the generation which had grown up together with the youthful art of printing. To the world of those days it was still like a newly acquired organ; people felt rich, powerful, happy in the possession of this 'almost divine implement.'" Huizinga, *Erasmus and the Age of Reformation*, 65. For its impact on Italy see Caponetto, *Protestant Reformation*, 18. Grendler examines literary aspects of religious restlessness in *Cinquecento* Italy. Grendler, "Religious Restlessness," 25–38.

75. So Fenlon opens his book *Heresy and Obedience in Tridentine Italy* with the memorable words, "At the close of the middle ages the condition of the Church was nowhere considered to be healthy . . . [it was] magnificent in everything except religion." His first chapter provides a helpful telling of this story. Fenlon, *Heresy and Obedience*, 1–23.

76. Jung suggests that this classic formula, "*reformandi sunt homines per sacra et non sacra per homines*," could be called the motto of *Evangelisme*. Jung, "On the Nature of Evangelism," 513.

77. Ortolani, "The Hopes of the Italian Reformers," 13. Ortolani is best known for his work on the Italian *Evangelisme* martyr, Pietro Carnesecchi (1508–67): Ortolani, *Pietro Carnesecchi*. Schutte offers a trenchant analysis of this history in her work, Schutte, "Lettere Volgari," 639–88.

78. Caponetto, *Protestant Reformation*, xviii. Bouwsma's examination of Venice is a fine example of how one region differed significantly from another. Bouwsma, *Venice and the Defense of Republican*, 124.

Erasmus piqued the interest of his contemporaries, motivating many to take up and read the sources they had neglected.[79]

This renewed focus upon the Bible could be seen, for instance, in the Benedictines of Santa Giustina of Padua, whose attention to Scripture paralleled the text-centered approach of Protestants.[80] Reading the Gospels served as an initial step toward studying the Pauline epistles and, eventually, discussing the doctrines of "justification, faith, works, papal power, purgatory, and a whole range of other theological issues."[81] While little more than embryonic, these developments represented a conscious re-appropriation of sacred resources in defiance of the ignorance, corruption, and superstitious practices of the early sixteenth-century clergy.[82]

In Spain, Erasmian ideas joined the existing current of *alumbrado* spirituality that was moving through educated aristocrats and simple *contadores* alike.[83] This movement emphasized "religious individualism founded on the illumination of the spirit as the sole source of truth, in opposition to the official doctrines of the Church."[84] Out of this milieu emerged reform-minded individuals such as Juan de Valdés (c. 1500–1541).

Although Simler's *Oratio* only refers to Valdés in passing, there is no doubt that the Spaniard exerted influence on Vermigli's theological development.[85] Simler assesses that "the first praise for this (Neapolitan) church is due to Valdés."[86] In this group of disciples were high-ranking Italian prel-

---

79. About these epistles, Erasmus advised his readers, "In primis autem Paulum tibi facito familiarem: hic tibi semper habendus in sinu, nocturna versandus manu, versandus diurna, postremo & ad verbum ediscendus" [In the first place, make Paul your intimate friend . . . keep him always in your bosom, turning it night and day . . . and learn (him) by heart]. Erasmus, *Enchiridion Militis Christiani*, 328.

80. Collett, *Italian Benedictine Scholars and the Reformation*, 127.

81. Church, *The Italian Reformers, 1534–1564*, 53.

82. Concerning this period's emphasis on Scripture, Gleason asserts, "Foremost was the focus on ethical and moral reform of the individual Christian who encountered God's word in the Bible, specifically the Gospels and Pauline epistles" Gleason, *Gasparo Contarini*, 191.

83. Erasmus exerted an especially strong influence in Spain, so much so that McNair uses the word "cult" to describe his popularity. McNair, *PMI*, 310.

84. Firpo, "Italian Reformation," 353–64. Erasmus also had direct influence on the peninsula. About this phenomenon, Grendler writes, "Joyful letters spread the message of Erasmus to Italy, and many men opened the Gospel and moved forward to the glory of Christ." Grendler, "Religious Restlessness," 29.

85. Firpo, "Italian Reformation," 353–64; McNair, *PMI*, 143; Valdés, *Valdés' Two Catechisms*. McLelland makes this case in "Valdés and Vermigli," 238–50.

86. Simler, "Oratio," in Vermigli, *Life, Letters, and Sermons*, 20. Salvatore Caponetto asserts, "Juan de Valdés (c. 1500–1541) was one of the most important Christian thinkers of the sixteenth century and one of the greatest writers in the Castilian language

ates, women of nobility, and *Literati* who gathered around Valdés to study the Bible with particular attention to justification by faith alone.[87] Pietro Carnesecchi, who was part of the Valdésian circle, described these gatherings as *"regno di Dio"* (the kingdom of God).[88] According to Simler, it was at this time that Vermigli acquired books by Martin Bucer and Ulrich Zwingli.[89] As study of Reformed teaching deepened, so did the friendship of Vermigli and Valdés.[90]

During this period, it was increasingly common for Protestant tracts, which questioned Catholic doctrine, to circulate through southern Europe. For instance, Juan de Valdés, in his *Dialogue in Christian Doctrine* (1529), quotes from the works of Luther, Melanchthon, and Oecolampadius.[91] Not only did Italian printing presses make possible a "diffusion of writings by northern reformers," they also unleashed a catalog of "works on religious subjects by Italians."[92] Schutte, in her meticulous study of Italian *lettere volgari* (letters written by famous people in the Italian vernacular during the mid-sixteenth century),[93] demonstrates that Protestant texts popularized Evangelical values, especially the doctrine of justification, beyond clerical circles and reaching into the lower social classes.[94]

---

prior to Miguel de Cervantes." Caponetto, *Protestant Reformation*, 63.

87. "Evangelism included a desire to reform abuses, emphasis on Scripture, and the primacy of justification through faith without the omission of good works." Grendler, "Religious Restlessness," 27. For more on this movement see Gilly, "Juan de Valdés," 257–58; Nieto, "The Changing Image of Valdés," in Valdés, *Valdés' Two Catechisms*, ed. Nieto, 51–125.

88. Nieto, *Juan de Valdés*, 148. Firpo describes Valdés's role in Naples as "spiritual director and proselytizer for a message capable making use of diverse instruments and approaches: from personal encounters and colloquies to the clandestine circulation of his writing, from the epistolary exchange to the spoken word from the pulpit." Firpo, "Italian Reformation," 359.

89. Simler, "Oratio," in Vermigli, *Life, Letters, and Sermons*, 20.

90. Benrath, *Bernardino Ochino, of Siena*, 62. Carnesecchi confirmed the nature of this friendship at his Inquisition trial, in which he stated that Valdés was *"molto amico."* Ortolani, *Pietro Carnesecchi*, 237.

91. Firpo, "Italian Reformation," 353–64. Firpo makes his case on the basis of Gilly, "Juan de Valdés," 257–305.

92. Gleason, "On the Nature of Sixteenth-century Italian Evangelism," 14; ibid., "Sixteenth-century Italian Interpretations of Luther," 168; Cargnoni et al., *Storia della spiritualità italiana*, 292–96.

93. Schutte, "Lettere Volgari," 639–88. With the exception of Rome, most letters in this corpus come from the northern half of the peninsula (ibid., 670). Nevertheless, our research confirms that the constituent elements of Italian *Evangelisme* in the north (ibid., 662) were also shared by the south, as in the work of Valdés and Benedetto.

94. "Many literate Italians had ample opportunity to acquaint themselves with Protestant ideas, since in the 1520s and 1530s a number of works by Northern Reformers

E. Italian *Evangélisme* and the Doctrine of Justification

The *Evangélisme* movement gained momentum between the years 1536 and 1540, particularly in cities such as Venice, Modena, Verona, Lucca, Siena, and Naples. The dissemination of reforming ideas was aided by travelling preachers, whose traditional values (e.g., prayer, repentance and devotional practice in the vein of *De Imitatione Christi*) and fresh, Protestant-friendly emphases, such as salvation grounded in faith alone, was embraced by the laity.[95]

It was at the grassroots that Italian religious renewal gained crucial indigenous recognition. For instance, The Oratory of Divine Love (also called the Theatines), an informal society of devout Catholics, dedicated themselves to improving moral life in Rome and beyond.[96] There were also the Barnabites, or Clerks Regular of St. Paul, whose members preached, heard confessions, and visited hospitals.[97] The Capuchins, which started as an attempt to renew the Franciscan Order, also arose during this period.[98]

What had started below was given a boost from the top when Pope Paul III proposed a papal commission on reform, *de emendanda ecclesia*,

---

circulated freely in Italy." Schutte, "*Lettere Volgari*," 643. McNair goes so far as to assert that, "Wherever the doctrine of Justification by Faith took root in pre-Tridentine Italy—whether in Lucca, Modena, Naples, Padua, Venice, or Viterbo—it was preceded by Lutheran, Zwinglian, or Calvinist tracts which the timely invention of printing had disseminated far and wide." McNair, *PMI*, 8. Perhaps a more balanced explanation, one that gives adequate attention to the indigenous elements of Italian reform, is Fenlon's statement: "Evangelism was not created by the Reformation; it was most certainly redirected by it." Fenlon, *Heresy and Obedience*, 19.

95. McNair, "New Light on Ochino," 290–300.

96. Founded by Gaetano di Thiene (1480–1547), this group was established as an official order by Pope Clement VII's 1524 papal bull, *Exponi nobis*. Members of this group included Gian Matteo Giberti (later Cardinal-bishop of Verona), Giacomo Sadoleto (Cardinal-bishop of Carpentras, France), and Gianpetro Carafa (Cardinal-bishop of Naples, later Pope Paul IV, prominent *zelanti* leader and catalyst of the Italian Inquisition). Church, *The Italian Reformers*, 21–22. There is evidence that co-founder Gaetano de Thiene (1480–1547) listened to Peter Martyr preach from the pulpit of San Pietro ad Aram in the years 1537 to 1540. Olin, *The Catholic Reformation*, 128.

97. Founded by Antonio Maria Zaccaria (1502–47) et al., the order was accepted by Clement VII in 1533 before Pope Paul III officially recognized them in 1535. Mullett, *The Catholic Reformation*, 73.

98. Ozment, *The Age of Reform,*, 404. The Discalced Carmelites and Society of Jesus also emerged during this era. While originating in Spain, their influence quickly traveled to Italy. The "Discalced" Carmelites ("without shoes," actually, they wore sandals) was a women's movement led by St. Teresa Avila (1515–82). Teresa influenced St. John of the Cross (1542–91) to found the first monastery of Discalced Carmelite Friars. Egan, "The Spirituality of the Carmelites," 50–62. For a helpful overview of the Jesuits during this period, see O'Malley, *The First Jesuits*.

which sought to strengthen the integrity of curial offices.[99] Through its main exponents, Cardinals Contarini, Cortese, Pole, and Morone, the commission influenced "the higher reaches of the Roman Church."[100] McNair even argues persuasively that Vermigli himself served as a theological consultant to Contarini and the Commission during this time (1536–37).[101] Meanwhile the urge to piously reform was also reflected in the upper echelons of the church hierarchy by the *Spirituali*, which included most of the above-mentioned prelates, as well as other intellectuals, noblewomen and ecclesiastical powerbrokers.[102] So significant was this group that none other than Michelangelo was converted through its ministry, particularly by the influence of Pole and Valdés.[103] These prominent leaders gathered at Pole's residence in Viterbo (the so called *Ecclesia Viterbiensis*), where they studied the Bible alongside the commentaries of Bucer on Matthew and Romans and of Luther on the *Psalms*,[104] and the *Beneficio di Cristo*.

Perhaps the most public exponent of Italian *Evangélisme* was Cardinal Gasparo Contarini (1483–1542). He is especially important in understanding *Evangélisme*'s interest in the doctrine of justification. While much can be said about his career as an imperial diplomat, his elevation to the cardinalate, his advocacy of the new Jesuit order, and his involvement in the

---

99. The commission issued a report on March 9, 1537 titled *Consilium de emendanda ecclesia* ("Plan for Reforming the Church"), which was later adopted as the group's name. Church, *The Italian Reformers*, 21–22. Gleason, *Gasparo Contarini*, 142–44.

100. Fenlon, *Heresy and Obedience*, 19.

101. McNair, *PMI*, 116–38.

102. While sometimes used as a synonym for "Evangelism," Prosperi and Bowd argue that it is anachronistic to employ the nomenclature of "Spirituali" to describe the movement of Italian reform prior to 1540. For an examination of the diachronic use of the term see Bowd, *Reform before the Reformation*, 144–45; Prosperi, *Tra evangelismo e controriforma*, 285–86, 314–15. Notable (clerical) members of the *Spirituali* were Cardinal Gasparo Contarini, Cardinal Reginald Pole, Cardinal Giacomo Sadoleto, Cardinal Giovanni Morone, Abbot Gregorio Cortese of San Georgio in Venice, Tommaso Badia (Master of the sacred palace), Bishop Gian Matteo Giberti of Verona, and Archbishop Federico Fregoso of Salerno. Background on each of these men is found in Church, *The Italian Reformers* and in Caponetto, *Protestant Reformation*.

103. Paoletti and Radke, *Art in Renaissance Italy*, 404. Antonio Forcellino contends that Michelangelo was a member of the *Spirituali*. Forcellino, *Michelangelo: A Tormented Life*, 8.

104. For an explanation of how members of the *Spirituali* like Carafa, who eventually championed the *Zelanti* cause, cooperated with more amiable advocates of reform among the *Spirituali* (i.e., Contarini and Pole) before the Italian Inquisition started in 1542, see Fenlon, *Heresy and Obedience*, 24–44.

Colloquy of Regensburg, we will confine ourselves to the parts of his story that most directly relate to the soteriological focus of *Evangélisme*.[105]

By the latter half of the 1530s, when Pope Paul III had made Cardinals of Contarini (1535) and Reginald Pole (1536), a commitment to justification by faith alone had solidified in these men and in several of their colleagues in the Roman Curia.[106] Central to this conviction was the notion, gleaned from the study of Scripture, of God's sufficiency in salvation.[107] As the study of the Bible increased, so too did the concern for the doctrine of justification, which sent people probing yet more deeply into the Bible.[108] This cycle fueled the engine of Italian *Evangélisme*. A suitable slogan arose among those so convinced, one that was familiar to Contarini and Pole: "*Dominus opus habet*."[109] It is God who works—the Lord is ultimately responsible for salvation, not men. At the end of the day, man would stand before God, "with only his faith in the cross and the merits of Christ to offer him hope of salvation."[110]

The seriousness of Contarini's view of salvation was tested in 1541 when Charles V convened a colloquy at Regensburg. On April 21, the Holy Roman Emperor announced the names of the Catholic and Protestant debaters. Philip Melanchthon, Martin Bucer, and Johann Pistorius presented the Protestant position, with John Calvin present on the sideline, while representing the Roman Catholic side were Johann Eck, Johann Gropper, and Julius Pflug. Also present but inactive was the Catholic Dutchman, Albert Pighius, who would become an important interlocutor of Peter Martyr on

---

105. For an overview of Contarini's life and major contributions, see Gleason, *Gasparo Contarini*; Mackensen, "Contarini's Theological Role at Ratisbon in 1541," 36–49; Matheson, *Cardinal Contarini at Regensburg*. Prior to Gleason's volume, the standard full-length work was by Franz Dittrich, *Gasparo Contarini, 1483-1542: Eine Monographie*.

106. Among the others were Federigo Fregoso (made Cardinal in 1539) and Gian Matteo Giberti (made Cardinal in 1543). Fenlon, *Heresy and Obedience*, 34–35.

107. Ibid., 31.

108. During the same year as the Colloquy of Regensburg, Contarini wrote his *Epistola de iustificatione* (1541) in which he articulated a *duplex iustitia* on justification that distinguishes righteousness that is credible in the sight of God from righteousness that is credible in the eyes of men. Hünermann, ed., "Cardinal Gasparo Contarini, Bishop of Belluno," 24.

109. This phrase was employed by Pole after it was first used by a certain Benedictine monk named "Marco," a lecturer from Padua who exercised particular influence on some of the *Spirituali* members. Ibid., 34.

110. Gleason, *Gasparo Contarini*, 275. James Ross summarizes Contarini's soteriological priorities in terms of a "firm belief in the total inadequacy of human penance, faith in the saving merits of Christ crucified, and hope in the loving mercy of God." Ross, "Gasparo Contarini and His Friends," 208.

the topic of justification.[111] Cardinal Contarini presided as papal legate on behalf of Pope Paul III.[112] The theological meeting, which started on April 27, came to be called the Colloquy of Regensburg.

A sufficient amount of material has been published concerning the Colloquy of Regensburg's aims and outcomes, so it is unnecessary to retell the full story here.[113] The primary lesson for our purposes concerns the agreement reached between Catholics and Protestants on the doctrine of justification, as reflected in the fifth article of the final Regensburg Book.[114] Such agreement illustrates the relative freedom with which Catholic theologians were allowed to consider and formulate the doctrine of justification in the early decades of the sixteenth century.[115] This was so at least until 1542, when the Italian Inquisition started, or, more definitively, until the first period of the Council of Trent (1545–47), during which the *Decree on Justification* was written (January 13, 1547).[116] In response to the question of whether justification is forensic (based upon an *iusitia alienum*) or an ongoing work of love and charity (based on an *iusitia inhaerens*), Regensburg asserted that it was both. In justification, the Regensburg Book asserted, God imparts righteousness by the Holy Spirit *and* he forensically imputes Christ's righteousness.[117] Such imputation is necessary to make one right before the throne of God's justice since the imperfection of one's inherent righteousness falls short of the divine standard. This clear statement of im-

---

111. James, "Complex of Justification," 45–58. Campi, James, and Opitz, eds., *Peter Martyr Vermigli*. Vermigli's main interlocutors in his writing on justification were Pighius, Richard Smith, and the Council of Trent.

112. Matheson, *Cardinal Contarini at Regensburg*, 93–94. Evidence indicates that Contarini originally asked Vermigli to represent the Catholic delegation at the Colloquy of Worms in 1540 before it was reconvened in 1541 to coincide with the Imperial diet. McNair, *PMI*, 197–99.

113. Eells, "The Origin of the Regensburg Book," 355–72; Gleason, *Gasparo Contarini*, 225–35; Lane, *Justification by Faith in Catholic-Protestant Dialogue*; ibid., "A Tale of Two Imperial Cities," 119–45; Lugioyo, *Martin Bucer's Doctrine of Justification*, 103–208; Mackensen, "Contarini's Theological Role at Ratisbon in 1541"; Matheson, *Cardinal Contarini at Regensburg*.

114. For a detailed analysis of the Latin text of Article 5 with commentary and English translation see Lane, "Calvin and Article 5 of the Regensburg Colloquy," 234. The Regensburg Book was written prior to the colloquy and used as a basis for the discussion, although it was also amended on the basis of those discussions.

115. Abigail Brundin and Matthew Treherne describe Catholics and Protestants both holding ardent positions of *sola fide*. Brundin and Treherne, eds., *Forms of Faith in Sixteenth-century Italy*, 3–4.

116. O'Malley, *Trent: What Happened at the Council*, 104, 108–9.

117. While the term *duplex iustitia* is not made explicit, the concept underlies the whole of the article.

putation is responsible for making the fifth article a significant concession by the Catholic side that was mostly acceptable to Protestants.[118]

Robert Ives suggests that the key statement of Article 5 is probably, *per fidem vivam & efficacem iustificari peccatorem*.[119] Here the living and efficacious faith of the sinner is defined as the movement of the Holy Spirit by which one enjoys the "remission of sins and reconciliation on account of the merits of Christ, through the free goodness of God."[120] Since the merit of Christ is the ultimate ground of justification, it is "not on account of our own worthiness or works."[121] Precisely because of this emphasis on Christ's righteousness, which is imputed to the believer, the Protestants at Regensburg could embrace the final version of Article 5.[122]

Although conservative Catholics such as Eck were not pleased with the Protestant flavor of the article, some from the Catholic camp approved. Foremost in this group was Contarini. Writing later to Contarini, his confidant Reginald Pole "likened the formula to a partly concealed pearl, always possessed by the Church, but now accessible to everyone."[123] Expressing wonder over the Catholic endorsement of the article, Calvin wrote to Farel on May 11, 1541,

> You will be astonished, I am sure, that our opponents have yielded so much. . . . Our friends have thus retained also the substance of the true doctrine, so that nothing can be comprehended within it which is not to be found in our writings.[124]

It is important to note that Article 5 does not teach *duplex iustificatio* (double justification). Some interpreters have confused this with the concept of *duplex iustitia* (double righteousness). Frank James makes this error when he asserts, "Pighius supported the doctrine of double justification as articulated

---

118. Lane agrees with Matheson and Fenlon on this point. *Justification by Faith*, 57.

119. Ives, "An Early Effort toward Protestant-Catholic Conciliation," 99–110. The Regensburg text may be found in Bucer, *Acta colloquii in commitiis Imperii Ratisponae habiti*, 6.

120. "Quod remissionem peccatorum et reconciliationem propter meritum Christi gratuita Dei bonitate acceperunt." Ibid.

121. In context, "Et sic fide in Christum iustificamur seu reputamur iusti, id est accepti per ipsius merita, non propter nostram dignitatem aut opera." Ibid.

122. Schenk, *Reginald Pole, Cardinal of England*, 102.

123. Ibid.

124. John Calvin to Guillaume Farel, 11 May, 1541, *Letters of John Calvin*, vol. 1, 260. Months later, Calvin wrote negatively about the overall Colloquy of Regensburg, but he mentions nothing of Article 5. Calvin to Viret, 3 or 13 August, 1541, (ibid., 278–79).

at the Colloquy of Ratisbon/Regensburg (1541), which he attended."[125] Unlike the standard *duplex iustificatio* of Catholic teaching, which is built upon initial justification of the sinner (*iustificatio impii*) by faith apart from preparatory works and a second justification (*iustificatio pii*) by works (*operum*)—expounded on the basis of the epistle of James, chapter 2—the final draft of Article 5 teaches that there is only *one* justification,[126] the ultimate ground of which is the merit of Christ (*accepti per ipsius merita*). Accordingly, justification is a work for which God is ultimately responsible, something he accomplishes by simultaneously imparting the Holy Spirit and imputing Christ's righteousness.[127] As we shall see, this is the essence of Peter Martyr's doctrine.

F. Vermigli's Doctrine of Justification

Only a modest amount of attention has been dedicated to Peter Martyr's doctrine of justification. Charles Schmidt, writing in the mid-nineteenth century, was among the first modern scholars to pay heed to it.[128] While Schmidt's treatment is general, he elucidates Vermigli's commitment to upholding the renewing work of the Spirit when he quotes the Italian reformer, "This doctrine [of justification] is the beginning, source and support of all *piety*."[129] More focused by comparison is the work of McNair, which evaluates Vermigli's doctrine from various encounters on the Italian peninsula, particularly with Juan de Valdés and members of the Italian *Spirituali* such as Contarini.[130] McNair argues that it was in this context that Peter Martyr originally accepted *sola fide*.[131] In fact, according to McNair, not

125. Vermigli, *Predestination and Justification*, 182n460. McGrath explains why it is incorrect to assign the term "double justification" to the position of Gropper and Pighius. "There is no question of a 'double formal cause of justification'; simply the recognition that both notions of righteousness are involved in justification." McGrath, *Reformation Thought: An Introduction*, 4th ed., 133.

126. Unlike the Catholic and Protestant varieties of *duplex iustificatio*, Article 5 teaches that indwelling and imputed righteousness occur "*simul*."

127. "Article 5," in Lane, *Justification by Faith*, 233.

128. A treatment of Vermigli's Romans *locus* on justification is found in Schmidt, *Peter Martyr Vermigli*: 113–17.

129. Ibid., 113. Emphasis added. "Diese Lehre ist Unfang, Quelle und Stüze aller Frömmigheit."

130. McNair, *PMI*, 139–79.

131. Ibid., 179. Thus McNair concludes his chapter with a memorable summary of Vermigli's Evangelical doctrine, "Though the man who set out for Ravenna [from Naples] in the spring of 1540 was half mortified by fever he was wholly justified by faith."

only did Vermigli embrace the idea, he proceeded to teach it publicly in the city of Lucca.[132]

While most of McLelland's research has focused on Vermigli's sacramental theology, he has argued that Vermigli's view of justification properly revolves around the notion of union with Christ:[133] "There is no doubt that this doctrine of union with Christ is the dynamic of Peter Martyr's theology."[134] In keeping with this emphasis, McLelland identifies in Vermigli's understanding of justification a two-fold righteousness in which an initial forensic declaration of imputed righteousness is its primary characteristic, followed by a "second righteousness" consisting of the sanctifying work of the Spirit.[135]

Klaus Sturm proposes a similar portrait of two-fold righteousness in his treatment of Peter Martyr's theology during the Italian's first stay in Strasbourg (1542–47).[136] Sturm's work represents the only thoroughgoing analysis of Vermigli's doctrine of justification from this period, particularly from his Genesis commentary.[137] Sturm argues that on account of Vermigli's upbringing in the Roman Church, "Martyr's soteriology, ecclesiastically developed, certainly has a distinct affinity for the basic ideas of Catholicism."[138] In fact, Sturm goes so far as to label Vermigli a "*Reformkatholic*" for the way he orients internal renewal under the aegis of justification.[139] With regard to this position, Sturm acknowledges that Martyr flatly repudiated the sort of two-fold righteousness that posits two *correlative* causes. Thus he writes, "Martyr expressly rejected this opinion in order to categorically avoid relativizing Christ's righteousness appropriated in faith, which God imputes for forgiveness of sins and to admit only one *causa* for justification: the mercy of God."[140] However, Sturm suggests that Vermigli maintained another sort of double righteousness, such that "in the final analysis . . . Martyr's doctrine of justification concurs with that of Contarini."[141] So Catholic-friendly was his view, according to Sturm, that it is "difficult to determine whether Mar-

---

132. Ibid., 229.
133. McLelland, *Visible Words of God*, 113.
134. Ibid., 142.
135. Ibid., 128, 144, 176.
136. Sturm, *Die Theologie Peter Martyr*.
137. Vermigli's Genesis commentary is also considered by Emidio Campi, "Genesis Commentary: Interpreting Creation," 209–29.
138. Sturm, *Die Theologie Peter Martyr*, 44.
139. Ibid., 69.
140. Ibid., 67–68.
141. Ibid., 69.

tyr's doctrine of justification would be justifiably condemned on the basis of Trent's canons on justification."[142] Our next chapter will examine whether this is in fact true.

Marvin Anderson briefly analyzes Vermigli's doctrine of justification in two articles, the substance of which also appears in his book, *Peter Martyr, a Reformer in Exile*.[143] Anderson's main contribution lies in identifying the patristic sources that undergird Vermigli's doctrine. Among his observations, he notes how Vermigli lines up numerous church fathers to support the notion of *sola fide*, especially Augustine and Chrysostom.[144] Anderson also emphasizes the pastoral thrust of Vermigli's doctrine of justification, which Anderson describes as "the gateway to a new life in Christ."[145] Finally, it is worth noting that Anderson locates Peter Martyr's doctrine of justification, particularly as it is expressed in his Romans commentary (1558), "as part of a conciliatory genre originating with Contarini, Cortese, Pole, Sadoleto, Seripando and other Paulinians of Sixteenth Century Italy."[146] This is consistent with the conclusions of our research.

Another treatment of Peter Martyr's doctrine of justification is found in Donnelly's book, *Calvinism and Scholasticism in Vermigli's Doctrine of Man and Grace*.[147] Concentrating exclusively on the Romans *locus* (instead of the smaller and less mature *loci* on justification from Martyr's Genesis and 1 Corinthians commentaries), Donnelly recognizes that "the doctrine of justification by faith alone is crucial for Martyr as for all the Reformers."[148] As the title of his monograph suggests, Donnelly is especially interested in analyzing the scholastic elements of Vermigli's doctrine.[149] In keeping with his overall thesis that Vermigli was a "Calvinist Thomist,"[150] Donnelly argues that Vermigli repudiated the Protestant doctrines of *simul iustus et*

---

142. Ibid.

143. Anderson, *Peter Martyr, a Reformer in Exile*, 601, 270–78, 323–26, 335–42, 346–53.

144. Anderson, "Peter Martyr on Romans," 405. He also highlights agreement between Vermigli and Cranmer on the subject based on their common patristic influences. Ibid., 414.

145. Ibid., 413.

146. Anderson, *Peter Martyr, a Reformer in Exile*, 274.

147. Donnelly, *Calvinism and Scholasticism*, 149–55.

148. Ibid., 149.

149. Ibid., 156. Of interest to us (for the way it contrasts with Newman's understanding) is Martyr's agreement with Aquinas on the functional value of hope as a "habit." We will examine this concept more closely in the next chapter.

150. Ibid., 197–207.

peccator,¹⁵¹ perseverance of the Saints,¹⁵² and irresistible grace, since he does not use the terminology.¹⁵³ However, James points out that Vermigli, like Calvin, maintains these doctrinal concepts, even though he does not employ the nomenclature.¹⁵⁴

It is noteworthy that Donnelly agrees with McLelland's thesis that Vermigli closely aligned the doctrines of justification and union with Christ.¹⁵⁵ In this connection, Donnelly recognizes in Peter Martyr's thought the distinctively Protestant doctrine of "imputed justice," while also observing a "second inherent justice."¹⁵⁶ Because this second form of righteousness, expressed through good works, fails to meet the divine standard of justice, it is buttressed by the imputation of Christ's righteousness. On account of this distinction, Donnelly acknowledges that, "In teaching a second justice or sanctification, Martyr fits easily into the mainstream of Protestant tradition."¹⁵⁷ On the other hand, because he reads Vermigli as rejecting *simul iustus et peccator*, perseverance, and irresistible grace, Donnelly regards his doctrine as retaining "many Catholic nuances which Luther and Calvin left behind."¹⁵⁸

James has dedicated the greatest amount of attention to Peter Martyr's doctrine of justification. His doctoral dissertation, *"De Iustificatione*: The Evolution of Peter Martyr Vermigli's Doctrine of Justification," shines a floodlight onto a relatively obscure subject.¹⁵⁹ He meticulously examines the development of Peter Martyr's thought on justification from Naples into the subsequent stages of his life and ministry by analysing Peter Martyr's three main writings on the topic (the *loci* from his commentaries on Genesis, 1 Corinthians, and Romans).¹⁶⁰ As a result, he demonstrates that Vermigli's

---

151. Ibid., 154.

152. Ibid.

153. Ibid., 159.

154. James, "The Complex of Justification," 51.

155. Ibid., 157.

156. Ibid., 160.

157. Ibid. Donnelly states that Martyr's doctrine of sanctification compares closely with that of Calvin (ibid., 119).

158. Ibid., 154. Donnelly also finds Vermigli's doctrine of perseverance less than Reformed and his position on irresistible grace to be "highly qualified" (ibid., 159).

159. This was James's second monograph on the doctrine of Peter Martyr, following his DPhil thesis at Oxford, "Peter Martyr Vermigli and Predestination: the Augustinian Inheritance of an Italian Reformer."

160. After tracing Vermigli's steps through Italy to his departure in 1542, James examines his years in Strasbourg (1542–47), during which he first addressed the doctrine of justification in his Genesis lectures. Next, James examines this doctrine from Vermigli's Oxford lectures on 1 Corinthians (1548–49) and then from his Oxford lectures

doctrine underwent a maturation process that mirrored the trajectory of other Protestant theologians.[161]

Throughout his investigation, James acknowledges that Vermigli's conception of justification owed much to the lessons he had learned in Naples. However, we will, in the next chapter, go further than James in order to maintain that Vermigli's Neapolitan influence not only established the foundation of Martyr's doctrine, but also *continued to define its shape into its most mature form*. Since James affirms the former but denies the latter, this is an appropriate place to establish our fundamental agreement on the preparatory role of Martyr's Italian background before examining our disagreement over its abiding significance.

Underscoring the Protestant character of Martyr's position before his exile, James rightly asserts,

> The moment Vermigli embraced the doctrine of justification in Naples, his fate was sealed.... It also led him to a career as a Protestant theologian and staunch advocate of the doctrine he described as the "head, fountain and summit of all piety."[162]

James also describes Vermigli's view of the sacraments before his departure from Italy.

> By the time of his Priorate in Lucca, [Martyr] evinced a Protestantlike soteriology and had probably rejected a traditional view of the sacraments, yet he was unwilling to abandon the Catholic Church, that is, until compelled by the Roman Inquisition.[163]

A final quotation from James on this point underscores the "unanimity" and "general consensus" of scholars on the question of whether the fundamental form of Vermigli's theology was established before he crossed the Alps.

> Virtually all the research of the last twenty-five years, despite differences of interpretation, have [sic] reached unanimity on one question, namely, that Vermigli's theology was fundamentally formed before he apostatized from Italy.... There has been also

---

on Romans (1550–53). A concluding chapter compares and contrasts Peter Martyr's mature doctrine of justification to other early Reformed theologians.

161. In addition to his dissertation, James addresses the topic in "The Complex of Justification," and "Peter Martyr in Bucer's Strassburg." A cogent introduction is found in *Predestination and Justification: Two Theological Loci*, trans. and ed. James, III. Finally, one should consult James's translation of Peter Martyr's justification *loci* (from his 1 Corinthians commentary) in "Justification and Faith," in *PMR*, 133–50.

162. James, "*De Iustificatione*," 2–3.

163. Ibid., 139.

a general consensus that, ever since Naples, he had embraced a Protestant-inspired doctrine of justification by faith alone.[164]

By "theology," in this context, James refers specifically to Martyr's doctrine of the Eucharist and the authority of Scripture. On the question of how Vermigli's mature doctrine of justification resembled his Neapolitan beginnings, for which, as James notes, there is a "general consensus," we shall argue that the logic of Vermigli's position was properly grounded in a twofold righteousness.

G. Peter Martyr at Oxford

With this new, Protestant theology, Vermigli moved northward in May of 1541 to become prior of the rich and influential monastery on Saint Frediano in the Republic of Lucca. It was there that he initiated a series of educational and ecclesiastical reforms which, in the words of Philip McNair, amounted to an "ideological revolution; [so that] Lucca came perilously near to civic reformation on the pattern of Calvin's Geneva."[165] But after a mere fifteen months of such reform, Pope Paul III hastened its demise by reinstituting the Roman Inquisition. Recognizing discretion as the better part of valor, Vermigli renounced his vows and made the difficult decision to flee his homeland.[166] When he finally crossed through the Rhaetian Alps and arrived in Zürich in the fall of 1542, he was welcomed by Heinrich Bullinger (1504–75), Konrad Pellikan (1478–1556) and Rodolph Gualter/ Gwalther (1519–16).[167] Unfortunately, there were no positions open in Zürich. After two days, Vermigli continued to Basel, where he remained for a month, enjoying the hospitality of Oswald Myconius (1488–1552) and the generosity of Boniface Amerbach (1495–1562), who provided Martyr with books and money. Since Basel was also without an open academic post, Vermigli accepted an invitation to teach in Strasbourg, where he succeeded the late Wolfgang Capito as professor of Divinity.

164. Ibid., 142–44. James cites McNair, who argued that Vermigli had embraced "the doctrine of justification by faith alone" in Naples. McNair, *PMI*, 179. Cf. Donnelly, *Calvinism and Scholasticism*, 172.

165. McNair, "Biographical Writings," 7.

166. It was on the basis of Matthew 10:23, which provides sanction for Christians to flee persecution that Peter Martyr and Bernardino Ochino chose to leave their beloved homeland. McLelland, *Visible Words of God*, 9. For an interesting treatment of Peter Martyr's theology of exile, see Jason Zuidema's recent article, "Flight from Persecution," 112–16.

167. James has pointed out that this warm reception probably followed careful theological scrutiny. James, *"De Iustificatione,"* 9.

Simler explains that it was "that good and learned man," Martin Bucer, who arranged for Vermigli's academic appointment to the College of Saint Thomas in Strasbourg.[168] The Italian exile was expected to "teach sacred letters," which he proceeded to do from the twelve books of the Minor Prophets, Lamentations, Genesis, Exodus, and a large part of Leviticus.[169] Of these lectures, only those on Genesis and Lamentations are extant, with the former containing Vermigli's *locus* on the doctrine of justification.[170] "Certainly, upon his arrival," James notes, "Vermigli's theological perspective was judged acceptable to the Reformers of Strasbourg—indeed, it was compatible enough that he was immediately invited to lecture on the Old Testament."[171] With regard to the quality of his teaching, it wasn't long before Vermigli ascended to the stature of Bucer, and, in the estimation of many, even surpassed him.[172]

Strasbourg was significant for another reason. It was there that Vermigli married a former nun from Metz named Catherine Dammartin, "a lover of true religion."[173] According to McNair, the wedding probably occurred in October 1544.[174] Known for her Christian virtue, Catherine was especially admired for her charity among the English, with whom she and Peter Martyr lived for most of their married life. After eight years of marriage, she died childless in February 1553. Peter Martyr would later marry his second wife, another Katie, in May 1559.[175]

---

168. Simler, "Oratio," in Vermigli, *Life, Letters, and Sermons*, 28.

169. Ibid. In a personal letter to Heinrich Bullinger in 1551, Vermigli corroborates Simler's account by mentioning these books vis-à-vis his Strasbourg lectures (except for Lamentations). About them he writes, "But if it please God to spare my life, and I should obtain leisure, I shall not object to publish them." Peter Martyr to Henry Bullinger, in *Original Letters Relative to the English Reformation*, vol. 2, 499.

170. Sturm analyzes the *locus* on justification from Vermigli's Genesis commentary in Sturm, *Die Theologie Peter Martyr*, 58–70. Martyr's locus centered on Genesis 15:6.

171. James, "*De Iustificatione*," 155.

172. In Simler's words, "[Vermigli] seemed in the judgment of all not just to match Bucer but to surpass him." Simler, "Oratio," in Vermigli, *Life, Letters and Sermons*, 29.

173. Metz was a Bishopric and Free Imperial City of the Holy Roman Empire until 1552, when King Henry II of France seized the city after the agreement, in the Treaty of Chambord, of the Protestant German princes—who were in rebellion against Charles V—to support his claim. With the exception of the period between the Franco-Prussian War and World War I, it has remained a French territory ever since. Presumably, Peter Martyr communicated with his wife in Latin.

174. McNair, "Early Writings," 9.

175. Ibid., 9–11. Martyr's second wife, Caterina Merenda of Brescia, bore him two children who did not survive infancy, and a daughter, Maria, who was born on March 6, 1563, after Peter Martyr's death on November 12, 1562.

After five fruitful years of teaching in Strasbourg, Vermigli recognized the threat of doctrinal censure within the Holy Roman Empire (which was soon enforced by Charles V through the Augsburg Interim).[176] Thankfully, liberation arrived in the form of an invitation from Archbishop Thomas Cranmer to help fortify the newly independent Church of England with Protestant theology. McNair suggests that Vermigli was also motivated to accept the invitation by "holy curiosity, the same impulse which was an ingredient in the compulsion that urged him to cross the Alps in 1542."[177] On November 4, 1547, with permission from the Strasbourg senate, Vermigli departed from nearby Basel, accompanied by his friend, Bernardino Ochino.[178] Their spouses eventually would follow them in the spring, escorted by their friend, Giulio Terenziano (known in England as "Julius").[179] McLelland explains how the Strasbourg period was "a decisive phase for Martyr's theology, for in England he was immediately put on the defensive and from that time until his death was engaged in drawing out the implications of his doctrine in the face of a variety of opponents."[180] Toward this end, the recently crowned King Edward VI (February 20, 1547) approved Vermigli as Regius Professor of Divinity at Oxford University and bestowed on him the honor of Doctor of Divinity.[181]

While we tend to think of Oxford University as old and venerable, it should be remembered that the Regius Chair of Divinity at Oxford had only been established a few years earlier in 1540,[182] and the charter foundation for Christ Church, the new college under whose aegis the chair fell, was issued on November 4, 1546, just one year to the day before Vermigli and

---

176. Charles V's victory at Mühlberg on April 24, 1547 over the Lutheran Schmalkaldic League was probably the writing on the wall. The religious settlement called the Augsburg Interim was temporarily imposed until the completion of Trent, becoming Imperial law on June 30, 1548.

177. McNair, "Peter Martyr in England," 89.

178. They arrived in London on December 20. Vermigli traveled under the aegis of John Abell, a merchant at Strasbourg. Ibid., 90. Diarmaid, MacCulloch, outlines details of this journey, including an important letter from Bucer to Cranmer, which Vermigli and Ochino delivered upon arrival, outlining their (Reformed) view of the Eucharist. MacCulloch, *Thomas Cranmer: A Life*, 380–83.

179. McNair, "Peter Martyr in England," 96.

180. McLelland, *Visible Words of God*, 13.

181. Cross, "Oxford and the Tudor State," 133–35.

182. This date is potentially confusing. McNair identifies 1546 as the founding of the Regius Chair of Divinity, with Richard Smith occupying it. McNair, *Peter Martyr in England*, 93. However, G. D. Duncan has it starting with Smith in 1540. Duncan, "Public Lectures and Professional Chairs," 343–47. The discrepancy is explained by the fact that, after its initial establishment in 1540, the chair had its financial oversight transferred from Westminster Cathedral to the newly re-founded Christ Church in 1546.

Ochino departed from Basel for London.[183] Thus, Vermigli found himself in a new country, at a new academic institution, under a new dean, among several new canons, and, perhaps most significantly, facing a new theological challenge.[184]

Under the rule of the boy King Edward VI and his Lord Protectors, Edward Seymour followed by John Dudley, it was "through Archbishop Cranmer himself that a distinct Evangelical stance entered England; this was eventually styled 'Reformed' Christianity."[185] Peter Martyr and Bucer (who arrived in the autumn of 1549 to occupy the Regius Chair at Cambridge)[186] were chosen for the expressed purpose of implementing this vision.[187] According to Diarmaid MacCulloch, "by late 1547, Martyr and Cranmer were already very close in theological outlook."[188] Even so, the challenge of their mission loomed large. In Martyr's words, "Indeed I took upon myself a weighty charge."[189] This was despite the fact that, according to S. L. Greenslade, "Peter Martyr was unquestionably the most learned" of the early holders of the Regius Chair in Divinity.[190]

When Peter Martyr took up his post at Christ Church, he supplanted Professor Richard Smith, who McLelland describes as a "model of inconstancy," and, quoting John Strype, "giddy and unstable," and of "a profligate conscience."[191] McNair is more gracious by comparison, suggesting that, reading Smith in depth, "it is hard not to feel a sneaking sympathy with him."[192] Whatever one's opinion of Smith's character, the fact is that he quickly became one of Peter Martyr's chief nemeses.

The *ad hominem* nature of Smith's opposition to Vermigli, as evidenced in several invectives and diatribes, gives one the impression that he harbored

---

183. It was officially incorporated as "the cathedral church of Christ in Oxford" of King Henry VIII College. For an overview of this history, including an explanation of its origins as Wolsey's Cardinal College, see McConica, "The Rise of the Undergraduate College," 32–42.

184. Strictly speaking, Christ Church is not a college, but a "foundation." Richard Cox, the first Dean, is believed to have written its new constitution. During this time, Cox also served as Chancellor of Oxford University. Ibid., 37.

185. MacCulloch, *Thomas Cranmer: A Life*, 173.

186. Cross, "Oxford and the Tudor State," 134.

187. McLelland, *Visible Words of God*, 16.

188. MacCulloch, "Peter Martyr and Thomas Cranmer," 176.

189. McLelland, *Visible Words of God*, 17.

190. Greenslade, "The Faculty of Theology," 315.

191. McLelland, *Visible Words of God*, 20.

192. McNair, "Peter Martyr in England," 97.

a certain amount of resentment toward Martyr for his demotion.[193] This first of these attacks came shortly after Smith left Oxford in 1549, in a treatise defending celibacy.[194] He followed this with further attacks in a second work that upheld the sanctity of monastic vows.[195] McNair points to the highly visible nature of these traditions of Catholic piety as the reason for Smith's selection of these topics.[196] In a letter to Bucer, Peter Martyr expressed the view that Smith's book was "stuffed so full with maledictions, accusations, and the bitterest contempt, that I think I never have heard before of any tongue so unbridled in abuse."[197] Eventually, Smith instigated the famous Oxford Disputation on the Eucharist.[198] A final demonstration of Smith's animus was his *Diatriba de hominis iustificatione . . . adversus P.M. Vermelinum*, published in 1550.[199] Andreas Löwe's comment on this work gives a sense of how significant the doctrine of justification had become in this period: "Smyth's 1550 publication primarily sought to address the doctrinal innovations of his home-country . . . [and] that England had been corrupted wretchedly by the infection of many heresies among which justification by faith featured prominently."[200] Peter Martyr's most significant response to Smith's opposition was his exposition of the New Testament book of Romans, to which we now turn.

193. Löwe, *Richard Smyth and the Language of Orthodoxy*. Löwe explains that Smith regularly attended Vermigli's lectures, taking assiduous notes and occasionally causing a disturbance (41).

194. Ibid., 152. This and the following treatise were published together in a volume entitled *De coelibatu sacerdotum liber vnus. Eiusdem de votis monasticis liber alter, nunc primum typis excusi.*

195. According to Löwe, Smith "frequently accused Vermigli of breaking his vows in order to marry: 'Who was released by breaking his vow (such a man is that Peter, who—they say—took monastic vows in Italy) to consider marriage unlwaful in his mind and not admit that it was any crime of his.'" Löwe, *Richard Smyth and the Language of Orthodoxy*, 153.

196. McNair, "Peter Martyr in England," 95-99.

197. Gorham, *Gleanings*, 153-54. The letter is dated 10 June, 1550.

198. The disputation grew out of Martyr's exposition of 1 Corinthians 10:16-17, in which he cast aspersions upon the traditional Catholic doctrine of the Lord's Supper. The history of how the debate developed along with a modern English version of the treatise has been translated and edited by McLelland in *The Oxford Treatise and Disputation on the Eucharist, 1549*, published in 2000.

199. While Smith's title has Vermigli in the crosshairs, it is actually Luther and Melanchthon who receive the lion's share of attention.

200. Löwe, *Richard Smyth and the Language of Orthodoxy*, 120.

H. Peter Martyr's *Locus* on Justification

Vermigli's nearly six years in England were full and fruitful.[201] He started to lecture on Romans in March 1550.[202] According to Anderson, whose article, "Peter Martyr on Romans," provides a general overview of the commentary's scope and sequence, "Martyr viewed his lectures as a means of reforming the English Church."[203] Toward this end, Vermigli sought to expound the text and explain its theological implications by means of two theological *loci*: one on the doctrine of predestination[204] and the other on justification.[205] The latter of these, *de iustificatione*, will be the object of our attention for understanding Vermigli's doctrine.[206] We will focus here, rather than on the earlier *loci* from his Genesis and 1 Corinthians commentaries, because the Romans *locus* is his most extensive and mature treatment.[207]

The *loci* method, which was experiencing a revival in Martyr's day, might be likened to a surgical procedure for its relatively narrow scope and logical precision.[208] More than any other figure, Aristotle (384–22 BC) is credited for having popularized the approach, followed by Cicero (106–43 BC), who had himself first encountered it in the Philosopher's *Topica*.[209]

---

201. Donnelly calls them "the most influential period of [Vermigli's] life." Donnelly, *Calvinism and Scholasticism*, 3. McNair identifies seven particular fronts on which Peter Martyr exerted influence during this period: (1) The Eucharistic Disputation of 1549; (2) Riots later the same year; (3) The Vestrian Controversy; (4) The second Book of Common Prayer, published in 1552; (5) The Ecclesiastical Laws (also in 1552); (6) The Forty-Two Articles of Religion of 1553; (7) The Reformation Settlement after 1558. McNair, *Peter Martyr Vermigli*, 87.

202. Peter Martyr indicates in the preface of his commentary that even though he had read the Romans commentaries of Melanchthon, Bucer, Bullinger, and Calvin, he felt that it was nevertheless important to write his own commentary. Vermigli, *Romanos*, Preface.

203. Anderson, "Peter Martyr on Romans," 403.

204. *De Praedestinatione* is located immediately after Vermigli's exegesis of Romans 9. For a study of this *locus* see McLelland, "The Reformed Doctrine of Predestination According to Peter Martyr."

205. *De Iustificatione* is located immediately after Vermigli's exegesis of Romans 11.

206. Vermigli, *Romanos*, 87–230. All references to Vermigli's Romans commentary will cite page numbers from the 1560 version (which is available on the *Digital Library of Classic Protestant Texts*) followed in brackets by pages from James's English translation. In his English text, James indicates the pagination of the original 1558 version.

207. Like Donnelly (*Calvinism and Scholasticism*, 149), James also takes this approach, "This is especially important because it establishes his understanding of justification toward the end of his life and career." James, "*De Iustificatione*," 275.

208. For an overview of its history and development, see McLelland, "A Literary History of the *LOCI COMMUNES*," 479–94.

209. The *Topica* of Aristotle is part of his *Organon*, a collection of logical works

This method also drew from the humanist tradition represented by the likes of Lorenzo Valla (1407–57), with its trenchant historical, grammatical, and rhetorical analysis.[210] In Vermigli's context, the writing of theological *loci* often amalgamated dialectical and rhetorical methodology.[211] With regard to the former, it was a way to systematically focus argumentation by granting, denying, and admitting proof (*concedo, nego, admitto casum*). Concerning the latter, it brought the tools of exegesis to bear upon texts.

There is a long and significant debate on the relationship of scholastic and humanist methodology in Peter Martyr's work, the origin of which is typically associated with Brian Armstrong's portrait of Vermigli in his work, *Calvinism and the Amyraut Heresy* (1969).[212] While an examination of the debate is outside the scope of this book, it bears mentioning. Armstrong argued that the Italian reformer, along with Theodore Beza and Girolamo Zanchi, modified the biblical vision of Calvin according to Aristotelian philosophy, resulting in a tradition of Reformed Scholasticism. It was nearly two decades until Richard Muller disputed Armstrong's thesis as overly simplistic, particularly in regard to the portrait of Calvin as the chief codifier of Reformed theology (ignoring the collegial involvement of Bullinger, Musculus, Vermigli, et al.) and the apparent equation of Aristotelian categories with full-blown "scholasticism."[213]

A few years before Muller's critique, Donnelly appropriated much of Armstrong's case, concluding that Vermigli was a "Calvinist Thomist."[214] On the other side of the spectrum from Donnelly was the position championed by Anderson, which stressed Vermigli's humanist orientation.[215] Between them is McLelland's mediating position, which summarizes Vermigli's method as a synthesis: "Pietro Martire Vermigli above all," he contends, "provides a case study in the interaction between humanism and scholasticism. [He was] a Florentine who studied at Padua."[216] McLelland's *via media*

---

addressing principles and methods of presenting proof.

210. Vasoli, "*Loci Communes*," 20–21.

211. Kristeller, *Renaissance Thought*, 92–119. This was the case, for instance, at institutions featuring a mixture of scholastic and humanist curricula, such as the University of Padua where Vermigli received his education, or Heidelberg University, from which Martin Bucer was influenced during his study at the Dominican monastery in Heidelberg. Greschat, *Martin Bucer*, 18–20

212. Armstrong, *Calvinism and the Amyraut Heresy*, 87.

213. Muller, *Post-Reformation Reformed Dogmatics*. See also, Schmitt, "Towards a Reassessment of Renaissance Aristotelianism," 159–93.

214. Donnelly, "Calvinist Thomism," 441–55.

215. Anderson, "Biblical Humanism."

216. McLelland, "Peter Martyr Vermigli: Scholastic or Humanist?," 141.

is the predominant view in contemporary Vermigli scholarship and the one that we find most convincing.[217]

The Romans lectures were presented between 1550 and 1552,[218] but it was six years after their completion, in 1558, that the commentary was published. Unlike previous *loci* on justification, the polemic of this exposition manifests a serrated edge, the principle targets of which are Richard Smith, and, to an even greater extent, the Dutch Catholic theologian, Albert Pighius.[219] Of these two interlocutors, Vermigli regards Pighius as far more serious,[220] calling him the "Achilles of the Papists."[221]

The other target of Vermigli's *locus* is the Council of Trent and its *Decree on Justification*, which had been released just five years earlier.[222] According to James, "The polemical tone in the Romans commentary should be seen against the larger backdrop of the Council of Trent."[223] Indeed, the thrust of Peter Martyr's *locus* is aimed at defending the doctrine of justification by faith alone (contra Trent); at the same time, there is an ethical orientation to his doctrine that clearly distinguishes it from the teaching of Luther. In this respect, Vermigli was very much like his colleague, Martin Bucer. The words

---

217. Baschera, "Aristotle and Scholasticism," 133–60.

218. According to James, Vermigli lectured on Romans in at least three different locations (possibly four) during his career. The first conclusive account is from Girolamo Zanchi who noted that he heard Peter Martyr lecture on Romans in Lucca (1541–42). A few years later, a Frenchman, Hubert de Bapasme of Lille, revealed in a letter dated March 10, 1546 that Vermigli lectured on Romans in Strasbourg. Finally, there was Martyr's lectures as Regius Professor of Divinity at Oxford (1550–52). A possible fourth occasion was during Vermigli's triennium in Naples, about which McNair enumerates several reasons in support before ultimately calling the evidence inconclusive. James, "Romans Commentary: Justification and Sanctification," 308.

219. Pighius, *Controversiarum praecipuarum in Comitiis Ratisponensibus*. For more on Pighius, see Jedin, *Studien über die schriftstellertätigkeit Albert Pigges*; Pfeifer, *Ursprung der katholischen Kirche und Zugehörigkeit zur Kirche nach Albert Pigge*; Bäumer, "Albert Pighius," 271; Feiner, *Die Erbsündenlehre Albert Pigges*.

220. Anderson suggests that Vermigli's opposition to Pighius may have been motivated by the latter's polemic against Calvin. Anderson, *Reformer in Exile*, 270. Pighius's reputation as a formidable theologian is demonstrated by the fact that Calvin wrote two works against him, in 1543 and 1552.

221 Vermigli, *Romanos*, 1231, 1264 [138, 172]. On page 1298 [204], Vermigli calls Pighius "Hercules."

222. The canons of Trent which anathematized Luther's doctrine of justification were issued in January 1547. The newest volume to date on Trent is O'Malley, *Trent: What Happened at the Council*. Classic sources on Trent include the eighteen volumes of the *Concilium Tridentinium*; Tanner, ed. *Decrees of the Ecumenical Councils*, 2 vols.; Bäumer, ed. *Concilium Tridentinium*; Jedin, *Geschichte des Konzils von Trient*, 4 vols.; Schroeder, ed. and trans., *The Canons and Decrees of the Council of Trent*.

223. James, "Romans Commentary," 309.

of Bucer's biographer, Martin Greschat, on this point may be equally applied to Vermigli: "If Luther emphasized the unsurpassed importance of the sinner's justification by God, Bucer stressed the intimate connection between justification and the gift of an ethically renewed better life all the more."[224] How exactly Vermigli held these two forms of righteousness together in the name of justification will be the central question of our next chapter.

I. Conclusion

Looking at the big picture of Italian *Evangélisme*, a variety of notable characters cross the stage: aristocratic ladies such as Vittoria Colonna and Giulia Gonzaga; Spaniards such as Juan de Valdés; for a period of time, at least, Cardinals Contarini, Pietro Bembo, Reginald Pole, Giovanni Morone, Jacopo Sadoleto, and Girolamo Seripando; those who eventually fled, such as Bernardino Ochino, Peter Martyr Vermigli, Piero Paolo Vergerio, and Girolamo Zanchi; and those who would become martyrs, namely Pietro Carnesecchi and Aonio Paleario.[225] The beliefs and agendas of these characters often diverged;[226] nevertheless, there was a basic theological core drawing these figures together, the constituent elements of which would remain with Vermigli for the remainder of this life.

Peter Martyr brought his doctrine of two-fold righteousness with him to Strasbourg and eventually to Oxford. Amidst his many accomplishments during his six-year tenure as Regius Professor of Divinity at Christ Church—from the Eucharistic Disputation (1549) to his contributions to the Second Book of Common Prayer (1552) and the Forty Two Articles of Religion (1553)—Vermigli's lectures on *Romans* and his subsequent commentary remain among his most significant theological achievements. The latter of his two *loci* from this volume, *de iustificatione*, represents his most mature thinking on the subject of justification and therefore constitutes the focus of our study.

---

224. Greschat, *Martin Bucer: A Reformer and His Times*, 31. An important work for understanding Bucer's doctrine of justification is Stephens, *The Holy Spirit in the Theology of Martin Bucer*. With regard to Bucer's doctrine of "threefold justification," see Fink, "The Doers of the Law Will Be Justified," 485–524.

225. Caponetto, *Protestant Reformation*; Firpo, "Italian Reformation," 353–64; Grendler, "Religious Restlessness," 27.

226. Grendler, quoting Delio Cantimori, notes the difficulty of distinguishing between *Evangelisme*'s "Catholic Reform, philo-Protestantism, or sympathy for Protestant ideas." This was especially true in the years leading up to 1542. Grendler, "Religious Restlessness," 25–38.

A summary of the doctrinal elements characteristic of both Italian *Evangélisme* in general and Peter Martyr in particular would have at the center *sola fide*, based upon a canonically informed exegesis of Scripture. And this saving faith, Vermigli and his co-adherents insisted, produced in the believer a life so closely identified with Christ that he enjoys the benefits of both a forensic imputation and the Holy Spirit who transforms the believer from within. Exactly how Vermigli develops this *duplex iustitia* and distinguishes it from the teaching of his Catholic interlocutors will be analyzed below; but, we first wish to let Vermigli speak to the matter for himself. In his final moments of life, according to Simler, Peter Martyr "was silent in deep personal reflection; then he turned to us and stated with a rather clear voice that he acknowledged life and salvation in Christ alone, who had been given by the Father to the human race as its only savior."[227] This phrase, "salvation in Christ alone," is an apt summary of Vermigli's doctrine of justification, a doctrine so deeply ingrained in his Italian background, his heart, and his mind that it found clear expression in his dying words.

---

227. Simler, "Oratio," in Vermigli, *Life, Letters, and Sermons*, 60.

Chapter 2: Peter Martyr Vermigli's Doctrine of Justification

A. Theological Contours of Vermigli's Doctrine of Justification

HAVING CONSIDERED THE HISTORICAL background to Vermigli's doctrine of justification, we will now evaluate its theological content. The primary source for our study (among Martyr's other works) is his justification *locus* from his Romans commentary, which appears at the conclusion of its eleventh chapter.[1] In contradiction of the Roman position (as represented by Vermigli's interlocutors), Martyr presents a classic Protestant doctrine which defines the formal cause of justification in the strict sense of a legal pronouncement grounded in the imputation of Christ's righteousness.[2] In making this case, Vermigli employs forensic terminology to underscore that the basis of justification belongs to the legal domain.[3] At the same time, he uses the language of justification to describe the renewal of sinners by the Holy Spirit resulting in a disposition (*habitus*) of righteousness.[4] In defending his position, Martyr's Romans *locus* on justification unfolds three propositions: (1) It is not by works, (2) It is by faith, and (3) It is by faith alone.[5]

Vermigli's doctrine posits forensic "justification" as a punctiliar event—an act in which God declares a sinner to be righteous. He also uses the language of justification to describe an ongoing process of sanctification. It must be noted, however, that this secondary sense is properly distinguished from the forensic use of the word, which is primary. With both of

---

1. Vermigli, *Romanos*, 1181–1324 (1182).

2. Vermigli does not use the language of *"iustitia aliena"* but he affirms the concept when he asserts that justification is grounded in the judicial transference of Christ's righteousness to the sinner. Vermigli, *Romanos*, 1182 [87], 1201 [107], 1314 [220].

3. "Verba est forense, quod ad iudicia spectat." Ibid., 1182 [87–88].

4. Ibid., 1182 [87].

5. Ibid., 1181–1253 [87–160]; 1253–1311 [160–218]; 1312–24 [218–30].

these in view, justification involves a two-fold righteousness that is forensic and also moral.[6] With regard to the former, Martyr speaks in eschatological terms, explaining how God's end-time judgment is currently rendered in the lives of his children.[7] The basis of this declaration is solely the imputation of Christ's righteousness.[8] Regarding the latter, there is an ongoing need for the moral chaos of sin to be reformed in sanctification.[9] For Vermigli, it is not sufficient to simply speak of forensic justification without also connecting it to the Holy Spirit's work of renewal. He thus recognizes "two meanings of the phrase 'to justify,' namely, in fact or in judgment or estimation."[10]

In reading Martyr's Romans *locus*, it is not long before one recognizes a confrontation with what he regards as "Pelagianism" in the Roman Church.[11] Donnelly takes issue with this critique and suggests that Martyr's portrait of Trent creates a "straw man."[12] As Frank James points out, however, "For an Augustinian like Vermigli, whose most basic theological presupposition was that all humanity after Adam's fall is *massa perditionis* (a mass of perdition), Pelagianism was intolerable."[13] Furthermore, for Vermigli, the "Pelagian" problem also posed a pastoral threat:

> Certainly no one understands except those who have experienced how difficult it is for a bruised heart, dejected and weary with the burden of sins to find comfort.... If we, like the Sophists, commanded a person to have regard for his own works, then he would never find comfort, would always be tormented,

---

6. One way in which Vermigli captures the legal and relational dimensions of justification is by describing divine acceptance in terms of "adoption." Ibid., 1232 [139], 1259 [167], 1280 [187].

7. Ibid., 1263 [171].

8. Ibid., 1194 [100].

9. An explanation of this emphasis is found below in section B., "Regeneration and Pneumatic Renewal."

10. Ibid., 1182 [88]. The latter of these, justification "in judgment," constitutes the formal cause. Immediately after making this statement, Vermigli explains why the renewal of the Spirit and "way of life acquired from good works" ultimately relies upon forensic imputation to accomplish one's justification, since such works remain "imperfect and incomplete."

11. After quoting the Council of Trent, Vermigli quips, "What else would Pelagius say if he were now alive?" Ibid., 1248–49 [156]. A more accurate reading of Trent, however, would recognize its gracious character. Chapter 8 of the Council's *Decree on Justification* explicitly states that justification comes as a "free gift," and does so on the perennial consent of the Catholic Church, on the basis of faith, "without which 'it is impossible to please God'" (Heb 11:6). *Decree on Justification*, in Tanner, *Decrees*, 2:674.

12. Donnelly, *Calvinism and Scholasticism*, 151.

13. James, *Predestination and Justification*, xxxv.

always in doubt of his salvation and finally, be swallowed up with desperation.[14]

It is not necessary to repeat here the careful explication of others. James, in his doctoral dissertation, "De Iustificatione: The Evolution of Peter Martyr Vermigli's Doctrine of Justification," traces the main lines of Martyr's doctrine through the development of his Protestant career.[15] He analyses Vermigli's three primary writings on the subject—*loci* on justification from his commentaries on Genesis (1542-47), 1 Corinthians (1548-49), and Romans (1550-52),[16] showing how his doctrine underwent a maturation process. James reveals how Vermigli covered essentially the same theological ground in each *locus*, with successive editions providing further detail and support.[17] None of these developments, however, changed the essence of Vermigli's position.

Vermigli's doctrine draws deeply from the well of Scripture. In keeping with the *sola scriptura* principle of Protestantism, he appeals to the Bible as his final authority.[18] Support from the church fathers and councils only carry weight insofar as they accord with Scripture. Speaking of the councils, for instance, he writes, "[T]hey should not be heard without selectivity and judgment. We ought to receive and reverence only those councils which have kept their doctrine within the rule of Holy Scriptures."[19] The council that occupies the lion's share of Vermigli's attention is naturally the Council of Trent (1545-63). What begins on an irenic note immediately changes to a sharp critique: "There those good holy fathers, that is, hirelings of the pope . . . ."[20] The polemic that follows unleashes an array of arguments around five

---

14. Vermigli, *Romanos*, 1208 [114].

15. James, "*De Iustificatione*."

16. These dates indicate the years when Vermigli lectured on these books. Initial publication occurred accordingly: the commentary on Genesis in 1569 (Zürich), the commentary on 1 Corinthians in 1551 (Zürich), and the commentary on Romans in 1558 (London).

17. Given the polemical setting in which Martyr wrote his Romans *locus*, the text displays a high number of biblical citations. He also gives considerable attention to the church fathers, whereas previous *loci* only occasionally referred to them.

18. Vermigli, *Romanos*, 1245 [152]. This is illustrated by the meticulous attention that Vermigli devotes to Hebrew, Greek, and Latin exegesis (1182-85 [87-91]), and also the profusion of biblical texts that he marshals throughout his commentary. McLelland puts an edge on this point when he writes, "Peter Martyr's quarrel with Rome may be summed up in the phrase, 'the Scriptures, and not the traditions of men.'" McLelland, *The Visible Words of God*, 125.

19 Ibid.

20. Ibid., 1249 [156].

basic topics: the priority of grace over works,[21] the efficacious nature of the Spirit's renewal of the heart,[22] opposition to a general grace which is supposedly accessible to all,[23] the causes of justification,[24] and the certainty that God delivers on his promises—the doctrine of assurance.[25] The aggregate of these critiques amounts to Martyr's overall argument against the notion that one "can merit and prepare for justification."[26] The following analysis will consider how these elements fit together.

B. Regeneration and Pneumatic Renewal

As already indicated, Vermigli was concerned to include the cultivation of virtue in his doctrine of justification, even as he clarified its secondary role after forensic imputation. It is noteworthy that at the very beginning of his *locus*, where he unpacks the meaning of the Hebrew verb *tsadac*, he starts by explaining how God endows believers "with his own Spirit and renews them fully by restoring the strength of their minds."[27] Such sensitivity to the Spirit's renewing work is fundamental to Vermigli's doctrine, as evidenced in his description of justification as "the summit of all *piety*,"[28] a work of God which necessarily leads the regenerate into an experience of godliness.

Unlike the Catholic understanding, which ultimately grounds justification in *gratia inhaerens*, Vermigli insists that justification is properly rooted in a forensic imputation of righteousness that is *extra nos*. At the same time, his doctrine of justification also includes the Spirit's work of internal renewal. Vermigli maintained that this forensic doctrine exists in a three-fold (*tres partes*) concept of justification, a position that he elaborates in his Genesis[29] and 1 Corinthians[30] commentaries' *loci* on justification.[31]

21. Ibid.
22. Ibid., 1249–50 [157].
23. Ibid., 1216–17 [123–24].
24. Ibid., 1251–52 [159].
25. Ibid., 1252–53 [159–60].
26. Ibid., 1252 [159].
27. Ibid., 1182 [87].

28. Emphasis added. Ibid., 1191 [96]. *Columen totius pietatis*: Calvin uses similar language to describe justification: "*quae pietatis est totius summa*" in Calvin, *Institutes* 3:15:7. Barth and Niesel, eds. *Johannis Calvini Opera Selecta*, 4:245.

29. Speaking of justification, Vermigli writes that it is "iustitia nobis collata à Deo, tres habet partes." Vermigli, *In primum librum Mosis*, 59.

30. "Sed Iustitia Dei, quando nobis ab eo confertur, tripartita est." Vermigli, 15. For an English translation, see Vermigli, *PMR*, 135.

31. Vermigli's *triplex iustificatio* differs from that of Martin Bucer, which consists,

The constituent elements of this conception—(forensic) justification, regeneration, and sanctification—could be distinguished, but never separated.³²

While Peter Martyr does not reiterate the same three-fold scheme in his Romans *locus*, he does so in his commentary on Romans, in which he reflects on the doctrine of justification. His summary there of the three aspects of righteousness mirror his Genesis and 1 Corinthians *loci* on justification in which righteousness not only consists in the forgiveness of sins; it also includes the presence of the Holy Spirit which renews the mind and disposition (regeneration) and produces a habit of virtue (sanctification). For example, in his commentary on Romans 1:17, he explicates,

> God declares his righteousness or goodness toward us by three things chiefly. First, he receives us into favor, forgiving us our sins: not imputing death to us for those sins we commit, but on the contrary, imputes to us instead the obedience and holiness of Christ. Second, he kindles in our heart a desire to live uprightly, he renews our will, illuminates our reason and makes us prone to live virtuously, although before we abhorred that which was just and honest. Third, he gives us pure and chaste conduct, good actions and a sincere life.³³

Martyr also unfolds Romans 3:21 according to this three-fold structure.

> The righteousness of God, as I have declared in other places, is threefold: the first is that we are received into favor through Christ, and our sins forgiven and the righteousness of Christ is

---

firstly, of divine election, secondly, of the remission of sins mediated by the Spirit and accessed by faith alone, and, third, by monergistic works in Christ which God enables one to perform. Bucer, *Metaphrasis et Enarratio*, 119.

32. Prior to his Romans *locus*, Vermigli employed the language of "impartation" with regard to the transference of forensic and actual righteousness. For instance, his 1 Corinthians *locus* says that God justifies us "by compassionately imparting (*impartiendo*) his mercy and promises." "Primum sane constituatur, deum esse qui nos iustificat, suam misericordiam et promissiones clementer impartiendo." Vermigli, *Ad Corinthios Epistolam Commentarii*, 18. For an English translation, see Vermigli, *PMR*, 143. By the time of Martyr lectures on Romans, however, he discontinues the language of "impartation." James suggests that Vermigli's work in England, which sought to achieve greater continuity with the Continent, likely motivated this revision. James, "De Iustificatione," 301.

33. "Declarat autem Deus hanc suam iustitiam, sive bonitatem erga nos tribus potissimum rebus. Primum nos recipit in gratiam, condonat peccata, non imputat ea, quae nos [note] admittimus, ad mortem: sed e diverso potius imputat Christi obedientiam & sanctitatem. Secundo accendit in animis nostris studium recte vivendi, instaurat voluntatem, illustrat rationem, nosque totos propensos facit ad recte vivendum, quum antea a iusto honestoque abhorreremus. Tertio loco donat puros & castos mores, probas actiones, & synceram vitam." Vermigli, *Romanos*, 50.

imputed to us. The second righteousness follows this, namely that through the help of the Holy Spirit, our mind is reformed and we are inwardly renewed by grace. Third, holy and godly works follow.[34]

In this scheme, Martyr places regeneration and sanctification side by side in the name of justification as gifts that come from the Holy Spirit to the elect, while clearly and emphatically reserving the place of priority for imputation.[35] As far as we can tell, this attentiveness to the Spirit's work of renewal had been part of Martyr's theological framework for nearly a decade by the time he lectured on Romans at Oxford in 1551 and 1552. Reaching back to his first published work, his exposition on the Apostles' Creed (1544),[36] he similarly emphasized the indwelling of the Spirit in generating the outward evidence of righteousness by which one is in some sense judged and rewarded on the last day: "From this [divine inheritance]" he teaches, "we learn that our salvation does not depend on us, but on that divine election by which grace, the Spirit and faith dwell within us."[37] Indeed, Martyr goes so far as to assert that,

> This is the very essence [*tutto il negozio*] of Christianity: to be ever renewed within, and do good to those around us as much as possible. The risen Christ did not cease to bring blessing to others, but poured out upon his own the most precious gift of the Spirit.[38]

While such an emphasis upon the internal renewal of the Spirit would have been rather natural for Vermigli in the year or two following his departure from Italy, owing to his rigorous training in Catholicism, it is remarkable to observe how this emphasis continued into the latter stages of his life, when he was a Protestant leader. For instance, his 1 Corinthians *locus*—which was

---

34. "Iustitia Dei, ut alias docui, triplex est. Prima, qua per Christum in gratiam recipimur, & condonantur peccata, & Christi iustitia nobis imputatur. Ad hanc altera consequitur, ut vi Spiritus sancti reformetur animus noster, totique intus per gratiam instauremur. Tertio consequuntur sanctae & piae exercitationes. nam, qui huc pervenerunt, magno studio flagrant bene operandi." Ibid., 179.

35. So, for instance, after unpacking the *tres partes* of righteousness from Romans 1:17, Martyr writes: "Sed primum horum trium, & capitale, & summum est, quod alia complectitur, & dicitur esse Dei iustitia, quae in nos ab illo provenit. Non enim viribus humanis eam acquirimus." Ibid., 50.

36. Martyr's work, *Una Semplice Dichiaratione sopra gli XII Articola della Fede Christiana*, surveys Christian doctrine from the viewpoint of the Protestantism that he had recently embraced.

37. Vermigli, *Early Writings*, trans. and ed. Di Gangi and McLelland, 53.

38. Ibid., 49.

published in 1551 but had been taught by Vermigli shortly after his 1548 appointment in Oxford—demonstrated Martyr's concern to include good works in his doctrine of justification.

> A different kind of justification follows this upright life of holiness by which we are clearly praised, approved or declared just. For although good works do not bring that first righteousness which is given freely, yet they point to it and show it is present. . . . And on this same basis we will be justified by Christ in the last judgment by the remembrance of good works, that is, we will be declared just, on the testimony of mercy shown to our neighbors.[39]

Martyr explains that such good works are buttressed by the imputation of Christ's righteousness, which restores what is lacking in our "weak and mutilated" works,[40] thus comforting the human soul and assuaging our existential pangs of guilt. In this way, one's upright life of holiness functions as the basis of future justification. Such holiness, in effect, is the vindication of one's justification.

While Vermigli maintains this three-fold understanding of justification in his Romans commentary, he does not, as we have noted, present the same formulation in his Romans *locus* on justification.[41] Here, he no longer places regeneration and sanctification under the rubric of justification. In a strict sense "justification" is limited to a forensic activity; yet, at the same time, Vermigli understands regeneration and sanctification to necessarily accompany forensic imputation. Interpreting the Romans *locus* on justification in the larger context of the *Romans* commentary reveals the two distinct levels of justification alluded to above. James helpfully summarizes:

> In sum, Vermigli embraces both a narrower and stricter forensic understanding of justification, as well as a broader moral understanding, which stresses the necessary relationship between

---

39. "Ad hanc rectam vitam sanctorum, consequitur quaedam alia species Iustificationis, qua scilicet laudamur, approbamur, & iusti praedicamur. Nam bona opera licet illam primam iustitiam quae gratis conceditur non afferant, attamen indicant, & illam adesse demonstrant . . . Et hac eadem ratione à Christo in extremo iudicio commemoratione bonorum operum iustificabimur, id est iusti declarabimur, ex testimonio misericordiae proximis exhibitae." Vermigli, *Ad Corinthios Epistolam Commentarii*, 19. For an English translation, see Vermigli, *PMR*, 147. Cf. Vermigli, *Romanos*, 1182 [88].

40. Vermigli, *PMR*, 147.

41. James suggests the reason why Vermigli uses the *tres partes* concept of justification in his commentary and not in his *locus* is probably based on later reflection in Zürich, when he made final revisions before publication in 1558. James, "De Iustificatione," 330.

forensic justification and its accompanying benefits of regeneration and sanctification. Forensic justification, which is based on the imputed righteousness of Christ alone, is necessarily accompanied by the regenerative work of the Holy Spirit, which produces a moral transformation in the sinner, which in turn inevitably produces sanctification and good works.[42]

Because Vermigli is particularly concerned with how justification leads to the development of tangible faith,[43] he posits "two inward movements" of the Holy Spirit in which God exerts influence upon one's mind and volition.[44] From this double movement, faith is "engendered."[45] Vermigli also conveys this idea—that God forgives those whom he has already enlivened—in his exposition of Romans 8:1–2, stating that "after the spirit will have first moved the hearts of those listening, so that they believe, then at last the Gospel obtains/shows its power to save (for saving)."[46] For this reason, Martyr describes the Holy Spirit as the "cause" of faith.[47] Following naturally from his deeply held Augustinian conviction that humanity is a *massa perditionis*,[48] Vermigli asserts that "Unless [one's heart] has been renewed by the Spirit," there can be no justifying faith.[49] The Spirit enlivens, which produces faith,[50] resulting in justification. Vermigli envisages such faith as growing out of the Spirit's initial work, resulting in a union with Christ.[51] He writes, "But now, delivered by the grace of God, we are joined with Christ by the Spirit, to Christ himself being raised from the dead. By this union we may bring forth fruit to God, and no more death and

---

42. James, "Romans Commentary: Justification and Sanctification," 314.

43. Ibid., 1182 [87], 1215–16 [122].

44. Ibid., 1249–50 [156–57]: "In iustificatione duos esse interiores motus: quorum alter ad rationem pertineat, quae, uti diximus, non tantum docenda sit, sed etiam persuadenda, traducendaque in sententiam spiritus sancti. Alteri autem ad voluntatem, ut illa flectatur ad ea omnia suscipienda que spiritus sanctus promittit et offert. Ea est fides, qua iustificamur, et per quam peccata nobis nostra condonantur."

45. Ibid., 1284 [191].

46. "At postquam spiritus corda audientium semel permoverit, ut credant, tum demum Evangelium vim suam ad servandum obtinet." Vermigli, *Romanos*, 609.

47. Ibid., 1284 [191]: "quoniam causa est fidei."

48. Ibid., 1196 [102].

49. Ibid., 1249 [157]: "Sed animus humanus nisi innovetur spiritu."

50. Martyr employs various phrases to describe this enlivening work: "God renews the heart of man," "the illumination of the Holy Spirit," "inspiration," and the activity of being "called and stirred by grace." Ibid.

51. Vermigli's understanding resembles that of Calvin. Calvin, *Institutes*, 3.16.1.

damnation."⁵² Vermigli does not develop the concept of union with Christ in explicit terms outside of this reference.

The necessity of the Spirit's enlivening work in Vermigli's doctrine can scarcely be overstated: "Those who are justified receive the Holy Spirit, for without him it is quite impossible to be justified."⁵³ After the Spirit produces faith, it is this faith that constitutes the direct link to justification. So Martyr asserts, "as soon as one believes, he is immediately justified."⁵⁴ In making this connection, Vermigli is not positing faith as the formal cause of justification; he is, rather, concerned to show the logical progression in which the enlivening work of the Spirit leads to faith that leads to justification and sanctification. In this sequence, faith functions as the *causa instrumentum* by which God's people apprehend forgiveness and new life,⁵⁵ a faith that is generated by the Holy Spirit.⁵⁶

In addition to producing faith, the work of the Holy Spirit also stimulates sanctification.⁵⁷ Accordingly, Vermigli applies the term "righteousness" in two distinct ways. When addressing the strict sense of justification, the word describes the forensic accrediting which results in one being regarded as righteous. This sense is the burden of Vermigli's Romans *locus*. At the same time, he also uses the word to describe the cultivation of righteousness in the believer's soul,⁵⁸ beginning with conversion and leading to "good and holy works," that is, sanctification.⁵⁹ Unlike the forensic declaration of righteousness, this tangible manifestation of righteousness is *not* accessed by faith alone, but rather through spiritual discipline.⁶⁰ Thus, Martyr draws

---

52. Vermigli, *Romanos*, 1196–97 [102]: "Sed iam nunc liberati Dei gratia, Christo per spiritum copulamur, Christo, inquam, excitato a mortuis, ex qua coniunctione iam Deo fructificabimus non amplius morti et damnationi."

53. Ibid., 1201 [107]: "Qui iustificantur, spiritum sanctum accipiunt, nam iustificari absque illo prorsus est impossibile."

54. Ibid., 1305 [210]: "Quam primum inquit homo credit, confestim, inquit iustificatus est." See also 1233 [139–40].

55. Vermigli, *Romanos*, 1260–61 [168]; 1290 [197]; 1320 [226].

56. Ibid., 1282 [190]: "Praeterea rixatur etiam de productione fidei, quaeritque, unde ea in nobis generetur. Nos uno verbo facilè respondemus a Spiritu sancto."

57. Ibid., 1272–73 [180–81].

58. Ibid., 1182 [87].

59. Ibid., 1305–6 [211]: "Postquam autem semel sumus iustificarti, non satis est ad obtinendam salutem dicere, Credo: Accedat etiam oportet sancta vita, et bona opera."

60. Ibid., 1318 [224]: "[W]e grant that Christ requires more of us than faith, for who doubts that he wants those who are justified to live uprightly and to practice virtue of all kinds."

a connection between the regenerating work of the Spirit and sanctification: "there is no fruit of sanctification except what follows regeneration."[61]

As we will discover in due course, comparison with Newman is interesting here. While Newman emphatically repudiates the Catholic notion of *habitus* (in favor of divine indwelling), Vermigli is quite comfortable with the idea of the progressive development of holiness, that is, a "habit" of righteousness in the context of sanctification. Precisely because regenerate ones are having their minds and wills renovated by the renewing work of the Holy Spirit, they "cooperate with the power of God."[62] Such co-operation grows in time and actually becomes a form of *iustitia inhaerente* that leads to further acts of piety.[63] This, in Vermigli's words, is the "inward righteousness which is rooted in us, which we obtain and confirm by leading a continually upright life."[64]

The other element of Vermigli's doctrine that might be mentioned with reference to the work of the Holy Spirit is the role of heavenly rewards for the one whose life produces good works—providing that such works are not understood as a debt owed.[65] In his commentary on 1 Corinthians, Vermigli underscores that one's good works, emerging from one's habit of righteousness, are accepted by God:

> In the third place [in the *tres partes* concept of justification], from the habit of good works a certain righteousness adheres [*inhaerens*] to our souls, whereby we can also be called righteous in our human conduct. Neither the things we do nor the righteousness thus acquired are rejected by God, since they come from a soul which is already regenerate.[66]

Such moral achievement results in rewards, which come to the faithful as a divine gift. According to Vermigli, "we will grant that God sets forth prizes and rewards whereby we are moved to live holy lives."[67] He is careful to indicate that this accomplishment leaves no room whatsoever for

---

61. Ibid., 1196 [102]: "Fructus autem sanctifatio nisi ibi est nullus, verum ipsam regenerationem sequitur."

62. Ibid., 1250 [158]: "et gratia, atque spiritu instauratus cum divina virtute una cooperatur."

63. Vermigli quotes Augustine with approval regarding "the righteousness that adheres in us" (Augustinum sensisse de iustitia inhaerente). Ibid., 1320 [226].

64. Ibid., 1299 [205]: "sed de illa intrinseca nobis inhaerente, quam recte vivendo perpetuo acquirimus, et confirmamus."

65. Ibid., 1194 [100].

66. Vermigli, *Ad Corinthios Epistolam Commentarii*, 136.

67. Ibid., *Romanos*, 1288 [195].

boasting.[68] Nevertheless, good works are expected to characterize one who has been justified, precisely because of the Spirit's activity of regeneration.[69] While Martyr states at the outset of his Romans *locus* that it is not his purpose to develop the subject of works that follow justification,[70] he asserts that "such works are profitable to the regenerate, for by living uprightly and orderly they are renewed and made perfect."[71] Quoting Augustine, Martyr states that in this way (by producing virtuous works) justified ones fulfill the law by the grace of the gospel.[72] Thus, in good Augustinian fashion, Vermigli safeguards the comprehensive nature of divine grace, while simultaneously promoting the cultivation of virtue. Both are made possible by a union with God "by the Spirit."[73] A summary statement of this relationship is found in the following:

> Since no one has fulfilled or can fulfill it [the command to love God with heart, soul, and strength], it follows that we should fly to Christ through whom we may be justified by faith. After being justified, we may in some way begin to do what is commanded, albeit imperfectly.[74]

The first part of this equation—flying to Christ to be justified by faith—is the subject to which will now turn our attention.

C. The Forensic Framework of Justification

Forensic justification is crucial to Vermigli's doctrine. In the very first paragraph of his Romans *locus* (before his Hebrew lexicography and discussion on the role of the Holy Spirit), he raises a question that indicates the

---

68. Ibid., 1289 [195]: After arguing thus, he concludes, "Therefore, we must take away all merit, not only in those who are not yet justified, but also in those who have been justified."

69. One way to see this emphasis on renewal and works in Vermigli is in his treatment of James 2:17–18. There are three such places in his Romans *locus*. In these comments he asserts that faith works (1187 [93]), it is accepted by God (1239-40 [146]), and by works one comes to a fuller knowledge of God (1311 [217]).

70. Ibid., 1189-90 [995].

71. Ibid., 1290 [196].

72. Ibid., 1239 [146]. Martyr quotes Augustine's work, *Against Julian*, book four, chap. three.

73. Ibid., 1196-97 [102].

74. Ibid., 1233 [139]: "quod quia nunquam quisquam aut praestiterit, aut praestare potest, nihil superest, nisi ut confugiamus ad Christum a quo per fidem iustificemur, deinde iustificari, id quod praecipitur, incipiamus ut cunque efficere."

trajectory of what will follow. "Are men justified by works or by faith?"[75] The binary nature of this question, as we shall see, is significant for the conclusion that Martyr will eventually reach.

> Since there are two meanings of "to justify," namely, in fact or in judgment or estimation, and since the same God is author of both, which of the two should we follow in the proposed discussion? The latter, in fact, because the renewal imputed by the Spirit of God and our righteousness, that is, the way of life acquired by good works, are still imperfect and incomplete.... Besides that, when debating the matter, Paul was influenced by the testimony of the history of Abraham in Genesis and by the authority of David; he used the verb "to be reckoned," and, with proper understanding, reasons in light of our present concern and question.[76]

Vermigli thus concludes the prolegomena of his *locus* by choosing imputation over spiritual renewal as the primary and fundamental ground of justification. In addition to providing readers with a synopsis of his position, the above also reveals the fundamental presupposition that undergirds his doctrine of justification: the sinfulness of humanity.[77] For instance, as an example of how the problem of sin impacts humanity, Martyr points to the transgression of Adam in Romans 5 where one observes "the cause of so great an evil."[78] Following from the first man's disobedience, humanity, including infants, is "lost and condemned."[79] Later in his *locus*, Vermigli asserts this point rather explicitly, "The works of unregenerate men are sins."[80] In other words, the unregenerate are incapable of producing works that are acceptable to God. Therefore, the basis of justification cannot possibly rest on human effort. Such logic is particularly clear where Martyr comments on Romans 10:3.

> Being ignorant of the righteousness that comes from God, and seeking to establish their own righteousness, they did not submit to the righteousness of God." These words mean nothing

75. Ibid., 1181 [87]: "Iustificentur ne homines operibus, ab fide."

76. Ibid., 1182 [88].

77. Ibid., 1196 [102]: "Omnes nascentes massa perditionis complectitur, a qua labe homines operibus suis emergere posse, et vendicare sibi iustificationem iuxta sacras literas fieri non potest."

78. Ibid., 1196 [101]: "Accedit adhaec, quòd tanti mali causa exprimitur."

79. Ibid., 1196 [102]: "iam inde à prima ipsa origine per primum hominem perditi sumus & damnati."

80. Ibid., 1301 [201]: "... opera hominum non renatorum esse peccata."

else but that those who attribute too much to their own righteousness, namely to works, depart from God's righteousness. So great is the contrast between grace and works that the effect that proceeds from the one cannot proceed from the other.[81]

The above line of reasoning, with its binary contrast between grace and works, is predicated on Vermigli's anthropology, a view that James has labeled "intensive Augustinianism."[82] According to James, "It is [Martyr's] profound conviction that the Adamic fall rendered all of humanity legally guilty before the divine judge and morally corrupt in their souls, thus bringing alienation and condemnation from God."[83] This conviction, perhaps more than any other, appears to be the driving force behind Vermigli's vehement opposition to what he perceives as the "Pelagianism" of his interlocutors.[84]

A clear focus on the problem of human guilt inherited from Adam, in turn, eventually leads Vermigli to affirm the concept of imputation (*imputatio*), which he understands as a judicial transference of righteousness to the sinner.[85] Simply put, God "confers" the righteousness of Christ upon a man so that he is considered or reckoned to be righteous *coram deo*.[86] Vermigli stresses that this only happens by divine initiative. Commenting on Romans 4:1–4, Martyr explains how "imputation" is entirely of grace, effectively undermining what he regards as the notion of merit. Paul postulates imputation, he argues, "as an antithesis to merit or debt, so that he to whom something is imputed neither deserves it nor receives it as debt."[87] Furthermore, this imputation is two-fold in the sense that the sinner receives the attribution of Christ's righteousness and also the non-imputation of his own sins.[88] Martyr recognizes such imputation as essential to a biblical understanding of justification.

---

81. Ibid., 1199 [105].

82. James, "The Complex of Justification," 52–53.

83. Ibid.

84. Vermigli, *Romanos*, 1248–49 [156]; Pighius, 1282–83 [190]; Smith, 1323 [229].

85. Ibid., 1182 [87]: "Interdum vero iustificat Deus absolvendo a peccatis, adscribendo et imputando iustitiam."

86. Ibid., 1201 [107]; 1314 [220].

87. Ibid., 1194 [100]: "nos ex operibus non iustificari. Quoque id magis persuaderet, verbum id logizein, quod dicimus imputare, adscribere alicui iustitiam, aut pro iusto aliquem habere urget, et vult habere antithesim ad meritum et debitum, ita ut is cui quippiam imputatur, id non mereatur, neque ut debitum accipiat."

88. Martyr makes this point by quoting Romans 4:5 and Genesis 15:6, asserting that God simultaneously forgives sins and credits those who believe with righteousness. Ibid., 1252 [159].

For Vermigli, imputation is *extra nos* in that it addresses one's legal status, and not a form of *iustitia in nobis*, which affects the soul. Contrary to medieval Catholic theology, Martyr asserts that justifying righteousness, "does not adhere [*inhaere*] to our souls, but is imputed by God."[89] Moreover, Martyr also articulates a reverse imputation in which the sinner's guilt is put upon Christ. Writing about the suffering servant of Isaiah 53, Martyr elucidates this point. "[Christ] also in a sense justifies those that he takes on himself and bears their iniquities."[90]

In his analysis of the diachronic development of Vermigli's doctrine of justification, James points out that, in his Romans *locus*, Vermigli specifically employs the term *forense* for the first time (even though the concept had appeared in previous *loci*).[91] James suggests that such terminology was probably invoked to draw more explicit continuity with the teaching of the continental Reformers.[92] This conceptual development is related to an even more novel feature of Martyr's work on Romans—his postulation of an inaugurated eschatology. Vermigli describes the virtuous works of the regenerate as demonstrating their "participation in eternal life"[93] and justification as "eternal life already begun in us *now*."[94] Accordingly, one's identification with Christ—resulting in two-fold imputation (Christ takes the sinner's guilt and offers his perfect righteousness) and the empowering presence of the Spirit—indicates that justification has been brought forward to the present.

Our final consideration of forensic imputation, before examining Martyr's view of faith, concerns two particular *results* of such justification for the sinner, starting with the guarantee of absolution.[95] This grace falls into the inaugurated eschatology schema mentioned above, in which a believer is fully and decisively forgiven by the non-imputation of his guilt and the imputation of Christ's righteousness.[96] In one sense, forgiveness has "already" occurred, but the delayed "not yet" dimension can be seen in the

---

89. Ibid., 1194 [100]: "Quibus ex verbis non solum ellicimus iustitiam, qua dicimut iustificari, non inhaere animis nostris, sed imputari a Deo."

90. Ibid., 1264 [172]: "atque ita, ut ipse in se suscipiat, et portet illorum scelera."

91. James, "De Iustificatione," 297. Vermigli, *Romanos*, 1182 [87]: "verba est forense, quod ad iudicia spectat."

92. Vermigli, *Romanos*, 1182 [87].

93. Ibid., 1290 [196]: "participatio aeternae vitae."

94. Emphasis added. Ibid., 1263 [171]: "Et re vera nihil aliud est Iustificatio, quàm aeterna vita iam nunc in nobis inchoate."

95. Ibid., 1182 [87]: "Deus absolvendo à peccatis."

96. Ibid., 1212 [119].

need for the justified to appeal to God for the forgiveness of ongoing sins while also pursuing a greater apprehension of love.[97]

Along with God's forgiveness, Martyr also sees forensic justification resulting in *Dei favor*.[98] Combining the previous consequence with this one, he writes: "Moreover, as to the remission of sins, a blessing promised to us, we should remember that the chief and principal point consists in this, that we are received into favor by God and our sins forgiven us."[99] He elucidates this notion in his explanation of God's providential choice of Jacob over Esau, in which God had mercy on the former over the latter. "The forgiveness of sins, in as much as men are received back into favor," Vermigli explains, "does not depend on their works, but on the pure and favorable good-will of God."[100] With such favor, a positive relationship is established between the defendant and the judge, resulting in the former's acceptance. This forgiveness is a singular event, already realized by the justified, and, at the same time, it is gradually apprehended in one's moral life. James helpfully explains:

> To [Vermigli's] mind, "forgiveness" is more than a simple, single, judicial act. Forensic justification is like a pebble dropped in a pond; it creates ripples throughout the lifetime of a sinner. Certainly, it does address decisively the legal matter of guilt derived from Adam. However, even after the judicial acquittal, there remains a moral need for the justified sinner continually to seek forgiveness for subsequent sins. . . . It is this ongoing need for forgiveness, even after justification has been pronounced, that requires a necessary relationship with sanctification.[101]

D. Faith Alone

Vermigli views faith as the means of justification.[102] After asserting that justification is "not by works" in his first proposition, he endeavors to convince readers that it is properly "received by faith." This second proposition

---

97. Ibid., 1207 [113].

98. Ibid., 1217 [123].

99. Ibid., 1274 [182]: "Quod autem attinet ad remissionem peccatorum, quum nobis promissa sit benedictio, cogitare debemus, caput, & principium eius esse, ut recipiamur à Deo in gratiam, utque nobis peccata condonentur."

100. Ibid., 1199 [105]: "condonationem peccatorum, utque homines in gratiam recipiantur, non pendere ab illorum operibus, sed a mera propitiaque Dei benevolentia."

101. James, "Complex of Justification," 51.

102. Vermigli, *Romanos*, 1253 [160].

is supported by an arsenal of biblical texts, especially from the letter to the Romans, where Martyr begins.[103] For much of his argument, Martyr has the work of Albert Pighius in his crosshairs.[104] It is in this section that Vermigli's rhetoric reaches new heights (or depths) of aggression, often *ad hominem* (i.e., "[Pighius] deserves to be laughed at").[105] One begins to discern in such comments a connection between the intensity of Martyr's acrimony and his adjudication of Pighius as a Pelagian.[106] Less frequently, he engages the ideas of his predecessor at Oxford, Richard Smith.[107]

Over against meritorious works, faith is recognized by Vermigli to function as the active *instrumentum* by which one is declared righteous.[108] Vermigli describes faith as that which actively "takes hold and receives" the promise of forgiveness.[109] And he sharply distinguishes this "most sure and certain" faith from a "dead faith," "historical faith," "human faith," "temporary faith," and "naked" faith.[110] It is "never alone but always draws along with it various motions of the mind," particularly "confidence, hope, and similar affections."[111] The absence of these qualities in a person calls into question whether he truly possesses justifying faith.[112]

---

103. Particular attention is given to Romans 4, with Martyr pressing Paul's statement, "To one who does not work but trusts him who justifies the ungodly, faith is reckoned to him as righteousness." Ibid., 1254–55 [161–62]. After surveying Romans up through chapter eleven, Vermigli proceeds to look at 1 and 2 Corinthians. He examines Galatians in some depth, and then looks at Ephesians, Philippians, Hebrews, 1 Peter, 1 John, the Gospels, Acts, and the Old Testament. Ibid., 1258–64 [165–72].

104. See especially his "Contra Pighius" section. Ibid., 1264–72 [172–80] and "Pighius Redux." Ibid., 1273–98 [181–204]. A helpful summary of Pighius's doctrine of original sin is found in Feiner's PhD thesis, entitled, "Die Erbsündenlehre Albert Pigges." Although Pighius disavows Pelagianism, in the final analysis his position bears a striking resemblance to it. The human will, according to Pighius, is weakened on account of sin, but not to the extent that it prevents one from choosing God. According to Feiner, this is the essential weakness of Pighius's position—while claiming to uphold original sin, he in fact locates the cause of human guilt in an individual's willful transgression. Feiner, 63, 66, 70, 74, 83.

105. Ibid., 1286 [193].

106. Ibid., 1287 [194]; 1289–90 [196]; 1292 [198]. In this last example, Martyr writes, "Here indeed I cannot restrain myself, but must say that Pighius lies badly."

107. Martyr's "Smith Redux" section is significantly smaller. Ibid., 1298–99 [204–5].

108. Ibid., 1261 [169] 1283 [190], 1292 [198], 1321 [227].

109. Ibid., 1262 [170]: "apprehendimus promissiones Dei."

110. Ibid., 1183 [89], 1187 [93], 1285–86 [192], 1271 [179], 1188 [93], 1266 [174].

111. Ibid., 1183 [89]: "id est, ut nunquam sit nuda, sed trahat secum semper multos ac varios animi motus."

112. Ibid., 1183 [89].

Vermigli affirms that faith is "a firm and certain assent (*assensus*) of the mind to the words of God, inspired by the Holy Spirit, leading to the salvation of believers."[113] This emphasis on assent is consistent with Martyr's previous *loci*.[114] In his Romans *locus*, however, Vermigli introduces for the first time the notion of *fiducia* (trust).[115] Precisely because it is the Holy Spirit who inspires faith, creating "a new heart and mind,"[116] it naturally includes, for Vermigli, a volitional impulse. "In this way," he reasons, "we say that the faith which is effective differs very much from historical assent, and that we are justified by the [enlivened] faith we have just described."[117] In saying this, Martyr has not jettisoned *assensus* as a constituent element of justifying faith;[118] he has simply broadened his definition to more thoroughly account for the activation of the human will.

The third and final proposition of Vermigli's *locus* concerns the necessity of *sola fide*, a doctrine that he staunchly defends.[119]

> This saying [*sola fide*] is proved by all those places of Scripture which teach that we are justified freely, as well as those that affirm that justification comes without works and also those that draw an antithesis between grace and works. I say that all these places truly prove that we are justified by faith only, even if this word "only" is not read in the Scriptures; but that is not of much weight, since its signification is derived from them by necessity.[120]

Martyr begins his argument for *sola fide* by expressing his disagreement with Richard Smith, whom he sarcastically describes as "the very light of divinity" (rarely does Vermigli miss an opportunity to take a swipe at Smith).[121] Like an airplane embarking on its final descent from the grand height of ten-thousand feet, Vermigli's treatise rushes to a conclusion in the third proposition. While the first proposition of his *locus* occupies

---

113. Ibid., 1184 [90]: "Est itaque firmus certusque animi assensus verbis Dei a spiritu divino afflatus ad salutem credentium."

114. James, "*De Iustificatione*," 307.

115. Vermigli, *Romanos*, 1183 [89]: "Iure igitur a professoribus purioribus Evangelij statuitur, credere, cum actione, seu motu fiduciae, spei, et similibus affectibus maximam habere coniunctionem: sed potissimum cum syncera firmaque fiducia."

116. Ibid., 1286 [193].

117. Ibid., 1286 [193].

118. Ibid., 1188 [94].

119. Ibid., 1312 [218].

120. Ibid.

121. Ibid.

seventy-two folio pages and proposition two has fifty-eight, the third troubled the typesetter for merely thirteen pages. Moving expeditiously through this final argument, Martyr cites an array of biblical texts and church fathers to support his position.

Vermigli's commitment to *sola fide* is born out of his belief that one's good works have no role whatsoever in causing justification.[122] In a rather distilled statement, he articulates the essence of this conviction.

> And when we say that one is justified by faith alone we obviously say nothing else than that one is justified only by the mercy of God and by the merit of Christ, which we cannot grasp by any other instrument than faith alone.[123]

Emphatic as he is, Martyr is quick to counterbalance such statements concerning the gratuitous nature of justification with his conviction that *sola fide* must never be at the expense of sanctification. Thus, faith functions as the instrument, but it must never be seen as the totality of what is expected of a person. Vermigli offers an analogy to underscore this point. "The eye cannot be without a head, brains, heart, liver, and other parts of the body, and yet the eye alone apprehends color and light."[124] All of the above members are essential for life, just as virtue is required for the completion of justification, for "Christ requires more of us than faith, for who doubts that he wants those who are justified to live uprightly and to practice virtue of all kinds."[125] Indeed, Vermigli questions whether one can actually realize eternal salvation without such (a living) virtue.[126]

In this closing segment, Vermigli offers a final word on two important concepts which have appeared throughout his *locus* and which have bearing on his understanding of *sola fide*: opposition to the claim that general grace

---

122. Ibid.

123. Ibid., 1321 [227]: "Cumque dicimus, hominem iustificari sola fide, nihil sane aliud dicimus, quam hominem iustificari sola Dei misericordia, et solius Christi merito: quae non alio instrumento apprehendere possumus, quam sola fide."

124. Ibid., 1312 [218]: "Ita oculus non potest esse sine capite, cerebro, corde, epate, & aliis partibus corporis: & tamen colorem, & lucem solus oculus apprehendit." Martyr offers a similar analogy a few pages later: "Surely the meat that we eat is distributed to all the members and into the whole body, and yet it is received with the mouth only and not with the whole body." Ibid., 1322 [228].

125. Ibid., 1318 [224]: "Quod ad primum attinet, fatemur, Christum plus a nobis requirere, quam fidem. Quis enim dubitet, eum velle homines iustificatos recte vivere, seseque per omnnia virtutum genera exercere."

126. Ibid., 1318 [224]: "alioquin ad aeternam salutem non perventuros?" Martyr follows this directly with the qualifier that such virtue is the "fruit" of faith and not its cause "Atqui fructus isti sunt fidei, & iustificationis effecta, non causae."

is accessible to all and support of the perseverance of the saints. In regard to the first of these, when Martyr accuses his opponents of maintaining a doctrine of congruent merit, he determines their position to be a form of Pelagianism that is foreign to the teaching of Scripture.[127] He outlines the Catholic teaching on merit in terms of the traditional categories of *de congruo* (that which precedes conversion on the basis of natural ability) and *de condigno* (merit that fully deserves a reward subsequent to conversion).[128] Martyr holds congruent merit in contempt, asserting that "They are worse than foolish who would say that we were converted prior to the aid of God. He first loved us before we began to love him."[129] He regards condign merit equally unsustainable from Scripture and, therefore, he discards the entire system as "directly repugnant to the word of God." [130] In his view, if redemptive grace is obtainable prior to regeneration and appropriated by the sinner through good works, even if such works are enabled by God, the justification that follows would ultimately be based upon human effort.[131] In his words: "They hold that there is a kind of general grace accessible to all and common even to the unregenerate, who are in a sense helped to merit justification and do works which please God. But in saying this, they fall into the heresy of Pelagius."[132]

It should be noted that Martyr does in fact recognize a distinction between "prevenient" grace and "subsequent" grace (*gratia subsequentem*). Simply put, the former is identified with the initial work of the Spirit that enlivens sinners, and the latter consists in sanctification. He asserts that prevenient grace "is nothing other than the same favor of God through Christ, which moves us beforehand to rightly exercise our will, and after we are regenerated, helps and stirs us up to live rightly."[133] As an example, Vermigli responds to his opponents' argument from the book of Jonah where it

127. Ibid., 1218–19 [125].

128. Ibid. [125–26].

129. Ibid., 1217 [123–24]: "Desiperet supra modum, qui diceret nos ad nostram conversionem praevenire auxilium Dei. Ille prius nos diligit, quàm à nobis diligi incipiat."

130. Ibid., 1219 [125]: "pugnare cum verbo Dei."

131. Pressed through the framework of his intensive Augustinianism, Vermigli cannot begin to countenance the idea that meritorious works of the unregenerate are somehow pleasing to God. Ibid., 1195 [101], 1199 [105], 1214–15 [121–2], 1235–36 [142–43], 1260–61 [168], 1288 [194], 1313–14 [219–20].

132. Ibid., 1216 [123]: "Est enim, inquiunt, gratia quaedam generalis omnibus exposita, & communis etiam hominibus non regeneratis, qua utcunque adiuti, possint mereri iustificationem, & facere opera, quae placeant Deo. Sed hoc quum dicunt, incidunt in haeresim Pelagii."

133. Ibid., 1217 [123].

says, "God regarded the works of the Ninevites." Martyr explains why these works were not prevenient. "Since they believed before they did any works, they were justified by faith and not by works, which followed afterwards, and God is said to have regarded their works because they pleased him."[134] Because Martyr regarded faithful Ninevites as regenerate, their works were therefore pleasing and acceptable to God.[135] This ability to please God, according to Vermigli, is on account of the regenerate's close association with Christ, in which his "incomplete obedience" as a justified person effectively "pleases God."[136] In this way, Vermigli limits *gratia praevenientem* to the Spirit's initial enlivening work and opens the door widely to *gratia subsequentem*.

In keeping with his conviction that man's best efforts to secure divine favor through good works are in vain (i.e., justification cannot be merited), Vermigli also maintains a doctrine of perseverance, which, in a sense, affirms the inverse (i.e., the justification of one who is in Christ is secure, even when he commits a serious sin).

> In general, it may be stated that faith cannot be completely extinguished because serious sins are committed by the justified and those destined to salvation. In such cases, faith is lulled to sleep and lies hidden and does not burst forth into action unless awakened again by the Holy Spirit. In such fallen ones, the seed of God remains, although for a time it produces no fruit.[137]

Martyr seems to be saying that when the regenerate lapses into sin, even serious sin, his justification remains secure ("the seed of God remains"). He acknowledges that "true faith," *fidem veram*, sometimes "slips" or is "lulled to sleep," but is not lost.[138] "Therefore those who seek God, to be justified by him through faith, as the apostle teaches, attain what they desire; but those who would be justified by works fall away from justification."[139]

Not everyone agrees that Vermigli's doctrine of justification contains the idea of perseverance, including Donnelly.

> Martyr does not hold the doctrine of perseverance of the saints as interpreted by many later Calvinists, that once man has

---

134. Ibid., 1127 [134].
135. Ibid., 1227–28 [134].
136. Ibid., 1229 [136].
137. Ibid., 1278 [186].
138. Ibid., 1302 [208]: "amitti ... aut ita consopiri ut suum."
139. Ibid., 1288 [194]: "Quare, qui quaerunt Deum ut ab eo iustificentur ex fide, quemadmodum Apostolus docet, assequuntur id, quod optant: Illi vero, qui iustificari volunt ex operibus, exicidunt a iustificatione."

received justifying faith, he never falls from grace and justification. On the contrary, Vermigli teaches that man can fall into sin and thereby lose justification, but as often as he truly assents to God's promises he recovers justification.[140]

In making this case, Donnelly points to a statement from Martyr's Romans *locus* which seems to suggest that justification can be lost and subsequently reclaimed: "Indeed justification is not only taken hold of once, but as often as we truly and effectually assent to God's promises, for since we continually slip and fall into sins, it is necessary that our justification should be repeatedly renewed."[141] James, in his doctoral dissertation *De Iustificatione*, takes issue with this, regarding Donnelly's proof to be less than convincing in Vermigli's context and also inconsistent with what Vermigli writes elsewhere on the topic.[142]

With regard to the context of Vermigli's statement, Martyr is answering Pighius, who had argued from the narrative of Abraham that the Patriarch was not justified by faith for the remission of sins in the Christian sense (since he lived centuries before Christ).[143] Vermigli responds by quoting Paul from Galatians 3, in which the Apostle assigns Christian content to Abraham's faith.[144] Vermigli then argues that like Abraham, who reconfirmed his faith, in Genesis chapter 15 (after his 'initial justification', recorded in chapter 12), Christians must likewise reassert their belief in the promises of God. This is so, according to Martyr, because "Our minds are so weak that unless the words of God are repeated and impressed upon us, we easily resist faith."[145] Then, immediately after this sentence, comes the controversial statement concerning the need for justification to be

---

140. Donnelly, *Calvinism and Scholasticism*, 154.

141. Vermigli, *Romanos*, 1275 [182]: "Neque vero iustificatio semel tantum apprehenditur, sed quoties promissionibus divinis, vere atque efficaciter assentimur. Nam quum assidue labamur, et incidamus in peccata, opus habemus subinde repetita iustificatione." Donnelly quotes from Vermigli's *Loci Communes* (1583), 545.

142. In footnote 319 on page 349 of his thesis, *De Iustificatione*, James mentions that Donnelly's *Calvinism and Scholasticism* "cites from the 1587 edition of the *Loci Communes*." In fact, it is the 1583 version from which Donnelly quotes. This is noteworthy since James takes Donnelly to task for referencing the wrong edition and incorrect pages. Even so, Donnelly's reference to a second statement by Martyr which purportedly undermines the doctrine of perseverance is still lacking (he cites page 491 of Vermigli's 1583 *Loci*, *Calvinism and Scholasticism*, 154n 91). There were fourteen editions of Vermigli's *Loci Communes* following the first edition in 1576, thirteen in Latin and one in English. McLelland, "A Literary History of the *LOCI COMMUNES*," 488–94.

143. Vermigli, *Romanos*, 1273–75 [181–82].

144. Ibid., 1273–74 [181–82].

145. Ibid., 1275 [182].

"taken hold of" more than once, owing to our continual slips and falls into sin, necessitating that "our justification should be repeatedly renewed."[146] After analyzing this context, James concludes, "It seems clear that the issue Vermigli is addressing is the weakness of human faith not the weakness of divine justification.

> Vermigli is admitting that even in the justified person, faith needs rekindling at times. But he is not at all suggesting that a person can fall out of justification, since justification is exclusively the work of God and not man, as Vermigli understands it. For him, divine justification is not subject to the weaknesses of fallen creatures, but is determined by the faithfulness of God. This is confirmed in the paragraphs immediately following our text, where Vermigli stresses that the power of justifying faith lies not in the faith of the individual, but in the object of faith, namely, Christ.[147]

The disagreement between Donnelly and James highlights the tensions within Vermigli's doctrine of justification. Let us recall James's statement with which we concluded our previous section: "justification is like a pebble dropped in a pond" creating ripples throughout the lifetime of the sinner such that one has an "ongoing need for forgiveness, even after justification has been pronounced." To the extent that justification entails this ongoing, future-directed movement that includes sanctification, Donnelly's suggestion that Vermigli believed one could fall away from justification on account of sin is sustainable. Furthermore, Donnelly is undoubtedly right that this position of Vermigli's differs from that of latter Calvinists, as such Reformed thinkers more clearly distinguish the categories of justification and sanctification in Calvin's *duplex gratia*.[148] However, the subtlety with which Vermigli defines justification in terms of a first righteousness, which, in a strict sense, is purely forensic, followed by the broader expression of righteousness in an ongoing development of virtue, makes it difficult to define his position on perseverance with quite as much clarity and precision.

After the nuances of Vermigli's doctrine have been observed and requisite qualifications have been made, we must ultimately disagree with Donnelly, if, by his assertion that "Vermigli teaches that man can fall into sin and thereby lose justification," he means to say that one loses his righteous state *coram deo*. Because Vermigli understands the formal cause of a believer's

---

146. Ibid.
147. James, "*De Iustificatione*," 351.
148. Calvin, *Institutes*, 3.2.11, 3.24.4–11.

justified state to be the imputation of Christ's righteousness,[149] those who have genuinely believed, according to Vermigli, must also realize future justification.[150] Such faith, says Martyr, "cannot be completely extinguished,"[151] even though the experience of sin necessitates Christians to repeatedly take hold of and renew the reality of their justification. In short, since Martyr understands God's redemptive activity to be immutable and efficacious, those whom he regenerates also persevere.[152]

There is precious little in Vermigli's Romans *locus* (or any of his *loci* on justification) on the role of the sacraments in mediating justifying grace. Martyr first addresses the issue in proposition one, in which he confronts the position of his opponents with regard to the role of ceremonies.[153] The Catholic position was, according to Vermigli, inconsistent for the way it ascribes "the forgiveness of sins and the bestowing of grace to the sacraments, just as in the Old Testament they were attributed to circumcision."[154] Apparently, his opponent's position was also to regard the ceremony of circumcision as having a continuing validity in the New Testament sacraments, so that it contained the "power of justifying."[155] In no uncertain terms, Martyr opposes this notion.

> Indeed, we utterly deny that any sacraments bestow grace. They do offer grace, but it is by signification. For in sacraments and words, and in the visible signs, the promises of God made through Christ are set before us. If we take hold of those promises by faith, we obtain a greater grace than we had before. And

---

149. Martyr expresses general agreement with the causal framework of Trent in terms of the "final" cause (the glory of God), the "efficient" cause (divine mercy), and the "meritorious" cause (the death and resurrection of Christ). After addressing each of these, Vermigli explains that the point of contention is the "*causam formalem*." Unlike Trent, which defines the formal cause in terms of the righteousness with which one is counted *and made* just, Vermigli limits the strict sense of justification to the forensic reckoning of righteousness. He thus concludes this section, "Therefore, we say that justification cannot consist in that righteousness and renewal by which we are created anew by God. For it is imperfect because of our corruption, so that we are not able to stand before the judgment of Christ." Vermigli, *Romanos*, 1251-52 [159].

150. So Vermigli's quotes John 6:40 and then concludes, "Therefore, we infer this: I believe in the Son of God; therefore, I have now and shall have what he has promised." Ibid., 1293 [1990], see also 1252 [159].

151. Ibid., 1278 [186].

152. Ibid., 1253-54 [160-61], 1292-93 [198-200], 1315-16 [221-22].

153. Ibid., 1208-9 [115-16].

154. Ibid., 1212 [118-19].

155. Ibid., 1212 [119]: "vim iustificandi."

with the seal of the sacraments, we seal the gift of God that we embraced by faith.[156]

In keeping with this statement, Vermigli explicitly rejects the Catholic doctrine of baptismal regeneration.[157] To make the point, he showcases Abraham who was justified by faith before receiving the sign of circumcision. Likewise, says Martyr, believers in Christ are justified before they are baptized, "for our baptism corresponds to the circumcision of the ancients."[158] He also repudiates the sacrament of penance: "Auricular confession also, derived from the papists, is completely superstitious; therefore we utterly reject it, for they impose it as something necessary for salvation and a reason why sins should be forgiven, which they are never able to provide from the testimonies of Scripture."[159] Ceremonies have no power to justify, according to Vermigli, any more than do the virtues of love and hope.[160] "So great is the opposition between grace and works," Martyr concludes, "that Paul says, 'If of grace then it is not now of works, and if of works, then it is not of grace.'"[161]

By the time Vermigli reaches the conclusion of his *locus*, he has forcefully argued that "justification exists by faith alone." All along, it has been the main idea toward which his treatise has driven, and, at his conclusion, it is where he lands. In light of this strong emphasis, it can be difficult to understand how Vermigli's doctrine of justification holds *sola fide* together with the sanctifying work of the Holy Spirit. In other words, what is the logical relationship between these two forms of righteousness? The answer to this question comes into focus when we analyze justification's formal cause.

---

156. Ibid. Later in his *locus*, in proposition three, Martyr makes a similar point: "As to the sacraments, we have often taught how justification is to be attributed to them, for they stand in relation to justification as does the preaching of the Gospel and the promise of Christ offered to us for salvation" 1318 [224].

157. Ibid., 1251 [158].

158. Ibid., 1251 [159]. See also 1315 [221]. Martyr envisages adult believers in his analogy to Abraham. In the case of baptized infants, it was the faith of one's parents extended covenantally to their children that constituted the justification which properly preceded baptism. For an explanation of Vermigli's view of baptism in the context of his covenantal theology, see Lillback. "The Early Reformed Covenant Paradigm," 70–96. McLelland also addresses this subject in *The Visible Words of God*, 152–59.

159. Ibid., 1230 [136].

160. Ibid., 1315 [221–22].

161. Ibid., 1316 [222].

E. Justification's Formal Cause and the *Duplex Iustitia*

Unlike Newman, who dedicates an entire lecture (number two) and a full appendix to the "formal cause" of justification, Vermigli only gives the terminology passing attention. The passage in which he explicitly addresses it is in proposition one, as he counters the claims of the Council of Trent.[162] After citing the Council's position on the "final," "efficient," and "meritorious" causes of justification, he analyzes its definition of the "formal" cause. Martyr affirms the forensic character of the Catholic position, which goes so far as to count one just through the extension of forgiveness. However, Vermigli strongly disagrees with the Catholic assertion that the actual righteousness of a believer, even though it is understood to be empowered by the Holy Spirit, also constitutes a ground of justification. Such a view, he argues, contradicts the teaching of Paul, David, and Abraham, each of whom posit imputation as justification's formal cause.[163] "Therefore," Martyr concludes, "we say that justification cannot consist in that righteousness and renewal by which we are created anew by God. For it is imperfect because of our corruption, so that we are not able to stand before the judgment of Christ."[164] For Peter Martyr, the imputation of Christ's righteousness is the only formal cause.[165]

Vermigli's intensive Augustinianism, as we have already seen, underlies his conviction that justification is properly grounded in the imputation of Christ's righteousness apart from meritorious works.[166] "'Christ is of no advantage to you,'" he summarizes, "for if you have justification as the fruit of your works, then Christ's coming, death, and shedding of blood would not have been necessary.'"[167] Throughout his *locus*, Martyr repeats this essential point, repudiating the notion that good works can serve as the formal cause;[168] whether such works consist in the observance of ceremonial

---

162. Ibid., 1252 [159]. For other references to the cause(s) of justification see 1228 [135] and 1253 [160], although neither of them specifically deals with justification's formal cause.

163. Ibid. Vermigli cites Romans 4:5, Psalm 32, and Genesis 15:6.

164. Ibid.

165. Ibid., 1182 [88]; 1251-52 [159].

166. Ibid., 1182 [88].

167. Ibid., 1203 [109]: "Atque adhuc magis quod dictum est, confirmavit, Christus vobis factus est ociosus: nam si iustificationem habetis, ut fructum operum vestrorum, Christi adventus, mors, et sanguinis effusio non fuerunt necessaria."

168. Ibid., 1195-96 [101]; 1201-2 [107-8]; 1213 [120]; 1238 [144-45]; 1279-80 [186-88]; 1312-13 [218-20].

laws,[169] moral admonitions,[170] or in virtues such as love, they all inevitably fall short.[171] Simply put, Martyr understands good works to be an *effect* of justification and not a *cause*.[172]

Since a positive statement of Vermigli's doctrine of justification would essentially replicate what we have offered above with regard to his forensic framework (i.e., *imputatio, coram deo, extra nos, forense, absolutio, dei favor*), we should approach the subject from a different angle, one that also addresses the question with which we concluded the previous section: what is the relationship between the imputation of Christ's righteousness accessed by *sola fide* (the formal cause) and the sanctifying work of the Holy Spirit which creates a habit of grace (which he calls a "different kind of justification")?[173]

One way to describe the relationship of forensic imputation and the actual righteousness wrought by the Spirit is in terms of a *duplex iustitia*. Klaus Sturm, for instance, makes this proposal when he evaluates Vermigli's doctrine of justification against the background of Italian *Evangélisme*. "In the final analysis," Sturm concludes, "it seems to me that Martyr's doctrine of justification concurs with that of Contarini."[174]

There is good historical reason for evaluating Vermigli's doctrine of justification in light of the *duplex iustitia* commonly associated with Contarini. After the Colloquy of Regensburg concluded (July 29, 1541), Contarini traveled to the Italian city of Lucca to attend a summit between Emperor Charles V and Pope Paul III.[175] Arriving for its start on September 7, Contarini found lodging at Vermigli's monastery of San Frediano.[176] Simler indicates that, during these days, "Martyr and Contarini held daily discussions

---

169 Ibid., 1189-90 [95-96]; 1202-3 [108-9]; 1209-10 [115-16]; 1251 [158].

170. 1209 [116]; 1224 [131]; 1315 [221-22]. Against those who argue that one can be justified by observing the moral law, Vermigli marshals a catena of biblical texts from Paul's epistles (especially from Romans) before finally concluding, "I would like to find out from these fellows why they remove the power of justifying from the works of ceremonies and so easily attribute it to our moral works." Ibid., 1211 [118].

171 Ibid. 1188-89 [94-95].

172. Ibid., 1228 [135]: "Illi enim semper statuunt bona opera causas esse iustitiae: cum ea re vera iustitiae effecta sint, non causae."

173. Vermigli, *PMR*, 147.

174. Sturm, *Die Theologie Peter Martyr Vermiglis*, 69.

175. Gleason, *Gasparo Contarini*, 259; Anderson, *Peter Martyr, a Reformer in Exile*, 46.

176. McNair, *PMI*, 233.

about religion" which revolved around the Regensburg debate.[177] McNair has little doubt that the specific topic of discussion was the *duplex iustitia*.[178]

In his chapter entitled "The Complex of Justification: Peter Martyr Vermigli Versus Albert Pighius," James acknowledges that the *duplex iustitia* of Contarini and other members of Italian *Evangélisme* influenced the early stages of Vermigli's doctrine of justification.[179] James argues, however, that a parallel between Vermigli and Contarini and the *Spirituali* with reference to *duplex iustitia* is "overdrawn"[180] and in danger of obscuring the Protestant character of Martyr's position.[181] According to James, after traveling north of the Alps in 1542, Vermigli eventually distanced himself from the doctrine of two-fold righteousness, which he had imbibed from such people as Contarini and Valdés in Italy, in exchange for Bucer's *tres partes* conception of justification, which he encountered in Strasbourg during the subsequent five years (1542–47).[182] While much of James's argument is persuasive, we shall argue that it is unwarranted to so sharply distinguish the Protestant Vermigli from the *duplex iustitia*. It is our contention that the Neapolitan influence not only established the foundation of Martyr's doctrine; it continued to define its shape into its most mature form. Thus, even though Peter Martyr doesn't explicitly describe his position with the term *duplex iustitia*, nevertheless, two-fold righteousness continues throughout his life to be the essential substructure of his doctrine of justification.[183]

James position deviates from both Sturm[184] and Donnelly,[185] who portray Vermigli's doctrine of justification as that of a "*Reformkatholik*."[186] One reason for their assertion is the close proximity of forensic justification with regeneration and sanctification in Vermigli's three-fold schema. Indeed, Sturm goes so far as to assert that it is "difficult to determine whether Martyr's doctrine of justification would be justifiably condemned on the basis

---

177. Simler, "Oratio," in Vermigli, *Life, Letters, and Sermons*, 24–25.

178. McNair, *PMI*, 234.

179. James, "Complex of Justification," 57.

180. Ibid.

181. Ibid., 56.

182. Vermigli, *In primum librum Mosis*, 59.

183. This is the position of Sturm who recognizes fundamental compatibility between Vermigli and *duplex iustitia*, even though Vermigli doesn't formally uphold the position. Sturm, *Die Theologie Peter Martyr*, 69.

184. Sturm, *Die Theologie Peter Martyr*, 62–68.

185. Donnelly, *Calvinism and Scholasticism*, 154.

186. James, "Complex of Justification," 45, 53, 55; Cf. Sturm, *Die Theologie Peter Martyr*, 62–68.

of Trent's canons on justification."[187] But James rejects the *Reformkatholik* label, and explains convincingly why Vermigli's doctrine of justification is best understood as "thoroughly Protestant."[188] Furthermore, James is correct to emphasize the development of Vermigli's complex of justification in basic agreement with Bucer. The problem with his argument is the way he seeks to distance the Italian reformer from the doctrine of *duplex iusitia* by means of pitting Vermigli against Albert Pighius.

In Peter Martyr's view, Pighius was "the chief spokesman for the Roman Catholic theology of grace, original sin, and free will," and, therefore, as we have noted, Martyr's Romans commentary engages him by name dozens of times.[189] More to the point, Vermigli regarded Pighius as the "champion of contemporary Pelagians,"[190] as did Calvin,[191] and Pelagianism was an error that they could not allow to go unopposed. In his argument against Sturm, James is quite insistent that it is the Augustinian anthropology of Vermigli that motivates him to refute Pighius's Pelagianism.[192]

Pighius's argument against *sola fide* challenges the notion that faith is considered the sole instrumental cause.[193] He contends that "love (*caritas*), instead of faith, justifies, because love is more noble and excellent virtue."[194] Vermigli elucidates the heart of this disagreement when he writes, "Here lies the whole controversy: to which of these virtues is justification to be chiefly ascribed?"[195] In no uncertain terms Martyr identifies faith over love as the proper instrument by which justifying grace is appropriated:

> Therefore, in this matter of justification, although there are many other works of the Holy Spirit in our hearts, yet none except faith leads to justification. Thus the apostle concludes,

---

187. Sturm, *Die Theologie Peter Martyr*, 69.

188. James provides evidence to this effect such as Vermigli's ardent opposition of Trent, and that he was acknowledged as a Protestant by opponents and supporters alike. James, "Complex of Justification," 56.

189. Donnelly, *Calvinism and Scholasticism*, 39.

190. Ibid., 105; James, "Complex of Justification," xxvii.

191. Calvin, *The Bondage and Liberation of the Will*, xx.

192. James, "Complex of Justification," 55.

193. In the context of this second proposition, Vermigli reflects on the causes of justification from Romans chapter 1. The efficient cause is God's power. The final cause is our [future] salvation, the instrumental cause is faith. Vermigli, *Romanos*, 1252–53 [160].

194. Vermigli, *Romanos*, 1276 [184].

195. Ibid., 1282 [189].

"neither circumcision nor uncircumcision is of any avail, but faith working through love."[196]

At the same time, Vermigli addresses Pighius's doctrine of original sin and preparatory works, as Calvin did, opposing what he regards as Pighian "Pelagianism."[197] Summarizing the logic of Pighius's position, Vermigli explains how the Dutchman was fond of using John 1:12, "God gave them power to become sons of God," to argue that one must exercise his will in the application of this divine empowerment in order to be justified. Such human effort, in Martyr's view, amounted to works righteousness. Thus, it was Pighius's insistence on these preparatory works and his failure to subordinate *iustitia operum* (operative righteousness) to the *iustitia fidei* (righteousness of faith) that roused Vermigli's ire against him.[198]

When Claus Sturm argues for Vermigli's *Reformkatholik* orientation, he emphasizes the Italian Reformer's close theological proximity to the *Spirituali*, especially to Contarini, Seripando, and Gropper, and to the notion of *duplex iustitia* espoused by the Colloquy of Regensburg.[199] At this point, James protests, describing Sturms's association of Vermigli with the *duplex iustitia* as an "interpretive problem," precisely because Vermigli placed Pighius in the crosshairs of his justification polemic. Since James labels Pighius a "moderate,"[200] who was present at Regensburg supporting Gropper and Contarini, the logical deduction is that Vermigli must have moved away from the *duplex iustitia*. The implication seems to be that by moving away from two-fold righteousness, Vermigli became less Catholic and more Protestant.

There are four reasons to question whether Vermigli did in fact move away from a doctrine of *duplex iustitia*. First, it is reasonable to doubt whether Pighius was indeed a "moderate" Catholic of Contarini's ilk. Edward Yarnold explains that while Pighius acknowledges one's dependence upon imputed justice, it was, for him, "more a matter of vocabulary than

---

196. Ibid., 1260 [167–68].

197. Vermigli makes essentially the same case against the Council of Trent. Ibid., 1249–53 [156–60].

198. Ibid., 192, 194–95. This position follows naturally from Pighius's anthropology: that in original sin Adam's offspring embraced guilt and death, but not corruption. For this reason, Pighius argued that man has the power to choose righteousness, leading to the appropriation of actual righteousness. In view of this emphasis, Jedin speaks of Pighius's "almost Pelagian view of human moral ability." Jedin, *Studien über die schriftstellertätigkeit Albert Pigges*, 11.

199. Sturm, *Die Theologie Peter Martyr*, 67; James, "Complex of Justification," 46.

200. James, "Complex of Justification," 46, 56.

of theology."²⁰¹ Contrary to Pighius, the Catholics at Regensburg, in their second draft, asserted that the ungodly are "justified freely without any preceding merit and without works of the law."²⁰² Such a view is out of step with Pighius's position, which recognizes in human volition the ability to secure justifying grace.²⁰³ Furthermore, the Catholic Church also had reservations about Pighius's orthodoxy, especially his explanation of original sin, as evidenced in the Council of Trent's rejection of his doctrine.²⁰⁴ The Council's opposition to semi-Pelagianism rendered Pighius's formulation untenable, and the Spanish Inquisition eventually put his *De libero hominis arbitrio* on the Index of forbidden books.²⁰⁵ Pighius may have attended Regensburg, but his ideas on the efficacy of grace were at odds with moderate Catholics.²⁰⁶

Second, some of the Catholics at Regensburg were apparently extending themselves in ecumenical solidarity with Protestants beyond the point of their actual belief. An account of this is found in the work of Brian Lugioyo. In his overview of the various drafts through which Article 5 passed before reaching its final version, Lugioyo describes the Catholic edition written by Gropper, submitted on April 29, which omitted the phrase *per fidem* and emphasized the role of works as the primary ground upon which the ungodly are justified.²⁰⁷ With this strong dependence upon works, the draft reflects what would become a more conservative Catholic position, as evidenced in just a few years by the Canons of Trent and the anti-Protestant polemics of Pighius.

Third, there is consensus on the compatibility of Bucer's and Calvin's doctrine of justification with the *duplex iustitia*.²⁰⁸ It must be remembered that Bucer co-authored the so-called Regensburg Book with Gropper.²⁰⁹ His *duplex iustificatio* included the remission of sins by imputation and an im-

---

201. Yarnold, "*Duplex iustitia*," 204–23.

202. Lugioyo, *Martin Bucer's Doctrine of Justification*, 189.

203. According to Vermigli, Pighius emphasized the obedience of God's commandments on the strength of one's will as the way to be justified. Vermigli, *Romanos*, 1273–82 [181–89]. See also Feiner, *Die Erbsündenlehre Albert Pigges*, 66.

204. Jedin, *A History of the Council of Trent*, 145, 153.

205. Schaff, *The History of Creeds*, 4th ed., 474.

206. While it is true that Contarini was shunned by Carafa and other rigid conservatives following Regensburg, it was not on account of heresy. Gleason, *Gasparo Contarini*, 257–76. Just thirty years later, the Sorbonne was to pronounce Contarini's position acceptable. Dickens, *The Counter Reformation*, 105.

207. Lugioyo, *Martin Bucer's Doctrine of Justification*, 190.

208. Ibid., 202–3; Matheson, "Martin Bucer and the Old Church," 5–16; McGrath, "Humanist Elements in the Early Reformed Doctrine of Justification," 5–20.

209. Eells, "The Origin of the Regensburg Book," 355–72.

partation of righteousness by the Spirit,²¹⁰ elements that are consistent with Vermigli's position.²¹¹ On account of the Holy Spirit, those who are justified by faith (*prima iustificatio*) will also be "justified" by works (*secundaria iustificatio*).²¹² These are different words to describe the essence of Peter Martyr's position.²¹³ Since Martyr's doctrine of justification was in principle in line with Bucer's, and Bucer's position remained compatible with Article 5, there is a logical harmony between Vermigli's doctrine of justification and the *duplex iustitia*.

Like Bucer's formulation, Calvin's doctrine of justification evinces the same general agreement to *duplex iustitia*, as Calvin's own statement to Farel confirms.²¹⁴ On this point, Lane sheds direct light:

> How does this doctrine of *duplex iustitia* compare with Calvin's teaching? The idea is fundamental to Calvin's theology of salvation although the actual term he used only in a negative sense, when opposing Osiander's teaching on justification (*Inst.* 3:11:11f. [1559]). The idea of *duplex iustitia*, in the sense that it is understood in Article 5, is found in his references to a *duplex gratia*, referring to justification and sanctification (*Inst.* 3:11:1 [1539], 6 [1559]).²¹⁵

Fourthly and finally, we find the doctrine of *duplex iustitia* in Vermigli's theological offspring, men such as John Jewel and Richard Hooker.²¹⁶

---

210. Bucer describes this impartation as "a certain persuasion of the Holy Spirit concerning the gospel," (*certa Spiritus sancti de Evangelio persuasio*). Bucer, *Metaphrasis et enarratio*, 425.

211. Vermigli conveys his adherence to *duplex iustificatio* when he contrasts the two meanings of justification: the present reckoning of imputation and the future realization of actual righteousness. Vermigli, *Ad Corinthios Epistolam Commentarii*, 19 [147]; Ibid., *Romanos*, 1182 [88]. McGrath suggests that a "doctrine of double justification", in the strict sense of the term (as it is encountered during the Tridentine proceedings on justification), is essentially a doctrine of a *double formal cause of justification*." McGrath, *ID*, 313. In this sense, Vermigli's doctrine (because it posits imputation as the single formal cause) is *not* a strict *duplex iustificatio*.

212. Bucer, *Metaphrasis et enarratio*, 232. We noted in our introduction Lugioyo's helpful point that "Bucer's use of *secundaria* hints not to a [temporal] following (*secunda*) but to an inferior or second-rate justification that highlights the superiority of the first." Lugioyo, *Martin Bucer's Doctrine of Justification*, 189.98n297.

213. This assertion, once again, is predicated on Vermigli's distinction between a present, forensic justification versus an actual realization of justification which occurs in the future. Vermigli, *Ad Corinthios Epistolam Commentarii*, 19 [147]; *Romanos*, 1182 [88].

214. Lane, *Justification by Faith in Catholic-Protestant Dialogue*, 56.

215. Lane, "Calvin and Article 5," 233–63.

216. McNair opens his Introduction of *Peter Martyr in Italy* describing Vermigli as

Jewel served as Vermigli's notary during the Oxford disputation, and then, following Mary's ascension to the English throne, he found refuge in the home of Martyr in Strasbourg and Zürich.[217] Like Vermigli, Bucer, and other Reformed thinkers, Jewel recognizes the need for twofold righteousness in the doctrine of justification. Quoting Thomas Aquinas, Jewel affirms "works are said to justify, not as justification is the procuring of righteousness, but in that it is an exercise or a shewing or a perfecting of righteousness. For we say a thing is done, when it is perfected or known to be done."[218]

Jewel's protégé, Richard Hooker, continued in this same trajectory.[219] Identifying one of the greatest merits of Hooker's soteriology, Corneliu C. Simuţ points to "the synthesis between justification and sanctification," which he credits to the influence of Martin Bucer and his theory of double justification.[220] In Hooker's words,

> Which thing being attentively marked, sheweth plainly how the faith of true believers cannot be divorced from hope and love; how faith is part of sanctification, and yet unto justification necessary; how faith is perfected by good works, and yet not works of ours good without faith: finally, how our fathers might hold, we are justified by faith alone, and yet hold truly that without good works we are not justified.[221]

Lee Gibbs, in his analysis of Hooker's *Discourse of Justification*, explains that, for Hooker, the gift of the indwelling Spirit includes the righteousness of sanctification (faith, hope, and love) and the forensic righteousness of Christ by imputation *in tempore*, that is, "at one and the same time."[222]

Jewel's theological father and as Hooker's grandfather. McNair, PMI, xiii.

217. Jewel remained an affectionate disciple thereafter, writing of his mentor, "Doctor Peter Martyr, of whom I cannot speak without great reverence." Jewel, *The Works of John Jewel*, vol. 3, 646.

218. Jewel, *The Works of John Jewel*, 300. Philip Edgcumbe Hughes describes how Jewel maintained a fierce commitment to *sola fide* without denigrating the necessity of works. Hughes, ed. *Faith and Works*, 39.

219. In addition to his connection to Vermigli through Jewel, Hooker may have learned about Peter Martyr from his Uncle, John Hooker, a historian and scholar from Exeter, who had lodged with Vermigli while studying at Strasburg. MacCulloch, *The Reformation*, 486. Gary Jenkins states that Martyr also influenced Hooker through his Puritan tutor, John Rainolds. Jenkins, "Peter Martyr and the Church of England," 47–69.

220. Simuţ, *Richard Hooker and His Early Doctrine*, 104.

221. Hooker, *The Works of the Learned and Judicious Divine*, vol. II, 309.

222. Gibbs, "Richard Hooker's *Via Media* Doctrine of Justification," 219–20. This notion of *in tempore* is roughly analogous to Calvin's great *simul*, *Institutio*. Calvin, *Institutionum Christianae religionis libri quatuor*, 210.

Both of these gifts are understood to be an outgrowth of the believer's union with Christ.[223] With those who have ears to hear, the reverberation of this theological complex echoes backward in time, even before Peter Martyr in Switzerland or Oxford, to the theological conventicles of Naples, Viterbo, and Venice.

Although Vermigli never uses the nomenclature of *duplex iustitia* to describe his doctrine of justification, it nevertheless serves as an accurate summary of his position; that is, assuming imputation is clearly designated as the formal cause. It must be noted however that because this designation was not always clearly explicated in theological discourse (i.e., the fundamental role of imputation in causing justification),[224] Vermigli regarded the *duplex iustitia* with suspicion and, at some points, he even criticized it. For instance, he writes in his Genesis commentary, "that [the *duplex iustitia*] view is wholly overthrown which says that we are justified by grace, yet in such a way that it attributes a role to works, since together with faith they actually lead to justification. I show that this is false."[225] In this vein, Sturm is correct that Vermigli avoided the position "in order to categorically avoid relativizing Christ's righteousness appropriated in faith, which God imputes for forgiveness of sins and to admit only one 'causa' for justification: the mercy of God."[226] In other words, Vermigli would not risk confusing his position with a variety of *duplex iustitia* that failed to clearly define the formal cause in terms of imputation. Nevertheless, with this formal cause properly designated, the doctrine of *duplex iustitia* is a helpful way to account for Martyr's inclusion of the Spirit's cultivation of actual righteousness in the broader conception of his doctrine of justification.

---

223. Simuţ, *The Doctrine of Salvation in the Sermons of Richard Hooker*, 117–18. Yarnold also describes Hooker as a proponent of *duplex iustitia*, emanating from Saint Paul's theology of Christological union. Yarnold, "*Duplex iustitia*," 204–23.

224. Lane, for example, analyses Contarini's *Epistola de Iustificatione* (a letter written from Regensburg on May 25, 1541 in which he defends his views against Messer Angelo, Cardinal Gonzaga's theological advisor) and concludes, "Because of the *duplex iustitia* and the double sense of justification, it follows that there is a double formal cause of justification: 'charitas et gratia Dei nobis inhaerens et iusticia Christi nobis donata et imputata' (29:1-4)." Lane, "Cardinal Contarini and Article 5 of the Regensburg Colloquy (1541)," 163–90 (179).

225. Vermigli, *In primum librum Mosis*, 61: "Quare illa opinio omnino evertitur, quae ita nos iustificari fide dicit, ut tamen operibus tribuat partem, quod scilicet una cum fide ad iustificandum concurrant."

226. Sturm, *Die Theologie Peter Martyr*, 67–68.

F. Conclusion

We have learned that the basic contours of Vermigli's doctrine of justification comprise the following elements. Recognizing that humanity after Adam's sin is under divine condemnation as a *massa perditionis*, Martyr looks through his "intensive Augustinianism" lens to confront the problem of "Pelagianism." With this threat in view, he employs the judicial language of *forense* to underscore the legal nature of justification, that is, the way in which God considers elect sinners to be in a state of righteousness. This reckoning is entirely *extra nos* and is not responsible for effecting internal renewal; *imputatio* is employed to explain how exactly this occurs. Such imputation consists of two movements: the accounting of Christ's righteousness, and the non-imputation of one's sin, the benefits of which are forgiveness and eternal life. In a few places, Martyr uses the language of "adoption" to capture the legal and relational aspects of this relationship.[227] Any suggestion that justification is caused by works is regarded by him as entirely unscriptural.[228]

In addition to his emphasis on forensic imputation, Vermigli includes regeneration and sanctification in the broader confines of justification. He calls this broader vision "a different kind of justification,"[229] insofar as it becomes part of the basis by which we are justified in the final judgment. In this sense, Vermigli maintains a form of *duplex iustificatio*.[230] Too weak and imperfect to withstand the scrutiny of divine holiness on its own, these works are buttressed by the imputation of Christ's righteousness and thereby made acceptable.[231] Such works are pleasing to God, and, while they are never meritorious, they are rewarded on the last day.[232] Furthermore, these works are an essential component of salvation. "And if these works are born of God then it is inevitable that they are justified *and regenerated* (emphasis added)."[233] Martyr is careful to distinguish these works from their proper cause, namely forensic imputation.[234] Works are the effect (or fruit) and imputation is the cause (or root).

---

227. Vermigli, *Romanos* 1232 [139], 1259 [167], 1280 [187].

228. Ibid., 1224 [131].

229. Ibid., *Ad Corinthios Epistolam Commentarii*, 19 [147].

230. Ibid.; *Romanos*, 1182 [88].

231. Ibid., *Ad Corinthios Epistolam Commentarii*, 19 [147].

232. Ibid., *Romanos*, 1222–23 [128–29],1227–28 [133–34], 1290–91 [196–97]. Ibid., 1194 [100]; Ibid., 1288 [195].

233 Ibid., 1232 [139]: "Quod si nati sunt ex Deo, necesse est, eos iustificatos, et regeneratos esse."

234. Ibid., 1128 [135], 1235–36 [142].

And Christ would want everyone to understand that none except the just are received into the kingdom of heaven. Therefore, he considers these external works so that it might be clearly understood by them that righteousness is imputed to men by faith. For no one can be so ignorant as not to know there are two principles of these: one by which they exist, the other by which they are known.[235]

In making the above distinction, Martyr posits a doctrine of justification that is "*of* works" (works validate one's initial justification) and, in the broader, secondary sense of the term, justification is also "*by* works" insofar as the future judgment necessitates the fruit of regeneration. This distinction will be valuable in chapter five when we compare the doctrines of Newman and Vermigli.

Faith is the instrument that appropriates two-fold righteousness (*duplex iustitia*)—forensic imputation and that which is wrought by the Spirit. In the former case, it is simply faith, while, in the latter, it is faith accompanied by the activity of the regenerated mind and volition. Such regeneration produces a habit of virtue (sanctification) in the course of a faithful life. In Vermigli's Romans commentary, the enlivening work of the Spirit serves as the context for justification, while the same Spirit directly instigates sanctification. Martyr employs the notion of *habitus* to describe the human disposition that produces good works. Such a disposition is an "inward righteousness which is rooted in us, which we obtain and confirm by leading a continually upright life."[236]

For Vermigli, one cannot properly address the cataclysmic crisis of original sin by limiting justification to the problem of guilt. In addition to the legal dimension, it is also necessary for salvation to engage the spiritual and moral consequences of Adam's transgression. To Martyr's thinking, one's union with the crucified and resurrected Christ, which results in a living faith, meaningfully addresses each of these consequences by bringing together forensic justification, regeneration, and sanctification. In this way, Vermigli offers a holistic view of justification that seeks to account for the comprehensive nature of human sin.

Having examined Peter Martyr's doctrine of justification in the context of his socio-religious milieu, our next chapter will transition into the life and times of the second figure with whom this study is concerned: John Henry Newman.

---

235. Ibid., 1228–29 [135].

236. Ibid., 1299 [205]: "sed de illa intrinseca nobis inhaerente, quam recte vivendo perpetuo acquirimus, et confirmamus."

Chapter 3: Newman's Historical Background

A. The Study of John Henry Newman

IN JANUARY OF 1864, the Anglican novelist Charles Kingsley published an article charging that the Roman Catholic Church in general, and John Henry Newman in particular, had little regard for truth. Failing to obtain either a retraction or so much as an apology from Kingsley, Newman composed seven pamphlets, which he published from April 21 to June 2. Recognizing his opportunity to offer a public defense of his Catholic faith, Newman reprinted five of the seven articles in a single volume entitled, *Apologia Pro Vita Sua* (1864). While lacking some personal details, such as the names of his parents, the *Apologia* gives an autobiographical account of Newman's theological pilgrimage. Imbued with a quality of existential transparency, the *Apologia* quickly became a bestseller in Britain and remains one of the greatest religious autobiographies of all time.

The *Apologia* was the first volume of what would eventually become a cottage industry of books dedicated to Newman's life.[1] Shortly afterward,

---

1. The most significant general biographies on Newman fall into three basic categories: those that are dedicated to his life, others that emphasize his thought, and those that do an adequate job of explicating both. The major works that fall into the first category include: Ward, *Young Mr. Newman* ; Ruggles, *Journey into Faith*; Bouyer, *Newman: sa vie, sa spiritualité* (Bouyer's work was translated into English in 1958 and recently reprinted by Ignatius Press under the English title, *Newman: His Life and Spirituality*); Newsome, *The Convert Cardinals*; Chisnall, *John Henry Cardinal Newman*; Short, *Newman and His Contemporaries*. The second category, emphasizing Newman's thought, include: Merrigan, "*Numquam Minus Solus, Quam Cum Solus*"; Harrold, *John Henry Newman*; Holloway, *The Victorian Sage*; Boekraad, *The Personal Conquest of Truth*; Dessain, *John Henry Newman*; Dulles, *John Henry Newman*; Ker and Merrigan, *The Cambridge Companion to John Henry Newman*; Sheridan, *Newman on Justification*. Biographies that sufficiently grapple with life and thought include: Bremond, *Newman : Essai de biographie psychologique* (translated into English under the title, *The Mystery of Newman*, trans. Corrance); Ward, *The Life of John Henry Cardinal Newman*; Middleton, *Newman at Oxford*; Trevor, *Newman: The Pillar of the Cloud*, vol. 1; Trevor, *Newman: Light in Winter*, vol. 2; Robbins, *The Newman Brothers*; Ker, *John Henry Newman*; Blehl,

Ann Mozley arranged Newman's letters and correspondence for publication.[2] The collection was eventually published in two volumes in 1890.[3] In 1891, the year after John Henry's death, his brother, Francis Newman, scandalized English-language readers with his *Contributions Chiefly to the Early History of the Late Cardinal Newman*.[4] It was an ugly screed, apparently intended to prove that John Henry was a thoroughgoing Papist long before his conversion in 1845. According to Robbins, it earned Francis a public rebuke. Six years later, when Francis himself died, an obituary in the *Athenaeum* referred to it as betraying "a theological unbrotherliness rarely met with in recent biography."[5]

It is outside of the purview of this study to survey the myriad of Newman biographies that have been written over the years. Our concern is to understand the historical development of Newman's doctrine of justification. Despite the modest number of monographs treating this aspect of Newman's thought, there are a few works that are especially helpful. The following overview will consider their particular contributions according to a three-fold taxonomy: Newman's treatment of Martin Luther, the general historical development of Newman's doctrine of justification, and uncreated grace in the context of his *via media*.

The relationship of Newman's doctrine of justification to that of Martin Luther has received considerable attention. In what is the most quoted and distilled expression of his grievance, Newman writes, "[Luther] found Christians in bondage to their works and observances; he released them by his doctrine of faith; and he left them in bondage to their feelings."[6] In his chapter, "Newman on Justification: An Evangelical Evaluation," Alister E. McGrath dismantles Newman's argument piece by piece before concluding that his "account of the doctrine of justification associated with Luther is seriously inaccurate, and at one point appears to demonstrate a standard of intellectual integrity which falls short of what one might have hoped to encounter."[7] McGrath's case, which he also makes in his *magnum opus*,

---

Pilgrim Journey; Turner, *John Henry Newman*. The centenary of Newman's death produced a handful of valuable volumes including Brown, *Newman: A Man for Our Time*; Foister, *Cardinal Newman 1801–90*; Ker and Hill, *Newman after a Hundred Years*.

2. The project started in 1884 before Mozley's first draft was presented to Newman in 1887.

3. Mozley, ed., *Letters and Correspondence of John Henry Newman* [to 1845], 2 vols.

4. Francis William Newman, *Contributions Chiefly to the Early History*.

5. Robbins, *The Newman Brothers*, vii.

6. Newman, *Jfc*, 340. The following citations from Newman's *Lectures* are from his third edition, unless indicated otherwise.

7. McGrath, "Newman on Justification," 94.

Iustitia Dei, is convincing.[8] Equally forceful is the article of Thomas Sheridan, SJ, "Newman and Luther on Justification" in which he agrees with McGrath that Newman is rightly criticized for his "unfair portrayal of Luther's teaching," and demonstrates that Luther's own doctrine had much in common with the position that Newman was defending.[9] In a similar vein, John F. Perry applies this historiography to contemporary ecumenical dialogue, by illustrating how badly wrong Newman got Luther, particularly in how Newman "deconstructed" a passage from Luther's *Commentary on Galatians*.[10] Also with an eye on modern ecumenism is the late Richard John Neuhaus's article, "Newman, Luther, and the Unity of Christians," which explains the far-reaching implications of Newman's ill-informed caricature of Luther upon subsequent generations of Catholics.[11] Other treatments include an article by Scott Murray, which analyses doctrinal similarities and differences of the two men according to various topics,[12] and a chapter by Joseph S. O'Leary examining Newman's treatment of Luther in the context of nineteenth-century Britain.[13]

Of the various works addressing the historical development of Newman's doctrine of justification, the single most important volume is the "theological biography" by Sheridan, *Newman on Justification*.[14] Sheridan carefully traces Newman's thought on the subject in eight chapters, covering Newman's childhood to the year 1835. A ninth and final chapter, "Final Synthesis and Conclusion," brings readers to 1837 when Newman's lectures were delivered in St. Mary the Virgin's Adam de Brome Chapel, and eventually to 1838 when the *Lectures on Justification* were first published. Peter Toon has a useful chapter in his book, *Evangelical Theology 1833–1856*, dedicated to the doctrine of justification in which he explains the backlash against Newman's position from within the Evangelical community.[15] Toon's

---

8. McGrath, *ID*, 295–307.

9. Sheridan, "Newman and Luther on Justification," 217. In the précis of his article, Sheridan concludes, "Newman wrongly attributed to Luther the idea that justification is by mere extrinsic imputation, and, while he correctly attributed Luther's insistence upon 'justification by faith alone' to the latter's rejection of any kind of human merit, he wrongly accused him of antinomianism" (217).

10. John F. Perry, "Newman's Treatment of Luther in the Lectures on Justification," 303–17.

11. Neuhaus, "Newman, Luther, and the Unity of Christians," 277–88.

12. Murray, "Luther in Newman's *Lectures on Justification*," 156–78.

13. O'Leary, "Impeded Witness," 153–93.

14. This was based on his doctoral thesis from the Institut Catholique de Paris, "Newman and Justification: A Study in the Development of a Theology" (1965).

15. Toon, *Evangelical Theology, 1833–1856*.

work is a helpful contribution, since his investigation is the only one of its kind. Less illuminating, by comparison, is his article "A Critical Review of John Henry Newman's Doctrine of Justification," which is more critical in its assessment of Newman than in its research.[16]

While the late Frank Turner's, *John Henry Newman: The Challenge to Evangelical Religion* has been rightly criticized for its excessive speculation into Newman's psychology, its emphasis on Newman's relationship to Evangelicalism sheds light on the formation of his doctrine of justification.[17] Ian Ker's biography has an extended section that puts Newman's doctrine on justification into its historical context, explaining the sequence of events that surrounded its composition.[18]

The Cambridge Companion to John Henry Newman, edited by Ian Ker and Terrence Merrigan, offers a general overview of Newman's thought, including a chapter on justification written by Sheridan.[19] This may be the single most helpful distillation of Newman's doctrine of justification available in print. A valuable primer on Newman's life and thought by Avery Cardinal Dulles, *John Henry Newman*, includes a brief overview of Newman's position on justification.[20] Similar in form and substance is Ker book, *Newman on Being a Christian*.[21] Finally, there is Henry Chadwick's excellent chapter, "Lectures on Justification," which examines Newman's position in the context of the Oxford Movement and the history of post-Reformation soteriology.[22]

The central importance of the category of *gratia increata* to Newman's doctrine of justification has also been a subject of some research. Charles Dessain, in his article, "Cardinal Newman and the Doctrine of Uncreated Grace," surveys Newman's pneumatology to see how it informed his *gratia uncreata*.[23] Dessain acknowledges that "On becoming a Catholic . . . Newman wrote little on the subject of Uncreated Grace."[24] In a similar direction, José Morales's chapter, "Newman and the Problems of Justification," analyses the logic of Newman's position, questioning whether it is in fact sustain-

16. Toon, "A Critical Review," 335–44.

17. Turner, *John Henry Newman*, 266–75.

18. Ian Ker, *John Henry Newman: A Biography* (Oxford: Oxford University Press, 2009), 149–57.

19. Sheridan, "Justification."

20. Dulles, *John Henry Newman*, 16–25.

21. Ker, *Newman on Being a Christian*, 52–58.

22. Chadwick, "The Lectures on Justification," 287–308.

23. Dessain, "Cardinal Newman and the Doctrine of Uncreated Grace," 207–29, 269–88.

24. Ibid., 285.

able.²⁵ Going further than Dessain, Morales argues that Newman jettisoned his *via media* on justification when he abandoned Anglicanism itself.²⁶ In particular, Morales questions the accuracy of Newman's assertion from the third edition of the *Lectures* that, "Unless the Author held in substance in 1874 what he published in 1838, he would not at this time be reprinting what he wrote as an Anglican."²⁷ Arguing from a sermon that Newman published in 1840, shortly after his original *Lectures*, Morales contends that Newman had by that point already moved away from locating the formal cause of justification in an uncreated grace in favor of an inherent deposit of righteousness.²⁸ Against this view, Thomas Holtzen, building on his doctoral dissertation from Marquette,²⁹ argues in his article, "Newman's '*Via Media*' Theology of Justification," that Newman's position on justification remained intact as a consistent *via media* owing to his doctrine of divine indwelling by the Holy Spirit.³⁰ Before examining Newman's *via media*, however, we will first consider the religious background in which it developed.

B. The World of John Henry Newman

"It was the best of times, it was the worst of times,"³¹ at least in the Church of England. Dickens's aphorism cogently describes the period of John Henry Newman's life on which the current chapter will concentrate, from his birth to the writing of his *Lectures on the Doctrine of Justification* (1801 to 1838). The reasons for this tumult were legion. Social and political upheaval across Europe, the growth of rationalism, the evolution of applied science, and Evangelical renewal movements associated with Wesley and Whitfield had given rise to, and voice to, a climate of crisis and reform. As a result, nineteenth-century Great Britain manifested three distinct Christian movements: revivalism within Anglican and nonconformist churches; a deeper commitment to ritualism in the same Anglican church; and, thirdly, a Latitudinarian (or Broad Church) form of liberalism. The first movement, so-called Evangelicalism, both stimulated and took shape in a groundswell

---

25. Morales, "Newman and the Problems of Justification," 143–64.

26. In the next chapter, we examine this argument and conclude that Morales is mostly correct.

27. Newman, *Jfc*, 9.

28. Morales, "Newman Today," 157. The particular sermon is "Righteousness, not of us, but in us," in Newman, *PMI*, 1041–49.

29. Holtzen, "Union with God and the Holy Spirit: A New Paradigm of Justification."

30. Ibid., "Newman's '*Via Media*' Theology of Justification," 64–74.

31. Dickens, *A Tale of Two Cities*, 3.

of missionary activity and social reform, while the second concentrated on a reviving of formal liturgy, whose sensational depth reached back to the early centuries of the church. The last was in some ways less of a movement than an intellectually respectable morality devoid of doctrinal substance, against which the other two more fervent strains could define themselves. Newman's life intersected with each of these traditions, as we shall see.

John Henry Newman was born in London on Saturday, February 21, 1801, the first of, in the end, six children. His father, John Newman, was a banker and an easygoing member of the Church of England. John Henry's mother, Jemina Foudrinier, was the daughter of a wealthy paper manufacturer who came from a French Huguenot background. The family lived at 80 Old Broad Street for two years before they moved to 17 Southampton Street (now Southampton Place), Bloomsbury. Decades later, Newman would recollect these childhood years as the starting point of his religious imagination.[32]

Newman's religious background has been described as "a conventional, non-sacramental middle-class one."[33] Before long, however, he was awoken from his religious slumber by reading the deist Thomas Paine and the skeptic David Hume.[34] Such reflection eventually led to his conversion to a sort of Evangelicalism that was "Calvinistic in character."[35] This occurred in the autumn of 1816 when Newman was fifteen.[36] Before analyzing the details of his conversion, the following section will briefly consider the larger Evangelical movement of the time.

In the "Introductory Essay" of her work, *The Evangelical and Oxford Movements*, Elisabeth Jay explains why nineteenth-century Evangelicalism has resisted clean-cut definition. She suggests that it is largely due to this variety of Evangelicalism's revivalist origins, in which elements of doctrine, piety, and organization were shaped by a wide array of personalities.[37] Accordingly, Jay writes, "The nickname 'Evangelical' was acquired by these

---

32. Newman, *Apo*, 2.
33. Gilley, "Life and Writings," 1.
34. Newman, *Apo*, 3.
35. Newman, *AW*, 29. For Newman the term "Calvinist" had few of the precise doctrinal elements that are common to continental Calvinism. The meaning for Newman comes into sharper focus by looking at the teaching of Evangelicals such as Thomas Scott, namely, the severity of sin, authority of Scripture, sufficiency of the cross, centrality of the new birth, power of the preached word, and necessity of holiness. Sheridan, *Newman on Justification*, 16.
36. Newman, *Apo*, 4.
37. Jay, *The Evangelical and Oxford Movements*, 1–19.

men because of the zeal they showed in spreading the Evangel or Gospel."[38] As David Bebbington,[39] David Newsome,[40] and Sheridan Gilley[41] have demonstrated, the broad range of leaders and circumstances to which this label was attached broadened the semantic range of the Evangelical label.[42] The following sampling of figures and contributions is simply intended to offer a sense of its general complexion and portray the contours of the tradition in which Newman's doctrine of justification initially took shape. Such background will also help us to identify the factors that drove Newman's reflection on justification into the *via media* and eventually into his *via Romana*.

According to Kenneth Latourette, "Taken as a whole, in 1815 [the year preceding Newman's conversion] the Church of England was far from healthy. It was rich in its endowments and its revenues, but it was closely bound to the existing order and its leaders were fearful of any change that would jeopardize their position."[43] But not all Englishmen were so tentative. There was a variety of dynamic movements, which emerged and came under the label 'Evangelical', both within and beyond the established Churches of England and Scotland, including non-conformist denominations and organizations.

To recognize Evangelicalism's aims and concerns requires one to consider the previous century, in which the Wesleyan revivals brought an increased emphasis on personal faith to both the rural population and the emerging working class of Britain. It was later, toward the end of the eighteenth century, when the upper class and segments of the established church were also affected by renewal. This was especially so between the years 1790 and 1830, when a "Calvinistic" brand of Evangelicalism acquired a significant following (often linked to Wesley's former colleague, George Whitfield). As the years passed, it was common for High Churchmen to condescendingly blame Calvinist Evangelicals for what they perceived as excesses in religion.[44]

38. Ibid., 3.

39. Bebbington, *Evangelicalism in Modern Britain*, 1–19.

40. Newsome, *The Parting of Friends*, 1–16.

41. Gilley, *Newman and His Age*, 47–53.

42. Bebbington has summarized Evangelical religion in terms of his so called "quadrilateral": conversionism, activism, biblicism, and crucicentrism. Newsome and Gilley identify common Evangelical traits such as denominational secessions, biblical literalism, chiliasm, and social justice. Newsome, *The Parting of Friends*; Gilley, *Newman and his Age*. Jay distinguishes between "essential" and "non-essential" features in her work, *The Religion of the Heart*, 51–105.

43. Latourette, *A History of Christianity*, rev. ed., vol. II, 1164.

44. Altholz, "The Mind and Art of Victorian Orthodoxy," 187.

Over against the "high-and-dry" church (Newman's favorite label for liberal clerics) and their followers,[45] early Evangelicals distinguished themselves with terrific stories of conversion. One such example is John Newton (1725–1807), the slave trader turned minister and hymn writer who penned, "Amazing Grace" and "How Sweet the Name of Jesus Sounds."[46] Newton eventually became a spiritual leader who influenced many others, including William Cowper (1731–1800)[47] and Thomas Scott (1747–1821).[48] As Newton's successor, Scott's books were best-sellers among Evangelicals, particularly *A Commentary on the Whole Bible* and *The Force of Truth* (1779). As we shall see, he was also the figure to whom Newman attributed the greatest amount of credit for his conversion. In Newman's words, "It was he who first planted deep in my mind the fundamental truth of religion," and "who made a deeper impression on my mind than any other, and to whom (humanly speaking) I almost owe my soul."[49]

Space will not permit a treatment of the many other individuals who contributed to Evangelicalism's impact. Some were scholarly such as Isaac Milner (1750–1820) and Charles Simeon (1759–1836), whose work infused Cambridge University with an Evangelical awareness. The so-called Clapham Sect, consisting of wealthy individuals including John Venn (1759–1833), Henry Thornton (1760–1815), and William Wilberforce (1759–1833), engaged in the enterprise of social reform, eventually achieving the abolition of the slave trade in the British Empire. In a similar vein was the prison reformer, John H. Howard (1726–90), and sometime afterward, the 7th Earl of Shaftesbury, Anthony Ashley Cooper (1801–85), who tirelessly served the poor and oppressed. Evangelicals created their own publications, such as the *Christian Observer*, *The Christian Guardian*, and the *Record*,[50] while also launching a host of missionary societies, starting most notably with the Baptists in 1792.[51] The famous Sunday school movement, initiated by Hannah More (1745–1833) and popularized by Robert Raikes (1735–1811), is also part of the Evangelical legacy. But while the list

---

45. Ker, *John Henry Newman*, 92.

46. Newton and Cecil, *Out of the Depths*.

47. Also a hymn writer, William Cowper is perhaps most noted for the poem "Light Shining out of Darkness" (from which the English language gets the idiom "God moves in a mysterious way") and the enormously popular hymn of that day, "There is a Fountain Filled with Blood." Harland, *William Cowper*.

48. Scott, *The Works of the Late Rev. Thomas Scott*.

49. Newman, *Apo*, 5.

50. For a history on each of these publications, see Toon, *Evangelical Theology*, 6–9.

51. Neill, *A History of Christian Missions*, 213–16.

of Evangelical contributions is long[52] and the movement was as varied as its participants, it drew men and women whose commonalities of thought shaped a common identity we can define.

According to the Evangelical Anglican Bishop of Liverpool, J. C. Ryle, it was "no written creed, no formal declaration of principles" that defined "Evangelical Religion."[53] With reference to Evangelical leaders who preceded him, particularly to those of the late eighteenth century,[54] Ryle enumerates five values that properly identify the movement:[55]

1. Absolute supremacy of Holy Scripture
2. Appreciating the depth and prominence of human sinfulness
3. Paramount importance assigned to the work and office of the Lord Jesus Christ.
4. The inward work of God's Spirit in the heart of man
5. Outward and visible work of the Holy Ghost

The English biographer, memoirist and Liberal politician, George W. E. Russell, offers a similar portrait. While he was a high churchman, Russell recollected his childhood experience of Evangelicalism, noting in particular how the religion of his youth generally divided humanity into two categories, the "converted" ones, who had "closed with the offer" (and were thus assured of their salvation), and those of "an unconverted character."[56] The distinguishing characteristic of the first category, the "real" Christian, according to Evangelical parlance, was one's heartfelt response to the gospel message. In Russell's words, "[I]f only we would accept the offer of salvation so made, we were forgiven, reconciled, and safe. The acceptance was 'Conversion.'"[57] This distinction between the converted and unconverted

---

52. Overton, *The Evangelical Revival in the Eighteenth Century*; Ryle, *Knots untied*; Moule, *The Evangelical School in the Church of England*; Mathieson, *England in Transition*; Mathieson, *English Church Reform 1815–1840*; Smyth, *Simeon & Church Order*; Reynolds, *The Evangelicals at Oxford, 1735–1871*; Toon, *Evangelical Theology*; Jay, *The Evangelical and Oxford Movements.*; Bebbington, *Evangelicalism in Modern Britain*.

53. Ryle, *Knots Untied*, 3.

54. Ryle does not identify these individuals by name. Despite the "low church" origins of the movement, with its emphasis on Scripture only, the priesthood of believers, and a general chilliness toward religious "tradition," it was indebted, according to Ryle, to "the Thirty-nine Articles, the Prayer-book fairly interpreted, the works of the Reformers, [and] the writings of the pre-Caroline divines" (v).

55. Ryle, *Knots untied*, 4–9.

56. Russell, *The household of faith*, 240.

57. Ibid.

was part of what drew Newman into Evangelicalism, and, as we shall see, it eventually repelled him.

C. Newman the Calvinist

Newman experienced his first religious conversion between August and December of 1816. A few months earlier, in March, his father's bank stopped payments in the aftermath of the Napoleonic Wars. Meanwhile, alone at Ealing School and shocked by the financial catastrophe afflicting his family, John Henry became ill.[58] This condition led to Newman's spiritual renewal under the influence of his schoolmaster, the Rev. Walter Mayers, who himself had recently converted to a Calvinistic variety of Evangelicalism. Mayers quickly became Newman's guide. This guidance was mainly expressed through the books that Mayers offered him, which, according to Newman, were "the human means of this beginning of divine faith in me" and "all of the school of Calvin."[59] It is important to note that while Newman's faith would change considerably over his lifetime, he never repudiated this conversion.[60]

Of the various authors that Mayers recommended to Newman, the most significant was Thomas Scott of Aston Sandford, John Newton's successor. In addition to appreciating Scott's doctrine and independence of mind, Newman valued his commitment to holiness:

> Besides his unworldliness, what I also admired in Scott was his resolute opposition to antinomianism, and the minutely practical character of his writings. They show him to be a true Englishman, and I deeply felt his influence; and for years I used almost as proverbs what I considered to be the scope and issue of his doctrine, "Holiness rather than peace," and "Growth the only evidence of life."[61]

Scott's emphasis on the holiness of the Triune God remained with Newman in perpetuity, as did his sober awareness of the problem of sin.[62]

---

58. This was the first of three serious illnesses which were accompanied by a profound spiritual crisis. Newman writes, "The first keen, terrible one, when I was a boy of 15, and it made me a Christian—with experiences before and after, awful and known only to God." Newman, *AW*, 150.

59. Newman, *Apo*, 5.

60. Ibid.

61. Ibid.

62. An especially distilled treatment of Scott's Trinitarian position is found in "The Personality and Deity of the Holy Spirit," in Scott, *Essays on the most important subjects*

On the matter of sin, Sheridan suggests that Scott was less than true to his Calvinist heritage by emphasizing personal transgression over the notion of total depravity.[63] This is questionable. Sheridan is correct that Scott was serious about the acuity of personal transgression. It is certainly the light in which Newman himself presents Scott when he writes, "All they whom God justifies, says Mr. Scott, are *considered as ungodly*" in view of their flawed attempts at piety.[64] The idea of him maintaining a stark contrast, however, between original and personal sin, with stress upon the latter, is hard to square with Scott's volume, *Remarks on the refutation of Calvinism*, wherein he is very much in step with Calvin, especially in his first chapter, entitled, "On Original Sin and the total Depravity of Human Nature."[65] Thus, if we were to identify two main pillars of Scott's creed, it would be the holiness of the Triune God juxtaposed with the utter depravity of human nature. This couplet, as we shall see, is especially important to Newman's doctrine of justification.

During this period, Newman also read Thomas Newton's *Dissertations on the Prophecies* (1754),[66] a work that persuaded him that the Pope is the antichrist predicted in Scripture. Of more significance for the substance of Newman's thought was Joseph Milner's *History of the Church of Christ* (1794), with which Newman reports being "nothing short of enamoured," especially "the long extracts from St. Augustine, St. Ambrose, and the other Fathers which I found there."[67] Then, in 1817, Mayers gave Newman a copy of Bishop William Beveridge's *Private Thoughts*.[68]

In a letter thanking Mayers for Beveridge's volume, Newman conveys confusion over a particular issue he had read about therein. The problem concerned the fate of infants who died apart from baptism. If, as Evangelicals such as Beveridge suggest, conversion is a conscious decision, therefore ruling out the efficacy of baptismal regeneration, on what basis can infants lay claim to Christian hope?[69] Here is how Newman put the question to Mayers:

---

in religion, 4th ed., 243–60.

63. Sheridan, *Newman on Justification*, 28.
64. Newman, *Jfc*, 115.
65. Scott, *Remarks on the Refutation of Calvinism*, 2nd ed., 1–51.
66. Newton, *Dissertations on the Prophecies*.
67. Milner, *The History of the Church of Christ*, 7. Milner's work presents a Calvinistic view in which the world is divided between the elect who are conscious of their justification by faith and the rest who are not.
68. Beveridge, *Private Thoughts upon Religion*.
69. The denial of baptismal regeneration was a touchstone of Evangelical orthodoxy, especially after the publication of Richard Mant's *Appeal to the Gospel* in 1812,

> There is a passage in the first chapter of the second part [of Beveridge] that I don't quite comprehend: it is on the Sacrament of Baptism. I had, before I read it, debated with myself how it could be that baptized infants, dying in their infancy, could be saved unless the Spirit of God was given them; which seems to contradict the opinion that Baptism is not accompanied by the Holy Ghost. Bp Beverage's opinion seems to be that the seeds of grace are sown in Baptism although they often do not spring up; that Baptism is the mean whereby we receive the Holy Spirit, although not the only mean; that infants, when baptized, receive the inward and spiritual grace without the requisite repentance and faith.[70]

Sheridan, in his book, *Newman on Justification*, analyses Mayers' answer to Newman in a letter dated April 14, 1817, and concludes that Mayers, like Beveridge, is comfortable affirming that regeneration may *possibly* be communicated in baptism, but not necessarily, as evidenced by the many "Christians" who constitute the visible church without actually belonging to the invisible church.[71] In keeping with the Evangelical tendency to identify who is of the "real" church, regeneration (or "conversion" or "new life in Christ") could only be known, in Mayers' understanding, by observing the "fruit of maturer years."[72] This answer seemed to have satisfied Newman, since it was not until September 29, 1820 that the subject of baptismal regeneration once again arose in his writing.[73]

Newman's correspondence with Mayers anticipates many of the concerns that re-emerge later in his life, particularly the question of Baptism's efficacy and its relationship to repentance and faith. Bound up in this question is the concern of Newman and his Evangelical forebears to define the source of "real" Christian life, whether it is properly derived from the sacraments or faith alone.

---

in which he repudiated the Evangelicals' missionary push for conversion in favor of an ecclesiology based upon baptismal regeneration.

70. Newman, *AW*, 152.

71. Sheridan, *Newman on Justification*, 38–42. According to Sheridan, the letter is found in the Archives of the Birmingham Oratory, Miscellaneous Letters (1816–24), no. 2.

72. Ibid., 40.

73. Ibid., 42.

D. Newman Questions His Evangelical Assumptions

When Newman was elected a fellow of Oriel College, Oxford in April of 1822, he expected that his Evangelical faith would be questioned.[74] He was right. After Richard Whately helped the "awkward and timid" John Henry crawl out of his introverted shell, his views were immediately challenged by the liberal atmosphere of the Oriel Common Room.[75] In the face of such scrutiny, the first piece of Newman's Calvinism to slip away was the doctrine of predestination.[76] But this was just the beginning. The Noetic triumvirate of Thomas Arnold (1795–1842), Richard Whately (1787–1863), and Edward Hawkins (1789–1882) would impose sustained pressure on Newman to step back and re-evaluate his religious assumptions.

Newman became a full fellow of Oriel on April 4, 1823, the same day as Edward Pusey and William Churton became probationer fellows. As Newman's relationship with Pusey grew, so did his estimation of Pusey's Christian faith. At first, Newman had regarded him as simply "moral."[77] Soon, Newman was expressing how impressed he was by Pusey's seriousness toward religion.[78] Finally, Newman confidently exclaims, "That Pusey is Thine, O Lord, how can I doubt?"[79] They spent much time together discussing religion, Newman contending for the doctrine of imputation, Pusey denying it, with Newman "inclining to separate regeneration from baptism, [and Pusey] doubting its separation."[80]

Despite his anti-Calvinist colleagues, Newman held fast to his Evangelical creed. Mayers, who remained a mentor until his death in 1828, persuaded Newman to take holy orders, and, in 1824, he was ordained deacon (the following year he would be ordained to the priesthood). After being appointed curate of Saint Clement's, a working-class parish in east Oxford, Newman engaged in pastoral work with great enthusiasm. It was in this context that Newman started to question a *sine qua non* of Evangelicalism: the distinction between "nominal" and "real" Christians.

The importance of this tenet among Evangelicals ran deep. As Newsome explains,

---

74. Newman seemed to have anticipated this when he explains his reticence as "the result of his Calvinistic beliefs." Newman, *AW*, 65–66.

75. Newman, *Apo*, 11.

76. Ibid., 4.

77. Newman, *AW*, 190.

78. Ibid., 190–91.

79. Ibid., 75.

80. Ibid., 203.

Time and time again, Evangelicals would stress that there were two kinds of Christian—the *nominal* Christian and the "truly religious" or "real" Christian, a distinction which gained currency with the publication of Joseph Milner's *Church History*, which appeared in stages during the 1790s and the following decade, and with Wilberforce's own *Practical View* . . . this distinction was soon recognized as stock Evangelical phraseology—and indeed its acceptance rapidly became a sort of party shibboleth."[81]

The question of whether such a distinction is theologically and pastorally defensible asserted itself in the summer of 1824. With many of the fellows away, Newman developed a closer relationship to Edward Hawkins, who advised the young protégé on his parochial duties, particularly on his preaching. Hawkins sharply criticized Newman's first sermon, which, by its Evangelical denigration of baptismal regeneration, "divided the Christian world into two classes, the one all darkness, the other all light."[82] According to Newman, Hawkins chided him by explaining,

> Men are not either saints or sinners; but they are not so good as they should be, and better than they might be. . . . Preachers should follow the example of St Paul; he did not divide his brethren into two, the converted and unconverted, but he addressed them all as "in Christ" . . . and this, while he was rebuking them for irregularities and scandals which had occurred among them.[83]

To drive his point further home, Hawkins gave Newman a copy of John Bird Sumner's *Apostolical Preaching*, which showed that Paul addressed the visible church as a collective body of Christians who categorically possessed the Holy Spirit (and not two distinct groups of converted and unconverted).[84] This work, coupled with an active routine of pastoral visitation, severely dented Newman's regard for the distinction between real and nominal Christians.[85] Working out this idea, especially in conversa-

81. Newsome, *The Parting of Friends*, 46.

82. Newman, *AW*, 77.

83. Ibid., 65.

84. Newman studied the work of Sumner, who was the Evangelical Bishop of Chester, early in his life before delving into his *Apostolical Preaching*. Later, after the writing of *Tract 90*, it was Sumner who was first to denounce the tract from the Episcopal bench for its deviation from justification by faith alone. Turner, *John Henry Newman*, 390–91.

85. About this experience, Newman writes (about himself in the third person): "It was during these years of parochial duty that Mr. Newman underwent a great change in his religious opinions." Newman, *AW*, 73. Later, in his memoir, he explains that "the

tion with Edward Pusey, would eventually lead Newman to question his commitment to the doctrine of imputation.[86] In his own words, writing in January of 1825, "I think, I am not certain, I must give up the doctrine of imputed righteousness and that of regeneration apart from baptism."[87]

While Hawkins reoriented John Henry's thinking on baptismal regeneration and imputation, he had yet another far-reaching influence, namely his stress upon the necessity of sacred tradition alongside of Scripture.[88] While ultimately unsatisfying to Newman from an Anglican point of view (his conversion to Catholicism turned on the Roman Church's ability to account for sacred tradition),[89] the tacit acceptance of tradition, which started in 1825, was a critical departure from his Evangelical background, as Newman himself explains,

> He [Hawkins] lays down a proposition, self-evident as soon as stated, to those who have at all examined the structure of Scripture, viz. that the sacred text was never intended to teach doctrine, but only to prove it, and that, if we would learn doctrine, we must have recourse to the formularies of the Church; for instance to the Catechism, and to the Creeds. He considers, that, after learning from them the doctrines of Christianity, the inquirer must verify them by Scripture.[90]

Newman's commitment to tradition would eventually create a doctrinal impasse. To the extent that he studied the history of doctrine, he was confronted by the universal practice of infant baptism. Newman reasoned that if baptism does indeed constitute the rite of initiation into Christ, and not simply the *visible* church, as Evangelicals were inclined to see it, it would therefore be possible for infants to be regenerated. He was not ready

---

religion which he had received from John Newton and Thomas Scott would not work in a parish; that it is unreal; that this he had actually found as a fact, as Mr. Hawkins had told him beforehand; that Calvinism was not a key to the phenomena of human nature, as they occur in the world" (79).

86. Ibid., 203.

87. Ibid.

88. Years later, Newman would refer to this as "the *quasi*-Catholic doctrine of Tradition." Ibid., 78.

89. Growing out of his study of the post-Nicene fathers, Newman grew uncertain about whether Anglicanism could be properly called "Catholic." These doubts took root in 1839, when he read an article by Cardinal Nicholas Wiseman in the *Dublin Review*, in which Anglicans were compared to African Donatists during the time of Augustine. Reflecting on this question over time, Newman began to correlate the Church of England with the heretical Arians of the fourth century. In Newman's mind, Anglicanism failed the Catholic test. Newman tells this story in his *Apo*, 127–237.

90. Newman, *Apo*, 9.

to accept this conclusion yet. Instead, he opted for the position of Beveridge and Mayers, which viewed baptism as planting the seed of grace. But make no mistake about it; as Newman modified his views on regeneration and the authority of tradition, he pursued a new religious path.

E. "Shreds and Tatters" of Evangelicalism

In addition to Sumner's *Apostolical Preaching*, Newman was also influenced by Joseph Butler's *The Analogy of Religion* (1736).[91] Above all, Butler's work cast aspersions upon the chief tenets of Evangelicalism, portraying it as "an emotional religion," with which Newman, as he later wrote, "could have little sympathy."[92] It was in the context of describing this book's influence that Newman also explained that he "had taken the first step towards giving up the Evangelical form of Christianity; however, for a long while certain shreds and tatters of that doctrine hung about his preaching."[93]

Recounting in his *Apologia* the factors most responsible for swaying him during this period, Newman highlights two. The first was his drift toward liberalism in which he preferred intellectual excellence to moral.[94] This movement, however, was only short-lived on account of his emotional breakdown as an examiner of schools and the sudden death of his favorite sister, Mary. The other factor was John Keble's *Christian Year* (1827), which brought to mind principles that he had previously learned from Butler. The first of these principles is especially relevant to the question of regeneration. "[It] was what may be called, in a larger sense of the word, the Sacramental system, that is, the doctrine that material phenomena are both the types and the instruments of things unseen."[95] Newman goes on to explain that sacraments are not simply a sign directing the faithful to the mysteries of faith; they are also the *instrumental means* by which one encounters them.[96]

As Newman rejected Evangelicalism's subjective criterion for church membership in favor of a supposedly objective sacramental assessment, there was a definite turning point in the development of his thought.[97]

91. Butler, *The analogy of religion*.
92. Newman, *AW*, 78.
93. Ibid. This step occurred shortly after his ordination to the priesthood on May 29, 1825.
94. Newman, *Apo*, 14. See also, Blehl, *Pilgrim Journey*, 77.
95. Newman, *Apo*, 18. The second principle that Newman learned from Butler is "probability [in the service of faith and love] as the guide of life" (19).
96. Ibid., 18.
97. Ibid., 49. Newman's sermon, "Holiness Necessary for Future Blessedness"

Velocity was added to this trajectory in 1831, when, having been relieved from his teaching duties, Newman accepted a commission to write a history of the church councils. It turned out that, instead, he wrote his first great work, *The Arians of the Fourth Century* (1833).[98] Research for this volume strengthened Newman's conviction with regard to the two aforementioned topics: regeneration understood in the context of sacramental objectivity and the authority of the church institution.[99] Newman's position on ecclesial authority after completing his study of the fourth century church, as Ker summarizes, was a firm embrace of traditional claims:

> Nor did the early Church use the Bible to teach the faith; it was the Church that taught what had to be believed, and it only appealed to 'Scripture in vindication of its own teaching'; heretics, on the other hand, like the Arians, relied on a 'private study of Holy Scripture' to elicit a 'systematic doctrine from the scattered notices of the truth which Scripture contains.' The parallel with the contemporary situation was obvious.[100]

Through this lens, Newman's reflection on baptismal regeneration led him to a renewed and optimistic vision of the sacramental Church. But, on the ground, the realities of the split between liberal and Evangelical camps, both of which were seeming increasingly alien to Newman, were thoroughly disheartening. Frustration over this problem (and general fatigue from research and writing) ran so deep that Newman needed a holiday. Recognizing this, he decided to accompany the Froudes on a Mediterranean voyage, a trip that would become another pivotal turning point for Newman.

It was in December of 1832 that Newman set sail from Falmouth with Richard Hurrell Froude and his father on a trip intended to enrich Richard's health. Visiting Corfu and then arriving in Rome by March 1833, Newman

---

(preached in 1826) makes explicit his repudiation of the Evangelical doctrine of sudden conversion: "It follows at once, even though Scripture did not plainly tell us so that no one is able to prepare himself for heaven, that is, make himself holy in a short time . . . there are others who suppose they may be saved all at once by a sudden and easily acquired faith." Newman, *PPS*, 10.

98. For an assessment of Newman's work, see Williams, *Arius: Heresy and Tradition*, 3–6, 147, 158.

99. It also introduced Newman to a third issue that would become important for his doctrine of justification—the Eastern notion of uncreated grace, which we will consider in due course. For a helpful explanation of how the fourth-century fathers, particularly Athanasius, applied the idea of uncreated grace to the doctrine of salvation, see Popov, "The Idea of Deification in the Early Eastern Church," 42–48.

100. Ker, *John Henry Newman*, 52.

took great pleasure in the beautiful sites.[101] When the Froudes returned to England in April, Newman decided to revisit Sicily. It was there, terribly ill with gastric or typhoid fever, that Newman's thoughts went to the liberal threat facing the church in the wake of the Reform Bill of 1832.[102] It was in light of these developments that he wrote in his journal, "God has still work for me to do."[103] After returning home by sea—during this voyage he wrote his famous poem "Lead Kindly Light"—he finally arrived in Oxford on July 9, 1833.[104] This was five days before Keble preached his assize sermon, later published as *National Apostasy*, which, in retrospect, Newman considered to be the beginning of the Oxford or Tractarian Movement.[105] The stage was now set for Newman to articulate his "middle way" or *via media*.

F. The Making of Newman's *Via Media*

By 1833, Newman had acquired the intellectual and spiritual raw materials with which he would construct his *via media*, including theological convictions he retained from his earliest years of piety, namely a commitment to the holiness of the Triune God and recognition of human depravity.[106] These convictions, which he originally imbibed from his Evangelical teachers such as Thomas Scott and Walter Mayers, would continue with Newman for the remainder of his life. You might say that the pursuit of holiness functioned as the engine that drove Newman's faith, and the doctrine of depravity was the governor that subdued his expectations for human achievement.

With the couplet of holiness and depravity in view, it is now time to examine the theological substance of Newman's *via media*. It essentially consists of three elements; the first two we have mentioned several times already—namely, regeneration understood in the context of sacramental objectivity and the authority of the church institution. Before getting to the

---

101. Newman, *Apo*, 32.

102. In the background of this legislation was the Roman Catholic Relief Act of 1829, which reduced many of the restrictions on Catholics. Newman and his contemporaries perceived this as a threat to the privileges of the Church of England.

103. Newman, *AW*, 127.

104. Newman, *Apo*, 35.

105. Keble's sermon underscored the struggle for Church identity in the face of government intervention, a theme that would remain central to the Tractarian movement. Rowell, *The Vision Glorious*, 4.

106. Michael Testa writes, "I have indicated that some Calvinistic tendencies remain with Newman throughout his life. One example is his profound sense of the sinfulness of humanity." Testa, "The Theological Anthropology of John Henry Newman."

third element, let us be sure we are clear on how Newman arrived at the first two conclusions.

Newman's view of regeneration and tradition were heavily influenced by his study of the fourth-century church fathers. With regard to regeneration, Newman consciously moved away from the Evangelical distinction that understood it to be a subjective experience accessed by faith alone and displayed in virtuous fruit among "real" Christians. Instead, he embraced the objectivity of the sacraments, through which one encounters the "real" presence of Christ in baptism and the Lord's Supper. Then, with a new appreciation for ecclesial authority, he moved away from the doctrine of Scripture alone to a combination of Scripture and tradition under the aegis of an authoritative church institution. In this way, he sought to safeguard the doctrinal fidelity of the contemporary Church of England (against doctrinal innovators and undue subjectivity) by appropriating the beliefs and practices of the ancient church vis-à-vis oral tradition and the efficacy of sacramental mediation.[107]

This development reflects a logic that inevitably led to the third element of Newman's refined position and to his *via media* on the doctrine of justification, namely, "uncreated grace" (*gratia increata*). Here is how it happened. By jettisoning the Evangelical distinction between "real" and "nominal" faith based on one's membership in the invisible church (step one), by embracing the sacrament of baptism as the necessary instrument by which one is regenerated (step two), and by insisting that the visible church is coterminous with the body of Christ (step three), Newman came to recognize the instrumental cause of justification in a way that was more consistent with the Roman Catholic position. If, at this time, Newman had converted to Catholicism, his course of action would have been simple—leave imputation and *sola fide* behind with Protestantism.[108] As long as Newman remained an Anglican (obligated to the Thirty-Nine Articles), however, such an abandonment was not an option. The eleventh article, which specifically defines justification by "Faith only," would not permit it. He therefore faced a conundrum, or at least he would have faced one, if not for a lesson that Newman had learned from his study of the fourth-century fathers—the doctrine of *gratia increata*.

The idea of grounding salvation in a form of *gratia increata* is the crowning development of Newman's soteriological reflection, and the one

---

107. Frederick H. Borsch explains how such an approach infused Tractarian spirituality with a measure of mysticism, often leading to an emphasis on the Eucharist. Borsch, "Ye Shall Be Holy," 356.

108. This is of course precisely what Newman did in 1845, when was received into the Catholic Church by Fr. Dominic Barberi of the Passionist Order.

that enabled him to finally develop his doctrine into a *via media* on justification. In keeping with the questions and concerns of the Alexandrian fathers, especially Clement, Athanasius, and Cyril, whose writings he devoured,[109] and also the French patristic scholar, Dionysius Petavius, SJ (1583–1652, or Denis Pétau),[110] Newman increasingly emphasized the inadequacy of human reason in grasping the divine presence (contra liberalism and Evangelicalism) in favor of sacramental mediation. At the center of this mediation was a mystical union with Christ,[111] in which, as Newman states, "true religion is in part altogether above reason, as in its Mysteries."[112]

Newman came to recognize that, by virtue of the church's sacramental union with Christ, believers possess the gift of the Holy Spirit, a gift which "pervades us (if it may be so said) as light pervades a building, or as a sweet perfume the folds of some honourable robe; so that, in Scriptural language, we are said to be in Him, and He in us."[113] The implication of this union shaped Newman's thinking about justification, as he continues to expound. "It is plain that such an inhabitation brings the Christian into a state altogether new and marvelous, far above the possession of mere gifts."[114] This fit naturally with Newman's growing regard for the sacrament of baptism, whereupon "each individual member receives the gift of the Holy Ghost as a preliminary step, a condition, or means of his being incorporated into the Church; or, in our Savior's words, that no one can enter, except he be regenerated in order to enter it."[115]

With the Alexandrian fathers, Newman recognized the divine presence to include the Father and the Son, along with the Spirit.[116] Joel Elowsky, quoting Cyril of Alexandria's explanation of this concept, illustrates the continuity of Newman's position with the fourth-century fathers, "When we thus receive the Spirit, we are 'proved sharers and partakers in the Divine Nature and we admit the Father himself into our hearts, through the Son and in the Son.'"[117] In such an economy, the Father declares sinful man to

---

109. Daley, "The Church Fathers," 31–41.
110. Dessain, "Uncreated Grace," 215.
111. Dessain, "Cardinal Newman and the Eastern Tradition," 95.
112. Newman, *PPS*, 242. This sermon was first published in 1835.
113. Ibid., 368. This sermon was first published in 1835.
114. Ibid.
115. Ibid., 655. This sermon was first published in 1836.
116. For a development of Newman's appreciation and usage of the Alexandrian fathers, see King, *Newman and the Alexandrian Fathers*.
117. Elowsky, "Bridging the Gap," 153.

be righteous, upon the merits and saving grace of Christ, by means of the inhabitation of the Holy Spirit.[118]

Michael Gorman, in his book *Inhabiting the Cruciform God: Kenosis, Justification, and Theosis in Paul's Narrative Soteriology*, offers some insight into the distinctive features of eastern theology that would have attracted Newman. In the opening pages, Gorman provides a Trinitarian definition of theosis with which Newman would have been most comfortable. "Theosis is transformative participation in the kenotic, cruciform character of God through the Spirit-enabled conformity to the incarnate, crucified, and resurrected/glorified Christ."[119] As our next chapter will examine, the reason for Newman's approval of this definition is largely indebted to his view of "Spirit-enabled conformity," in which justification is conceived of as a participatory and transformative experience closely tied to sanctification and holiness. In the words of his role model, Thomas Scott, many of whose ideas Newman retained for the remainder of his life, "Holiness rather than peace."[120]

The main contribution of Dionysius Petavius to Newman's doctrine was the concept of the Spirit's substantial indwelling in the regenerate soul, a notion that Petavius helped to reintroduce among Catholic scholars in the seventeenth century.[121] With a Trinitarian synthesis similar to Newman's, Petavius promoted the role of the Holy Spirit as the *gratia increata* of justification, that is, the formal cause upon which one is declared (and also made) to be righteous.[122] Expressing his approval in the advertisement to the third edition of his *Lectures on the Doctrine of Justification* (1874), Newman explains that "Petavius speaks of another, or fifth [form of justification], viz. the substantial Presence of the Holy Ghost in the soul."[123]

Our next chapter will examine more specifically how Newman constructed his doctrine with the resources of eastern thought. The main idea to grasp at this point is the influence of such ideas upon Newman's

---

118. Newman, *Jfc.*, 147 [163–64].

119. Gorman, *Inhabiting the Cruciform God*, 7.

120. Newman, *Apo*, 5.

121. Rondet, *The Grace of Christ*, 366–73.

122. Ibid., 367; Holtzen, "Union with God," 35. For an explantion of how Petavius used the eastern fathers, see King, *Newman and the Alexandrian Fathers*, 119–21.

123. Newman, *Jfc*, xii. Mark Medley examines the relevance of theosis for contemporary reflection on the doctrine of justification in his essay, "Participation in God." Medley provides an assessment of several modern Baptist theologians who, by applying the category of uncreated grace, have challenged concepts on justification that appear to reduce the doctrine to a legal-forensic activity. *Theosis: Deification in Christian Theology*, ed. Kharlamov, 207.

theological reflection. In keeping with the bent of his character, Dessain points out, "[Newman] could never have been satisfied with thinking of grace merely as a quality in the soul or a strengthening force or a refreshing water."[124] And as this was personally true for Newman, it also applied to the Oxford Movement in general, as Ralph Townsend comments, "The core idea of Tractarian spirituality is that we may become by grace what Christ is by nature; we are transfigured by the divine indwelling."[125]

G. The Oxford or Tractarian Movement

After describing the conclusion of his Mediterranean journey, Newman opens chapter two of his *Apologia* with these words: "When I got home from abroad, I found that already a movement had commenced, in opposition to the specific danger which at that time was threatening the religion of the nation and its Church."[126] The threat to which Newman refers was a perceived attack by the new Whig government (after nearly four decades of Tory rule) on the structures and revenues of the Protestant Church of Ireland.[127] Newman's response, in collaboration with such figures as Edward Bouverie Pusey, John Keble, Richard Hurrell Froude, William Palmer, Robert Wilberforce, and Isaac Williams became the context in which his *via media* emerged. While a great deal can be said about very small parts of this narrative, to say nothing of the overall Oxford Movement, we will focus our attention on those elements that elucidate Newman's doctrine of justification.[128]

Following Keble's assize sermon, "National Apostasy," from the pulpit of St. Mary's on July 14, the Oxford Movement initiated its campaign in September of 1833 with brief articles issued under the title, *Tracts for the Times*. The Tracts had two primary targets: the "High and Dry" establishment

---

124. Dessain, "Uncreated Grace," 215.

125. Townsend, "The Catholic Revival in the Church of England," 465.

126. Newman, *Apo*, 36.

127. The Irish Church Temporalities Bill 1833 was the immediate occasion for Newman's reaction. Herein lies a fascinating irony: the Oxford Movement's defense of a defiantly Protestant established Church of Ireland against Catholic adversaries who sought to reduce its power, eventually resulted in much of the movement crossing the Tiber into Catholicism.

128. Helpful works on the Oxford Movement include: Brilioth, *The Anglican Revival*; Chadwick, *The Mind of the Oxford Movement*; Chadwick, *The Spirit of the Oxford Movement*; Church, *The Oxford Movement*; Cox, *Recollections of Oxford*; Dawson, *The Spirit of the Oxford Movement*; Edgecombe, *Two Poets of the Oxford Movement*; Faber, *Oxford Apostles*; Mozley, *Reminiscences*; Nockles, *The Oxford Movement in Context*.

which sought to promote the marriage of State and Church, and the nonconformist churches, which, consisting largely of Evangelicals, had grown in membership throughout Britain. Of these two targets, liberalism initially occupied the foreground. So involved in the project did Newman become that he would eventually edit, publish, or contribute to thirty of the ninety tracts. Like Athanasius of old, Newman regarded himself as taking a stand against heresy—the liberal heresy of Erastianism and the subjective heresy of Evangelicals.[129]

Of all the criticisms leveled against the *Tracts*, the most common was its agenda to undermine the Protestant character of the Church of England. John Bowden, for example, had warned Newman in a letter dated July 14, 1834, that the Oxford Tracts "will be one day charged with rank Popery," and recommended that a tract be published to preempt the charge.[130] In response to this critique, Newman composed two tracts (numbers 38 and 41) suggesting that the Church of England had become more Protestant than it had previously been. The proper trajectory of Anglicanism, argued Newman, is a *via media* between Protestantism and the Roman Catholic Church.[131] His argument came to a head in 1837 with his *Lectures on the Prophetical Office of the Church* (first published on March 11, 1837), a work that systematized the teaching of Anglican Divines of the seventeenth century, originally delivered in Adam de Brome chapel of St. Mary's Church.[132]

The foundation of Newman's *via media* distinguished the so-called "episcopal tradition," which grew out of the Catholic creeds and was passed through generations by a succession of bishops, from the "prophetical tradition," which was thought to exist in the broader development of the Church's theological reflection.[133] In his *Lectures on the Prophetical Office*, Newman

---

129. Dulles, *John Henry Newman*, 5. Newman narrates his role in the movement up to his eventual disenchantment with the *via media* in his *Apo*, 101–46.

130. Newman, *Letters and Diaries of John Henry Newman*, Vol. 4, 304.

131. Unlike other expressions of Anglo-Catholicism, which borrowed wholesale from the Roman Catholic Church, the Tractarians were more cautious in such identification. Pickering, *Anglo-Catholicism*, 41.

132. In December 1876, Newman organized this work into a two-volume set entitled, *The Via Media*. The first volume consisted of the third edition of the *Lectures on the Prophetical Office of the Church*. The second volume comprised eleven more occasional pieces including his tracts on the Church Missionary Society of 1830, documentation of Tract 90, and his retraction of anti-Catholic statements in 1841. Newman wrote a new preface, which serves as his last word on the concept of an Anglican *via media*. Newman, *The Via Media of the Anglican Church*.

133. Newman, *Lectures on the prophetical office*, 304–13. In Newman's thought, these generally corresponded to the *lex credendi* (the episcopal tradition's dogmatic formulations) and the *lex orandi* (the prophetical tradition's development of doctrine).

emphasizes the vital necessity of this prophetical tradition. In addition to drawing attention to the growth and development of Christian teaching beyond the primitive creeds, this emphasis also had the effect of conceptually moving the range and scope of apostolic faith closer to Roman Catholicism. Statements such as the following illustrate how Newman's logic drove him in this direction.

> What is meant by the Church Catholic at this day? Where is she? What are her local instruments and organs? How does she speak? When and where does she teach, forbid, command, censure? How can she be said to utter one and the same doctrine every where, when we are at war with all the rest of Christendom, and not at peace at home? In the Primitive Church there was no difficulty, and no mistaking; then all Christians every where spoke one and the same doctrine, and if any novelty arose, it was at once denounced and stifled. The case is the same, indeed, with the Roman Church now; but for Anglo-catholics so to speak, is to use words without meaning, to dream of a state of things long past away from this Protestant land.[134]

It is noteworthy that in this second edition of the *Lectures on the Doctrine of Justification* (1838), following the above logic, Newman renamed "Anglicanism," "Anglo-Catholicism." Through this way of thinking, Newman and his fellow Tractarians were prompted to contend that it was necessary to look back before the sixteenth-century context of Cranmer, Latimer, and Ridley in appreciation of the Catholic scope of the early church.[135] With such a vision, Newman sought to strengthen the church to withstand the dangers of the moment by inculcating an informed commitment to "Apostolical Succession" and "the Liturgy."[136] The primary vehicles of communication driving this campaign were diverse. In addition to the *Lectures on the Prophetical Office*, print media included the *Tracts for the Times*,[137] Froude's

---

134. Ibid., 317–18.

135. Newman's infamous opposition to the construction of the Martyr's Memorial, the broad contours of which are helpfully outlined by Ker, bears eloquent testimony to this fact. Ker, *John Henry Newman*, 172–73.

136. Sheridan, *Newman on Justification*, 214.

137. The *Tracts* defined their positions in contrast to non-conformist churches (which Tractarians categorically rejected since they lacked bishops and were therefore considered to be illegitimate) and the Erastian elements of the established Church (which were thought to undermine the supernatural character of Christ's body). With the accession of Edward Pusey in late 1833, the *Tracts* acquired a greater degree of thoroughness.

Remains,[138] and the *British Critic*, a paper with a circulation of approximately 1,200, which Newman himself edited, starting in 1838.[139] Other platforms included the pulpit of St. Mary's Church, from which Newman preached weekly[140] and the Adam De Brome chapel where he lectured.[141]

The question naturally arises, to what was Newman reacting when he formed his *via media*? Sheridan, arguing from Newman's *Apologia* (1864), asserts that it was primarily the threat of liberalism, so that in *The Arians of the Fourth Century*, "Newman could not help but compare in his own mind the Church of which he was reading in the writings of the fourth century Fathers and the Church as he knew it in the England of his day."[142] Sheridan is not alone in recognizing this tendency. Rowan Williams, in his volume on Arius, makes a similar point; Williams, however, also highlights the role of Evangelicalism in provoking Newman's polemic. His argument illuminates the connection between Newman's writing of *The Arians*, the Oxford Movement, and Newman's growing critique of Protestantism.

> However, setting aside for the moment the distasteful rhetoric of [Newman's] exposition, it should be possible to see something of what his polemical agenda really is. *The Arians of the Fourth Century* is, in large part, a tract in defence of what the early Oxford Movement thought of as spiritual religion and spiritual authority. It works with a clear normative definition of Christian faith and practice, in which ascetical discipline goes hand-in-hand with the repudiation of Protestant biblicism (and Protestant rejection of post-scriptural development in teaching and devotion). . . . Newman's version of the fourth-century crisis, then, rests upon a characterization of Arianism as radically

---

138. Edited by Newman and John Keble in two volumes two years after Richard Hurrell Froude's untimely death on February 28, 1836, this work revealed the Tractarians' hostility toward Evangelicalism and the Protestant heritage from which they drew inspiration. Froude, *Remains of the late Reverend Richard Hurrell Froude*, ed. Newman and Keble.

139. Turner, *John Henry Newman*, 313–14.

140. The legendary status of Newman's pulpit was memorably captured by Matthew Arnold's retrospective evocation of "the charm of that spiritual apparition, gliding in the dim afternoon light through the aisles of St. Mary's, rising into the pulpit, and then, in the most entrancing of voices, breaking the silence with words and thoughts which were a religious music,—subtle, sweet, mournful." Ker, *John Henry Newman*, 90. For a concise review of the six volumes that comprise Newman's *PPS*, see Chadwick, *Newman*, 18–23.

141. Particularly the *Lectures on the Prophetical Office of the Church* (delivered in the spring of 1836) and *Lectures on the Doctrine of Justification* (the first of which was delivered on April 13 and the final on June 1, 1837).

142. Sheridan, *Newman on Justification*, 206.

"other" in several respects. It is the forerunner of stolid Evangelicalism, Erastian worldliness ("carnal, self indulgent religion"), and—by 1874 [when he revised his *Lectures on Justification*], anyway—the new style of university theology.[143]

Standing beside Williams, on the other side of the spectrum from Sheridan's interpretation, is the view of Frank Turner, who argues that the structure of the *Apologia* was purposefully designed to conceal Newman's antipathy for Evangelicals, "a dislike bordering on hatred that had been the single most energizing force in his thought and theology during the 1830s and early 1840s."[144] Turner provides credible evidence that in the *Apologia*, "Newman assiduously recast that Tractarian assault on Evangelical religion into a struggle against liberals and liberalism whose victim he claimed to have been."[145] Such a strategy, argues Turner, promised to recast Newman as a champion of dogmatic religious truth during the controversial years of the 1860s when he was *persona non grata* in most religious circles. The strength of Turner's case is tarnished, however, by his tendency to subject Newman to psychological analysis, even at the level of his subconscious motives, an approach which has met with a negative reception, not least among some well-established Newman scholars.[146] Nevertheless, Turner seems to be on to something when he points out the significance of Evangelicalism as a fundamental force of provocation for Newman during his Tractarian period.

There is a way of reading Newman that can retain the worthwhile element of Turner's insight—that Evangelicals indeed occupied the foreground with liberals in motivating the *via media*—without necessitating Turner's full-blown theory. This fact comes when we recognize that, in Newman's view, Evangelicalism tended toward liberalism.[147] Notice, for instance, how Newman makes this connection in his *Lectures on the Prophetical Office*.

143. Williams, *Arius: Heresy and Tradition*, 5.

144. Turner, *John Henry Newman*, 9.

145. Most of Turner's case turns on evidence that supports the intensity of Newman's opposition to Evangelicalism during the 1830s and 1840s. For example, he cites the Unitarian theologian, James Martineau, who recalled Newman having "assailed the Evangelical party with every weapon of antipathy which could be drawn from the armory of imagination or logic, Scripture or history." Ibid. Turner also offers a rhetorical analysis of Newman's appendix, added to the *Apologia* in 1865, in which he redefines the meaning of "Liberalism." Ibid., 10–11.

146. It is noteworthy that among the thirteen essays in *The Cambridge Companion to John Henry Newman*, which was published seven years after Turner's work, there is not a single mention of Turner.

147. Ker's research supports this connection. In the context of describing Newman's opposition to the inroads of Rationalism, he writes, "The result was that 'idea of

> Before Germany had become rationalistic, and Geneva Socinian, Romanism might be considered as the most dangerous corruption of the gospel. . . . But at this day, when the connexion of Protestantism with infidelity is so evident, what claim has the former upon our sympathy? And to what theology can the serious Protestant, dissatisfied with his system, betake himself but to Romanism, unless we [Anglo-Catholics] display our characteristic principles, and show him that he may be Catholic and Apostolic, yet not Roman?[148]

In this statement Newman manages to portray contemporary Protestantism as fostering unbelief like the rationalistic Germans (i.e., liberals) and the theologically minimalist Socinians.[149] The place where this was most obvious, from Newman's point of view, was in the Evangelical emphasis upon "private interpretation,"[150] a concept that he regarded as open to absurdity.[151] For example, Newman, in his sermon entitled, "Unreal Words" (published in 1840), exclaims his frustration with the myriad religious voices claiming to pronounce authoritatively upon issues of doctrine. "Let us avoid talking, of whatever kind; whether mere empty talking, or censorious talking, or idle profession, or descanting upon Gospel doctrines, or the affectation of philosophy, or the pretence of eloquence."[152]

As Newman was troubled by the subjective impulse of Evangelicalism, the feeling of suspicion and opposition was eventually reciprocated.[153] In its first review of the *Tracts* in 1833, the *Christian Observer* described

---

Mystery' was 'discarded', and religion took on a subjective rather than objective character. The blame is laid squarely on Evangelical Christianity, which directs 'its attention to the heart itself, not to anything external to us." Ker, *John Henry Newman*, 122. Ker makes the same point later in his volume when he described John Henry's frustration with the Evangelical faith of his younger brother, Francis Newman (199).

148. Newman, *Lectures on the prophetical office*, 25.

149. "Socinianism," in the context of nineteenth-century inter-denominational rhetoric, had more to do with "minimally dogmatic Christianity based on reason and toleration" than adherence to a particular set of doctrinal tenets. Turner, *John Henry Newman*, 14.

150. Ibid., 262.

151. So Newman writes in his *Lectures on the Prophetical Office of the Church*, "Scripture is not so clear—in God's providential arrangement, to which we submit—as to hinder ordinary persons, who read it for themselves, from being Sabellians, or Independents, or Wesleyans" (180). This appears in "Lecture Six" titled "On the Abuse of Private Judgment," (175–204).

152. Newman, *PPS*, 987.

153. It is sometimes overlooked that many Evangelicals recognized a degree of kinship with Tractarians in the early phase of the Oxford Movement. Newsome, "Justification and Sanctification," 33–34.

the publication as coming from "a Society formed at Oxford, the members of which, professing themselves to be the most orthodox upholders of the Church, have begun to scatter throughout the land publications which, for bigotry, Popery, and intolerance surpass the writings even of Laud and Sacheverall."[154] This was among the first public shots that would eventually develop into a full-scale doctrinal battle.

In response to opposition from the *Christian Observer*, specifically after its castigation of Pusey's tracts on baptismal regeneration,[155] Newman promised to publicly address the doctrine of justification in order to demonstrate that the teaching of the *Tracts* in general and these tracts in particular were in fact consistent with the Articles of Religion.[156] After submitting two letters of response for publication,[157] Newman decided to deliver a lecture series on the doctrine of justification in Adam de Brome's chapel at St. Mary's, Oxford. It was spring of 1837.[158]

Significant as the attack on Pusey was, there were additional factors motivating Newman to address the doctrine of justification. Evangelical critics of the *Tracts* proceeded to cast aspersions on what they viewed as the Oxford Movement's desire to revive the Roman doctrine of infused righteousness.[159] An opportunity for Evangelicals to assert this contention came when George Stanley Faber published his work *The Primitive Doctrine of Justification Investigated* (1837). Faber, a thoroughgoing Evangelical, endeavored to prove against Alexander Knox (an Irish lay theologian), and against Joseph Milner (Newman's favorite Evangelical church historian), that the Protestant doctrine of justification by faith was rooted in the teaching of the early fathers before it was corrupted by the medieval scholastics. When a review of Faber's work asserted that "we see no substantial

---

154. Turner, *John Henry Newman*, 173.

155. Pusey's three tracts, numbered 67, 68, and 69, were entitled, "Scriptural Views of Holy Baptism as Established by the Consent of the Ancient Church and Contrasted with the Systems of Modern Schools." The *Christian Observer* leveled a personal attack upon Pusey, concluding with the question, "Will any approver of the Oxford Tracts answer in Print?" Perry, "Newman's Treatment of Luther," 308.

156. Toon, *Evangelical Theology*, 141.

157. The first, dated January 11, 1837, argued for baptism as a gift particular to the Second Testament. The second letter, dated March 3 of the same year, clarified that Pusey had not written all that the *Observer* had accused him of. Newman then demanded to know what in Pusey's tract had violated the Thirty-Nine Articles. Perry, "Newman's Treatment of Luther," 308–9.

158. Chadwick, "The Lectures on Justification," 288.

159. Toon, *Evangelical Theology*, 141.

difference between the doctrine of Trent and the doctrines of Mr. Knox and the Oxford Tracts," a quarrel erupted.[160]

On account of his appreciation for the writing of Alexander Knox (d. 1831), Newman's attention was drawn to the dispute.[161] Newman's interest centered on Knox's essay, "On Justification," written in 1810, which belonged to a volume of Knox's letters and papers entitled the *Remains*. Originally prepared by the Rev. James John Hornby in 1834, Newman edited the updated edition in 1837.[162] Scott Murray summarizes the basic thrust and effect of the essay when he writes, "Knox argued that the Church of England no longer held justification as an *usus forensis* but rather as a moral renovation. This article apparently brought to boiling point a simmering controversy between the High Churchmen and the Evangelicals in the Church of England."[163] Against this backdrop, Newman's *Lectures on the Doctrine of Justification* was intended to set the record straight.

H. The *Lectures on the Doctrine of Justification*

Newman's *Lectures on the Doctrine of Justification* was (and still is) a lightning rod. On the positive side, Chadwick calls it "a book that deserves to be ranked at least on a par with any of his more widely read writings on theology."[164] Ker describes it as "a pioneering classic of 'ecumenical theology.'"[165] According to Alfred Plummer, the German historian J. J. Döllinger "always spoke of Newman's Justification as the greatest masterpiece of theology that England had produced in a hundred years."[166] With similar approbation, the Swedish historian Yngve Brilioth regarded the *Lectures* as "perhaps the chief theological document of the Oxford Movement."[167] On the other hand, there have been a fair number of detractors. Faber, mentioned above, found Newman's volume to be "confused and confusing."[168] Richard Holt Sutton dismissed the work as "somewhat straw-chopping and dry."[169] Most signifi-

---

160. Toon, *Evangelical Theology*, 142.
161. Ker calls Knox "the Irish forerunner of the Tractarians" in his *John Henry Newman*, 115.
162. McGrath, *ID*, 296.
163. Murray, "Luther in Newman's *Lectures*," 155.
164. Chadwick, "The Lectures on Justification," 287.
165. Ker, *John Henry Newman*, 157.
166. Chadwick, "The Lectures on Justification," 289.
167. Brilioth, *The Anglican Revival*, 282.
168. Ward, *The Life of John Henry*, 432.
169. Hutton, *Cardinal Newman*, 2nd ed., 83.

cantly, Bishop Charles Pettit M'Ilvaine of Ohio, whose lineage and personal interests belonged to Britain, was so disturbed by Newman's position that he published a refutation in the form of a book of over five hundred pages, entitled *Oxford Divinity compared with that of the Romish and Anglican Churches with a special view of the doctrine of Justification by Faith* (1841). Whatever one's perspective, the *Lectures on Justification* generally elicits a forceful and definite response.[170]

Newsome suggests that the *Lectures on Justification* may also be viewed as a clarification of sermons which Newman preached in the previous decade at St. Mary's, in which he sought to disprove the Protestant doctrine of justification by faith only.[171] Unlike his sermons, however, the *Lectures* speak with a strongly polemical tone in repudiation of the beliefs that he had once held as an Evangelical. Precisely because the doctrine of justification was so central to popular Protestantism, with its axiomatic focus upon a spiritual conversion, this subject was for Newman more than personal or theological; it was symbolic. Henry Chadwick is correct to point out that, "Without a treatment in some depth of the issue of justification, his statement of the *via media* must be gravely incomplete."[172] Now, at the age of thirty-six, Newman was evidently ready to conduct such a treatment.

The *Lectures* were initiated in Adam de Brome chapel on April 13, 1837. They were revised and published on March 30, 1838.[173] Newman's primary object for writing, according to Sheridan, "was to show how the Church of England understands the axiom 'justification by faith only.'"[174] Newman presented the position of Rome on justification as mostly true, but in some respects "defective."[175] The "ultra-Protestant" position (i.e., Evangelicalism), however, he denounces as simply "erroneous."[176] Even though Newman was meticulous in editing the *Lectures*,[177] it makes no pretense of

170. Toon, *Evangelical Theology*, 141–70.

171. Newsome, "Justification and Sanctification," 33. Many of these messages were published in the first three volumes of the *PPS* (originally published in 1834, 1835, and 1836, respectively).

172. Chadwick, "The Lectures on Justification," 289.

173. Newman dedicated his *Lectures* to Richard Bagot, Bishop of Oxford, hoping to receive an endorsement, and was heartbroken when Bagot had reservations. Gilley, *Newman and His Age*, 176–77.

174. Sheridan, *Newman on Justification*, 247. Newman writes as much himself in his *Apologia*, "I wrote my Essay on Justification in 1837; it was aimed at the Lutheran dictum that justification by faith only was the cardinal doctrine of Christianity." Newman, *Apo*, 72.

175. Newman, *Jfc*, 2.

176. Ibid.

177. Ker, *John Henry Newman*, 149–50.

being a systematic treatment of the subject.[178] So Sheridan writes, "[W]hile the overall picture is clear enough, the synthesis of the *Lectures* is far from complete in secondary details. There are some loose ends that do not fit into the complete pattern."[179]

The Lectures should be understood as part of the larger project of Newman's *via media* with his *Lectures on the Prophetical Office of the Church, Parochial and Plain Sermons, Tracts for the Times*, and Froude's *Remains*. Thus, Newman opens the advertisement to the third edition:

> These Lectures on the doctrine of Justification formed one of a series of works projected by the Author in illustration of what has often been considered to be the characteristic position of the Anglican Church, as lying in a supposed *Via Media*, admitting much and excluding much both of Roman and of Protestant teaching.[180]

Newman states his chief contention with Protestantism when he writes that "the Church considers the doctrine of justification by faith only to be a *principle* and the religion of the day takes it as a *rule of conduct*."[181] The tragic effect, as Newman saw it, was to reduce Christian faith to a subjective experience and to discard the urgency of obedience in favor of antinomianism.[182] Facing such a crisis, Newman's endeavored to steer a middle course between what he perceived as the extremes of solafideism (which he associates with "Lutherans who opposed Melanchthon") and works-righteousness (namely, "Vásquez, Caietan, and other extreme writers of the Roman school").[183] Against these extremes, Newman occasionally identifies his position with

---

178. It should be remembered that Newman was simultaneously editing Froude's *Remains* when he was getting his *Lectures on Justification* ready for publication. Ker, *John Henry Newman*, 147–49. Froude's infamous animosity for Protestantism, coupled with Newman's intense emotional attachment to his recently deceased friend, may have further sharpened the edge of Newman's polemic.

179. Sheridan, *Newman on Justification*, 239.

180. Newman, *Jfc*, ix.

181. Ibid., 333.

182. We are reminded of Scott's influence on Newman, which instilled a robust commitment to holiness and an antipathy for lawless faith. Sheridan, *Newman on Justification*, 26–29.

183. Newman, *Jfc*, 2. Newman's reading of Catholic authors was equally facile. Bellarmine and Vásquez receive only a passing quotation. Newman evidently believed the Catholic Church to teach that believers are justified on account of their renewal. Newman, *Jfc.*, 154. It is precisely this assumption that Newman clarifies in the third edition of his *Lectures* (1874), *Jfc.*, ix–xiv.

the "English divines," by which he largely meant the "Caroline divines,"[184] in grounding justification in the instrumental causation of faith *and* works.[185]

Aware of the controversy crouching at his door, especially among Evangelicals, the footnotes of Newman's *Lectures* mainly refer to Protestant authors. While Bishop George Bull (1634-1710) and Jeremy Taylor (1613-67) are occasionally presented as precursors of Newman's position,[186] a strong emphasis upon such infamous anti-Calvinists would not have served him well.[187] Instead, he gives more attention to Richard Hooker (1554-1600) and a less occasional reference to John Davenant (1606-68).[188] McGrath exposes the problematic way in which Newman connects the dots from Anglican history to his own position.[189] After examining these historical movements, McGrath concludes,

> Newman's use of the later Caroline divines to determine what constitutes an authentically Anglican doctrine of justification is deeply problematic. The theology of justification of the post-Restoration divines, such as Bull and Taylor, by no means

184. Ibid., 3. The "Caroline" divines (from *Carolus*, the Latin name for Charles) are the primary Anglican theologians and devotional writers during the reigns of Charles I (1625-49) and Charles II (1660-85). For an introduction to the general theological contributions of the Caroline Divines see Guyer, *The Beauty of Holiness: The Caroline Divines*. For a closer look at what these divines taught on the doctrine of justification, particularly John Davenant, William Forbes, Henry Hammond, Jeremy Taylor and George Bull, see Bryant, "Bishop George Bull's Doctrine of Justification."

185. Newman, *Jfc*, 275-76. In affirmation of Bull, Newman asserts, "By faith, according to Bishop Bull, is meant *fides formata charitate et operibus*, or the obedience which is of faith," (358). Newman looked chiefly to George Bull's *Harmonia Apostolica*, an Anglican attempt to reconcile Paul and James by stating that we are justified by faith *and* works.

186. Passing references to these men are found in Newman, *Jfc*. vii, 13, 16, 159, 358.

187. For an explanation of how Anglican theology moved from its "Classical" form (i.e., Hooker, Davenant, and Ussher) to the anti-Calvinist, "Caroline" variety (i.e., Taylor, Bull, and Barrow), see Allison, *The Rise of Moralism*. For an account of how this history unfolded before it is appropriated by Newman, see McGrath, *ID*, 277-83.

188. Most of these references are found in Newman's Appendix. He pits Davenant against Calvin, for instance, to argue with Davenant that Christ's righteousness is not a personal possession of the believer. Newman, *Jfc*, 362. Hooker appears with more frequency. Ibid., 125, 375, 378, 382-84, 400-404.

189. McGrath explains how Newman was at variance with some of the pre-Commonwealth divines and therefore concludes his *Lectures* with reference to three Anglican luminaries, Hooker, Taylor, and Barrow. In Newman's words, "I will appeal in conclusion to the three who have sometimes been considered the special lights of our later Church, Hooker, Taylor, and Barrow; of whom two will be found to sanction me, and the third, though apparently pronouncing the other way, to withdraw his judgment while he gives it." Newman, *Jfc*, 400. McGrath explains why this claim is fallacious, *ID*, 282-84.

represents a unanimous or even the majority opinion within contemporary Anglicanism.[190]

The biggest historiographical error in Newman's *Lectures,* however, is his treatment of Martin Luther. Newman gets Luther badly wrong, ostensibly collapsing his doctrine of justification into nineteenth-century Evangelicalism.[191] Newman's relative ignorance of Luther's Reformation, his inability to read German, and a poor translation of Luther's 1533 *Commentary on Galatians* (which was purged of anything that smelled Roman), worked against him.[192] It is telling that Newman quotes from the John Gerhard's *Loci Theologici* more than from Luther and Melanchthon.[193] Most troublesome is that Newman quotes Luther with selective omissions that have the effect of altering the meaning of Luther's doctrine.[194] McGrath conducts an analysis of the most egregious of these instances and charitably concludes that the fault is probably owing to inadequate English translations of Luther.[195]

Newman's most severe critique of Luther (and by extension the Evangelicals whom he represents) is reserved for the final chapter entitled, "On Preaching the Gospel." By this point Newman has made his case. According to the "Advertisement to the Third Edition" (1874), his argument hangs together according to the following outline.[196] (1) The first two lectures delineate the Protestant and Catholic doctrines of justification. (2) Three lectures—the third, fourth, and fifth—inquire into the meaning of

190. McGrath, *ID*, 299.

191. We all have lenses, and there is no such thing as a view from nowhere. In Newman's case, however, the issues of his day exercised an excessive degree of control over his interpretation. This was true, for instance, of Newman's works on *The Arians of the Fourth Century*, where Newman portrays Antiochene devotion, on account of its literal interpretation of Scripture, as inferior to the spirituality of the Alexandrian tradition. The correlation to Evangelical literalism of his own day is thinly veiled. Williams, *Arius: Heresy and Tradition*, 4–5, 158.

192. Chadwick, "The Lectures on Justification," 294. In footnote 19 Chadwick suggests, "Much of what Newman knew is likely to have come through J. Milner's *History of the Church of Christ* . . . where Luther dominates the account of the Reformation and is given a pietist face."

193. Johann Gerhard (1582–1637), a scholastic scholar and Lutheran pastor, was the most popular Lutheran theologian in England during the nineteenth century. Guyer, *The Beauty of Holiness*, 22. Newman concentrates on volume 3 of Gerhard's *Loci Theologici, De Justificatione Per Fidem*.

194. Newman, *Jfc*, 331–33. McGrath examines the most grievous example of misquotation in which Newman cites Luther to prove that justification is in some sense based on works, when, in fact, the omitted section asserts that justification is by faith alone. McGrath, *ID*, 305–6.

195. McGrath, *ID*, 306–7.

196. Newman, *Jfc*, xiv.

the term, "justification." (3) The next four—the sixth, seventh, eighth, and ninth—determine what "real thing" is denoted by the term, "justification." (4) In the tenth, eleventh, and twelfth, the office and nature of faith is examined in relation to justification. Additionally, a sixty-one-page appendix is devoted to understanding justification's formal cause from the history of Christian thought.[197] However, in between lecture twelve and the appendix is lecture thirteen, where, in Newman's words, "practical application is made of the principles and conclusions of the foregoing Lectures, to the mode of preaching and professing the Gospel, popular thirty or forty years since, called Evangelical."[198] Here Newman the pastor pulls out all the superlatives and speaks with an extraordinary degree of candor.

The point of this chapter, as Newman's clever turn-of-phrase states, is to respond to the "imputation of legalism" from Evangelical detractors. Newman spins the Protestant argument on its head by insisting that it is not creeds, rites, and works that inculcate self-righteousness and superstition; rather, it is Luther's position of "faith only." In addition to communicating the concern of this chapter, it also gives voice to the fundamental burden of Newman's overall *Lectures*.

> Men congratulate themselves on their emancipation from forms and their enlightened worship, when they are but in the straight course to a worse captivity, and are exchanging dependence on the creature for dependence on self.
>
> I observe, then, that what the Jews felt concerning their Law, is exactly what many upholders of the tenet of "faith only," feel concerning what they consider faith; that they substitute faith for Christ; they so regard it, that instead of being the way to Him, it is in this way; that they make it a something to rest in; nay, that they alter the meaning of the word, as the Jews altered the meaning of the word Law; in short, that, under the pretence of light and liberty, they have brought into the Gospel the narrow, minute, technical, nay, I will say carnal and hollow

---

197. Newman's appendix originated in his first edition (1838). A few additional comments, however, indicated in brackets, appear in the third edition (1874). These appear on pages 31, 73, 96, 101, 154, 186, 187, 190, 198, 201, 226, 236, 260, 343, 348-349, and 353. Newman provides a helpful introduction to such changes when he writes, "The purpose of this Appendix is to show that the cardinal question to be considered 1   cs and Protestants in their controversy about Justification is, What is the   ? When this is properly examined, it will be found that there is little or no   view between the disputants, except when the Protestant party adheres to Luther:—'Sola fides, non fides formata charitate, justificat: fides justificat   ritatem,' and refuses to assign a formal cause," 343 [391].

198.   n, *Jfc*, xiv.

system of the Pharisees.... And thus faith and (what is called) spiritual-mindedness are dwelt on as ends, and obstruct the view of Christ, just as the Law was perverted by the Jews.[199]

After the original version of Newman's *Lectures* was released in 1838, a second edition was published in 1840 with simple formatting changes. It was in 1874, five years before he was elevated to the Catholic Cardinalate, that Newman published the third and final edition. His stated reason for doing so appears in the opening page of the advertisement to the third edition, "Unless the Author held in substance in 1874 what he published in 1838, he would not at this time be reprinting what he wrote as an Anglican; certainly not with so little added by way of safeguard."[200] This resembles what Newman says in his *Apologia*: "What I held in 1816, I held in 1833, and I hold in 1864."[201] In our next chapter, after summarizing the substance of Newman's position, we will consider whether his claim to consistency is in fact justified.

I. Conclusion

We have considered how Newman's religious background led him from "a conventional, non-sacramental middle-class" experience of faith,[202] to a Calvinistic variety of Evangelicalism (1816–27), through a brief flirtation with liberalism (1828), and eventually into the so-called Oxford Movement (1833–38). The high point of Newman's *via media* came in 1841 when he composed his famous Tract 90, at which time his Tractarian balloon began to deflate until October 9, 1845, when he was received into the Catholic Church by Fr. Dominic Barberi of the Passionist Order.[203] There were, as we have seen, a number of crucial points in this development of Newman's religious thought between 1816 and 1838.

From Thomas Scott, Newman acquired a deep appreciation for the holiness of the Triune God and the utter depravity of human nature, values that remained with him to the end of his life. In 1823, when Newman became a fellow at Oriel College, the Calvinist orientation of his faith fell under siege. Edward Pusey pushed on Newman's doctrine of imputation. Edward Hawkins challenged his bifurcation of humanity between "real" and

199. Ibid., 323–26.
200. Ibid., ix.
201. Newman, *Apo*, 49.
202. Gilley, "Life and Writings," 1.
203. Ker, *John Henry Newman*, 316–21.

"pseudo" Christians and instilled an appreciation for the church fathers. After months of such influence and study, particularly of the fourth-century fathers, Newman started to reconsider his position on the authority of tradition and the objectivity of the sacraments. He eventually abandoned the Evangelical doctrines of *sola scriptura* and *sola fide* in exchange for an affirmation of the authority of oral tradition and baptismal regeneration. Thanks to the doctrine of uncreated grace, which he imbibed from the Alexandrian fathers and Petavius, Newman regarded himself to be in subscription to the Thirty-Nine Articles.

The year of 1833 was significant. According to Newman, Keble's assize sermon, "National Apostasy," marked the beginning of the Oxford Movement. From it developed the revival of the notion of Anglicanism as a *via media* between Roman Catholicism and Protestantism. Through various means, starting with his *Lectures on the Prophetical Office* (1837), Newman worked this position out in terms of the development of the church's "prophetic tradition." Realizing that he would eventually need to address his *via media* to the doctrine of justification—a central tenet of Evangelicalism—the conflict surrounding Alexander Knox was just the right occasion in which to articulate his position.

The first lecture on justification was delivered on April 13, 1837 and the final on June 1 of the same year. The general purpose of their composition was "to show how the Church of England understands the axiom 'justification by faith only.'"[204] His answer to this question is perhaps best summarized in the most frequently quoted sentence of his volume: "Justification comes *through* the Sacraments; is received *by* faith; *consists* in God's inward presence; and *lives* in obedience."[205] The precise meaning of this statement will be the subject of our next chapter.

---

204. Sheridan, *Newman on Justification*, 247; Newman, *Apo*, 72.
205. Newman, *Jfc*, 278.

Chapter 4: John Henry Newman's Doctrine of Justification

A. Theological Contours of Newman's Doctrine of Justification.

HAVING EXAMINED THE BACKGROUND to Newman's doctrine of justification, we will now analyze the substance of his position. The leading edge of our inquiry is concerned with how he identified the fundamental ground for justification, the formal cause by which Newman understood God to remove guilt and impart righteousness to sinners.

Like Vermigli, Newman refuses to drive a wedge between the options of justification as a legal declaration and the process of internal renewal. In this way, Newman stands in close proximity to the Reformed tradition by holding a forensic action (based upon an *iustitia alienum*) in simultaneous harmony with the ongoing impartation of love and charity (*impertita iustitia*). Defining the precise manner of this internal work will require careful attention.

Newman highlights the forensic nature of justification by distinguishing the declaration from the gift that it declares. While unified in a single act, the two are regarded as notionally distinct, starting with the "Voice of the Lord" that pronounces one to be righteous:

> Justification is the "glorious Voice of the Lord" declaring us to be righteous. That it is a declaration not a making, is sufficiently clear from this one argument that it is the justification of a *sinner*, of one who *has been* a sinner; and the past cannot be reversed except by *accounting* it reversed.[1]

Motivating this legal pronouncement is "a real and gracious act on God's part towards us sinners."[2] Following Augustine, Newman highlights the

---

1. John Henry Newman, *Jfc*, 67 [71–72].

2. Ibid., 72 [77]. One of Newman's most distilled statements on the sufficiency and efficacy of grace is near the conclusion of his sermon "The Mystery of Godliness,"

initiative of grace, occasioned by the human problem of guilt, the impious nature in which sinners are naturally born, and according to which they are justly condemned.[3] To deny this or to rely upon one's own righteousness, says Newman, amounts to the sin of pride—a vice that he routinely opposed in the liberalism of his day.[4] But unlike Augustine, Newman recognizes the need for an "*imputing* righteousness,"[5] an "estimation of righteousness [in Christ] vouchsafed to the past, and extending from the past to the present as far as the present is affected by the past."[6] In other words, since the problem of human guilt is exhibited before the judgment seat of God, a particularly *judicial* action is therefore supposed.[7]

Newman read the Evangelicals of his day as holding that justification consisted in a *mere* imputation and he therefore devoted roughly the first third of his *Lectures* (1838) to showing the distinction, but no separation, between justification and renewal.[8] His problem is not with "imputation" per se; what he rejects is a "mere" imputation.[9] In this way, Newman concedes that justification "viewed relatively to the past is forgiveness of sin, for nothing more it can be; but considered as to the present and future it is more, it is renewal wrought in us by the Spirit of Him who by His merits completes what is defective in that renewal."[10]

Newman is equally insistent on the internal work of the Spirit. "The Voice of the Lord," he states, "is mighty in *operation* . . . it has a sacramental power, being the instrument as well as the sign of His will."[11] Concerning the content of this activity, Newman continues, "Imputed righteousness is the coming in of actual righteousness," since God's word never returns to him void, but accomplishes what he pleases.[12] Reaching beyond a mere legal

---

published in 1840, in which he insists, first quoting Titus, "'Not by works of righteousness which we have done, but according to His mercy He has saved us.' We are reminded that we can do nothing, and that God does everything." Newman, *PPS*, 1020.

3. Walgrave, *Newman the Theologian*, 42–44. Newman explains how divine grace overcomes the unrighteousness of original sin in Newman, *Jfc.*, 88–91 [95–96].

4. Bouyer, *Newman: His Life and Spirituality*, 19.

5. Newman, *Jfc.*, 67 [72].

6. Ibid., 68 [72–73].

7. Ibid., 72 [76–77].

8. Ibid., 63.

9. Ibid. Newman explains his understanding of imputation at some length, 67–78 [72–83].

10. Ibid., 36 [38].

11. Ibid., 79–80 [86].

12. Ibid., 80 [86].

declaration into the realms of history and ethics, justification establishes new creation by means of the indwelling presence of God.

> He [God] imputes, not a name but a substantial Word, which, being "ingrafted" in our own hearts, "is able to save our souls. . . . God's word, I say, effects what it announces. This is its characteristic all through Scripture. He "calleth those things which be not, as though they are," and they are forthwith. Thus in the beginning He *said*, "Let there be light, and there *was* light. Word and deed went together in creation; and so again 'in the regeneration.'[13]

In Newman's *et . . . et* approach, insisting on both a forensic *and* an operative justification, he presupposes a *duplex iustitia* in which accounting righteous and making righteousness are bound together in an organic unity. Throughout his *Lectures on Justification*, Newman explains this pattern with the datum of redemptive history, where the one vindicated by God is also renovated, insisting that the two activities go hand-in-hand. In one of the more commonly known quotes from Newman's *Lectures*, he argues,

> We may, if we will, divide this event into parts, and say that it is *both* pardon *and* renovation, but such a division is merely mental, and does not affect the change itself, which is but one act. If a man is saved from drowning, you may, if you will, say he is *both* rescued from the water *and* brought into the atmospheric air; this is a discrimination in words and not in things. . . . In like manner, there is, in fact, no middle state between a state of *wrath* and a state of *holiness*. In justifying, God takes away what is past, *by* bringing in what is new. He snatches us out of the fire by lifting us in His everlasting hands, and enwrapping us in His own glory.[14]

In this particular analogy, it is difficult to see how deliverance from the suffocating water unto the freedom of atmospheric air illustrates the movement from justification (salvation from divine wrath) unto sanctification (an increased realization of holiness). Both of these images signify the initial point of justification when one is delivered from the imminent danger of God's judgment. Since Newman means by sanctification the development of actual righteousness, his analogy would benefit from something other than the liberating presence of fresh air. Air, it turns out, is an excellent analogy for Newman's concept of divine presence—something *extra nos* that reaches

---

13. Ibid., 80–81 [86–87].
14. Ibid., 101–2 [112].

one's interior and from there provides life. Actual righteousness, however, in terms of manifesting good works, is better represented by an actual activity such as an impressive swim stroke.

Another way to describe Newman's approach is in terms of the "both/and" relationship of justification and sanctification. Newman regards their distinction, which was so often argued by the Evangelical party of the Church of England, as "technical and unscriptural."[15] This "unreal righteousness," says Newman, is an aberration.

> Away then with this modern, this private, this arbitrary, this unscriptural system, which promising liberty conspires against it; which abolishes Christian Sacraments to introduce barren and dead ordinances; and for the real participation of the Son, and justification through the Spirit, would, at the very marriage feast, feed us on shells and husks, who hunger and thirst after righteousness. It is a new gospel, unless three hundred years stand for eighteen hundred.... [I]f men are bent on seducing us from the ancient faith, let them provide a more specious error, a more alluring sophism, a more angelic tempter, than this.[16]

After critiquing the Evangelical party, Newman levels a similar charge at the Roman Catholic position. His aim is not focused upon any official statements of the Church, but rather on some unnamed theologians who appeared to be reducing justification to the habit of obedience that results from God's favor. Such an approach, argues Newman, replaces a properly Christ-centered vision with unhealthy introspection (*incurvatus in se*).[17]

Newman added a footnote in the third edition (1874) of his *Lectures*, which embellished upon his disagreement with the Catholic position and identifies the particular theologians that he had in mind:

> This school is elsewhere called in these Lectures ultra-Roman or extreme Romanist. Such Catholic divines as Caietan, Vasquez, and Bellarmine were intended by this title, who, by making justification consist in the habit of charity or again in good works, not in sanctifying grace as an initial and distinct gift from above, seemed to the writer to fix the mind, equally with Anglican Arminians, not on a Divine inward Presence vouchsafed to it, but on something of its own, as a ground to rest upon and take

---

15. Ibid., 41 [44].
16. Ibid., 57 [61].
17. Ibid., 190 [220].

satisfaction in. Of course, such a judgment seems to him now unreal and arbitrary.[18]

Newman's qualification clarifies his point of disagreement with the Catholic position. Due to what he perceived as a reduction of justification to a religious transaction—an exchange of "the [mere] influence of grace, not as the operations of a living God, but as something to bargain about, and buy, and traffic"—Newman expressed reservations about the phrase "inherent righteousness."[19]

> If the Presence of Christ is our true righteousness, first conveyed into us by Baptism, then more sacredly and mysteriously in the Eucharist, we have really no inherent righteousness at all. What seems to be inherent, may be more properly called *adherent*, depending as it does, wholly and absolutely upon the Divine indwelling, not ours to keep, but as heat in a sickly person, sustained by a cause distinct from himself.[20]

With this taxonomy, Newman lays the groundwork for his *via media*. While "righteousness" is in the first place God's forensic declaration, the essence of justification, for Newman, consisted in the indwelling of the divine presence. Therefore, what Protestants commonly call "justification" (the judicial pronouncement) and sanctification (internal renewal) are, Newman reiterates throughout his Lectures, joined as one:

- "Justification and sanctification were [are] in fact substantially one and the same thing . . . [they are] parts of one gift, properties, qualities, or aspects of one."[21]
- "Justification, then, *as such*, is an imputation; but the actual Gospel gift called justification is more, it is renewal also."[22]
- "Justification renews, therefore I say it may fitly be called renewal."[23]
- "It is a parallel mode of speaking, to say that justification *consists* in renewal, or that renewal *constitutes* justification."[24]

---

18. Ibid., 190 [statement contained in Footnote 1 of the Third Edition, absent from the 1838 version].
19. Ibid., 186–87 [216–17].
20. Ibid., 187 [217].
21. Ibid., 63 [112].
22. Ibid., 66 [71].
23. Ibid., 86 [93].
24. Ibid., 86–7 [93–94].

- "[Justification] consists of *two* parts, acceptance and renewal."[25]
- "Again, we speak of being *baptized* with God's *grace*; and thus we may allowably say that we are *justified* or accepted by *obedience*. And we might of course with propriety urge that *baptism* is not a mere outward rite, but an *inward* power; and so we may say that *justification* is a *change of heart*."[26]
- "I have been arguing from the essential union between justification and renewal, that they are practically convertible terms."[27]

Even though Newman's *Lectures* portray justification and sanctification as one, they also state that justification is in some sense the beginning of sanctification: "Justification tends to sanctify." [28] The elasticity of these terms enables Newman to affirm the Thirty-Nine Articles, when it says, "We are accounted righteous before God, only for the merit of our Lord and Saviour Jesus Christ by Faith, and not for our own works or deservings."[29] How exactly this works, particularly with reference to the formal cause or ground of justification, is the critical question. It will be taken up by considering the constituent elements of Newman's position and their arrangement, and evaluating its theological integrity.

B. Incarnation

Instead of regarding justification as the *articulus stantis et cadentis ecclesiae*, Newman considered "incarnation" to be the chief tenet of Christian doctrine,[30] what he called "the central truth of the Gospel, and the source whence we are to draw out its principles."[31] To some degree this reflects the historical and existential realities of Newman's religious journey as expressed in his *Apologia* (1864) and in works like *Loss and Gain* (1848), in which ecclesial and sacramental categories are asserted with such force and

25. Ibid., 88 [95].
26. Ibid.
27. Ibid.
28. Ibid.
29. Church of England, "Articles of Religion, XI," in *The Book of Common Prayer*.
30. Ker, *Newman on Being a Christian*, 39.
31. Newman, *An Essay on the Development of Christian Doctrine*, 6th ed., 324. Elsewhere, Newman identifies the fundamental components of apostolic faith, doctrines that he himself sought to promote, as the Trinity, Incarnation, Atonement, original sin, the necessity of regeneration, supernatural grace mediated through the sacraments, apostolic succession, the necessity of faith and obedience, and the eternal scope of divine judgment. Newman, *Certain Difficulties Felt by Anglicans*, 128.

definition that they function as an organizing principle for his theology in general and for soteriology in particular.

On account of its central importance in Newman's thought, the concept of Christ's incarnation is a suitable place to begin a study of his doctrine of justification. Newman's principle of incarnation grows out of his own personal religious struggle, which may be summarized as a desire to commune with the living God—a value that can be traced from his early days as an Evangelical into subsequent years, when he lived in the full embrace of monastic values and settings. This melodic line runs through the whole of Newman's religious experience and is even captured in the slogan of his coat of arms, "*cor ad cor loquitur.*"[32] What is the ultimate heart to which a human heart can ever hope to speak? Newman provides the answer through the heroine of his novel, *Callista* (1856), who points to the divine heart of God: "[T]here was a higher beauty than that which the order and harmony of the natural world revealed and a deeper peace and calm than that which the exercise whether of the intellect or the purest human affection can supply."[33] To commune with God is the highest and most desirable end, and the incarnation makes this possible.

Newman's view of Christ's incarnation owes much to his reliance upon eastern fathers, a reliance he acquired in 1827 when he began to read a collection of patristic writings which Edward Pusey obtained for him in Germany.[34] This study led to Newman's first book, *The Arians of the Fourth Century* (1833), in which principles of the Alexandrian school, such as a high regard for the invisible presence of God and the inadequacy of human cognition for apprehending that presence, are developed and applied to the religious sociology of England in general and Oxford in particular.[35] Emerging from these principles are themes that shaped Newman's theological vision for the remainder of his life, particularly the importance of preserving divine "mystery," *totus Christus*, and the sacramentality of the universe.[36] The aggregate of these tenets may be expressed in terms of

---

32. Dessain, *The Spirituality of John Henry Newman*, 33–34.
33. Newman, *Callista*, 254.
34. Flanagan, *Newman, Faith and the Believer*, 29.

35. The Alexandrians are generally considered to represent the Oxonian Platonists (whom Newman supports), while the Antioch school is a not so thinly veiled reference to so-called rationalists, such as Evangelical literalists.

36. Daley, "The Church Fathers," 29–46. One might add to this list the *disciplina arcani* (withholding central mysteries of the Christian faith from catechumens) and the development of oral tradition as a supplement to Scripture.

union with Christ and the saving effects that such solidarity produces.[37] In Newman's words,

> The sanctification, or rather the deification of the nature of man, is one main subject of St. Athanasius's theology. Christ, in rising, raises His saints with Him to the right hand of power. They become instinct with His life, of one body with His flesh, divine sons, immortal kings, gods. He is in them, because He is in human nature; and He communicates to them that nature deified by becoming His, that them It may deify.[38]

Thinking with the eastern tradition, Newman focuses on the persons of the Triune God to understand how divine life condescends in redemption. He concludes that it is in the Son of God "who came down on earth, and who thus, though graciously taking on Him[self] a new nature, remained in person as He had been from everlasting, the Son of the Father."[39] Accordingly, the Son, precisely because he possesses the same nature as the Father and the Spirit, is never considered in abstract isolation from the members of the Godhead (as popular Evangelicalism was susceptible to doing); rather, the triune deity is the starting point for understanding the person and mission of the incarnate Christ. So, Newman posits, "In truth His Divine Sonship is that portion of the sacred doctrine, on which the mind is providentially intended to rest throughout, and so to preserve for itself his identity unbroken."[40]

The scope of Newman's incarnational theology is enhanced by the teaching of St. Ignatius of Antioch, which upholds the centrality of the incarnation with the atonement in salvation, as events that are not simply in the past, "but as present facts, in an existing mode, in which our Saviour comes to us."[41] Here one sees how the principle of incarnation naturally leads to *totus Christus*, the embodiment of Christ's person in his members. For example, in his sermon titled "The Mystery of Godliness" (published in 1840), Newman asserts,

> He has taken our nature, and in and through it He sanctifies us. He is our brother by virtue of His incarnation, and, as the text

---

37. Dessain, "Cardinal Newman and the Eastern Tradition," 95.
38. Newman, *Development of Christian Doctrine*, 140.
39. Newman, *PPS*, 1224–25. This sermon was published in 1842.
40. Ibid., 592.
41. Dessain, *The Spirituality of John Henry Newman*, 67. Newman explains how the atonement is "continually" being applied to the church in *Jfc.*, 202–4 [233–35].

says, "He is not ashamed to call us brethren;" and, having sanctified his nature in Himself, He communicates it to us.[42]

When Newman uses the plural "us," he wishes to stress, in contradiction of his many Evangelical contemporaries, the community of God's people, and not simply the individual Christian. What is more, unlike the Evangelical conception of the real church as invisible, Newman insisted that Christ's body also has institutional dimensions.[43] This "Communion of Saints" or "Kingdom,"[44] as Newman described it, is inherently sacramental, which inevitably defines the character and structure of justification.[45]

C. The Sacramental Framework of Justification

Newman assigned instrumental value to the sacraments. Accordingly, "Justification comes *through* the Sacraments; is received *by* faith; *consists* in God's inward presence; and *lives* in obedience."[46] Against the low-church Evangelicals of his day, who tended to regard sacramental instrumentality as a "yoke on the necks of the disciples," that "obscures the free grace of the Gospel,"[47] Newman contends that sacramental rites actually inculcate Christian faith.[48] In arguing this case, he cites a catena of biblical examples, including the empowering presence of angels, Naaman bathing in the Jordan, the Brazen Serpent, and the Mount of Transfiguration.[49] In each of these instances, divine grace is imparted through a tangible form and effects actual change in the recipient, not simply a legal fiction. From this premise, Newman argues that Protestants fail to understand how justifica-

---

42. Newman, *PPS*, 1014.

43. His sermon, "The Visible Church an Encouragement to Faith," a message published in 1836, makes this point. Newman, *PPS*, 633-43. See also Newman's sermon "The Communion of Saints." (ibid., 839-49).

44. Newman understood the church and the Kingdom of God to be synonymous. Flanagan, *Newman, Faith and the Believer*, 285, 311.

45. Dessain, *The Spirituality of John Henry Newman*, 54-55.

46. Newman, *Jfc.*, 278 [318].

47. This charge cannot be fairly leveled against Luther, despite Newman's insistence on Luther's general culpability. Luther maintains that *sola fide* should in no way diminish one's appreciation for the sacraments. Althaus, *The Theology of Martin Luther*, 349. Bellarmine corroborates this point with respect to Martin Chemnitz and John Calvin, who "teach that faith alone ought not to be opposed to the sacraments in the business of justification, as it is not opposed to the grace of God and the merits of Christ." Bellarmine, *De Sacramentis in Genere*, 99-100.

48. Newman, *Jfc.*, 280-82 [320-22].

49. Ibid., 285-87 [325-27].

tion is properly mediated and manifested, a fact that is allegedly betrayed by their inadequate exegesis of James's teaching on the necessity of "works" in justification.[50]

Controversy surrounding the sacraments was a major reason for Newman's composition of the *Lectures on Justification* (1838). The "Advertisement" to the original edition cites disagreement over their proper form and function, particularly their God-ordained role as instruments of grace, as a primary purpose for delivering the lectures and composing the volume.

> The present Volume originated in the following way: It was brought home to the writer from various quarters, that a prejudice existed in many serious minds against certain essential Christian truths, such as Baptismal Regeneration and the Apostolical Ministry, in consequence of a belief that they fostered notions of human merit, were dangerous to the inward life of religion, and incompatible with the doctrine of justifying faith.[51]

It is noteworthy that Newman refers to the issue as consisting of "essential" Christian truths, and that he capitalizes "Baptismal Regeneration" and "Apostolical Ministry." Because these rites emerge from Christ's incarnation and in some mystical sense possess divine character, they are, for Newman, essential. When Newman reached this conclusion, his doctrine of justification changed drastically, moving from a Calvinist orientation to a growing emphasis on the efficacy of the sacraments.[52] According to Sheridan, Newman first went public with this belief in 1828, preaching at St. Mary's on the spiritual influence of baptism.[53] In the following years, Newman became more confident of his position and by 1833 his theological shift was complete.[54] No longer could "faith alone" exclude sacramental instrumentality.

The challenge for Newman as an Anglican was the Thirty-Nine Articles' eleventh article, which asserted that "we are justified by *Faith only*," along with the Book of Common Prayer's Homily of the Passion for Good Friday, which stated that "Faith is the *one mean and instrument* of justification."[55] Newman accepted these statements at face value, agreeing that genuine faith is the sole instrument by which one is justified over other graces such as love and hope. He then made a further clarification that had the effect of thwarting the Anglican position of *sola fide*, and, to his thinking, sanctioned the

50. Ibid., 291–93 [331–33].
51. Newman, *Lectures on Justification*, v.
52. Gilley, "Life and Writings," 2–3.
53. Sheridan, *Newman on Justification*, 153–54.
54. Walgrave, *Newman the Theologian*, 21.
55. Newman, *Jfc.*, 223 [256].

practice of baptismal regeneration. Faith, he asserted, is "the sole *internal* instrument, not the sole instrument of any kind."[56] Such a distinction is an important underpinning to Newman's doctrine.

> There would be nothing inconsistent, then, in Faith being the sole instrument of justification, and yet Baptism also the sole instrument, and that at the same time, because in distinct senses; an inward instrument in no way interfering with an outward instrument. Baptism might be the hand of the giver, and Faith the hand of the receiver. However, this is not the exact relation of Faith to baptism, as is plain for this reason—that Baptism occurs but once, whereas justification is a state, and Faith "abides." Justification, then, needs a perpetual instrument, such as faith can be, and Baptism cannot. Each, then, has its own office in the work of justification; Baptism at the time when it is administered, and faith ever after.[57]

The Anglican Newman was prepared to accept and even use the language of "faith only" as a "lively mode of speech [figurative] for saying that we are justified neither by faith nor by works, but by God only."[58] He found this usage in Philip Melanchthon, in the Homilies, and in Bishop George Bull, for example, but he believed that "it is more suited to the Schools, than to the taste of a people like the English at the present day."[59] Be that as it may, Newman's interpretation of *sola fide* is a definite departure from the classic formulation, first expressed by Luther, "*propter Christum per fidum*"—a position aimed at safeguarding justification by *iustitia aliena*. In Newman's vision, faith is more than the means by which one grasps Christ (*fides apprehensiva*);[60] it represents, rather, a complex set of activities that include the sacraments, love, and obedience.

> While then we reserve to Baptism our new birth, and to the Eucharist the ultimate springs of the new life, and to Love what may be called its plastic power, and to Obedience its being the atmosphere in which faith breathes, still the divinity appointed or (in other words) the mysterious virtue of Faith remains. It

---

56. Ibid., 226 [259].

57. Ibid.

58. Ibid., 244 [279].

59. Ibid., 246–47 [281]. The internal and external distinction of faith is Newman's second response to those who accused him of violating article eleven, after the caveat that justification initiates sanctification.

60. Newman explicitly rejects the notion, attributed to Luther, that faith is the "primary instrument" of justification. *Jfc.*, 244 [279].

alone coalesces with the Sacraments, brings them into effect, dissolves (as it were) their outward case, and through them unites the soul to God.[61]

Quoting Hebrews 11:1, Newman defines faith as "the substance of things hoped for, the evidence of things not seen."[62] This "substance" of faith, according to Newman's protracted exposition, is predicated on the "unseen" and "hoped for" end, and therefore resists simple definition. In other words, faith remains undefined until it seizes upon its proper object, which, for the Christian, is the living Christ.[63] For the patient reader, it eventually becomes clear that this is the burden of Newman's argument: to connect faith with the presence of Christ.[64] Thus, faith is not mere assent of the mind (*assensus*), as Catholics defined it; nor is it simply trust (*fiducia*) as promulgated by Luther—it is union with Christ.[65] Whether this union comes through baptism, the inward instrument of faith (following baptism), or by the symbols that represent grace (i.e., obedience and hope), faith is manifest communion with Christ.[66] After a great deal of parsimony, the closest Newman comes to explicating a positive definition is, "Salvation by faith only is but another way of saying salvation by grace only."[67] What may seem unnecessarily opaque and subtle in Newman's definition, is more intelligible in the light of his doctrine of justifying presence.

D. Justifying Presence

To understand how the Sacraments mediate righteousness with a view to manifesting faith and obedience, one must grasp a vital connection between Newman's doctrine of incarnation and what he calls, "Justifying Presence." Predicated on the conviction that the living word became flesh not simply to deliver sinners from guilt (as Newman read Protestantism), nor, on the other extreme, for one to formulate a doctrine of justification "exclusively on the *effects* of grace" apart from a righteous state (as Newman read Catholicism),[68] Newman begins his *via media* by elevating the justi-

61. Ibid., 236–37 [271].
62. Ibid., 252 [288].
63. Newman is keen to point out that evil spirits also have faith; therefore, faith must consist in more than mere belief. Ibid., 253–54 [289–90].
64. Ibid., 266–73 [304–13].
65. Ibid.
66. Ibid., 251 [286].
67. Ibid., 283 [324].
68. Ibid., 182 [211–12].

fied sinner to fellowship and communion with the divine.[69] In this union, according to Newman, the justified receives a gift that *exceeds* the impartation of divine grace, the very presence of God. The notion is elucidated in Newman's famous hymn, *Praise to the Holiest in the Height*:

O wisest love! That flesh and blood
    Which did in Adam fail,
Should strive afresh against the foe,
    Should strive and should prevail;
And that a higher gift than grace
    Should flesh and blood refine,
God's Presence and His very Self,
    and Essence all-divine.[70]

Once again, Newman's indebtedness to the eastern doctrine of theosis is evident. It was early in 1835 when Newman applied this concept specifically to the doctrine of justification in a sermon titled "Human Responsibility." "The grace of Regeneration," he argues, ". . . is a definite and complete gift conveyed, not gradually, but at once; and it is a state distinct from every other, consisting in the Sacred presence of the Spirit of Christ in soul and body."[71]

When Newman speaks of the divine presence, he is explicit about its Trinitarian personhood. "The essential feature of Newman's understanding of the nature of justification," McGrath explains, "is his insistence upon the real presence of the Trinity within the soul of the justified believer, conceived in broadly realist terms, which undoubtedly reflects his interest in and positive evaluation of the Greek fathers such as Athanasius."[72] This is, according to Jose Morales, the "most outstanding merit" of the *Lectures*, the place where "Newman comes face to face with a mystery of faith."[73] Such a positive assessment is due to the way Newman correlates the roles to each of the divine persons in justification and sanctification. Accordingly, the Father declares sinful man to be just, upon the merits and saving grace of Christ, by means of the inhabitation of the Holy Spirit.[74] With this

---

69. Ibid., 182–88 [211–18].
70. Newman, *Verses on Various Occasions*, new ed., 363–64.
71. Newman, *PPS*, 437. This sermon was published in 1835.
72. McGrath, *ID*, 297.
73. Morales, "Newman and the Problems of Justification," 146.
74. Newman, *Jfc.*, 147 [163–64].

Trinitarian framework in view, Newman concludes, "This is to be justified, to receive the Divine Presence with us, and be made a Temple of the Holy Ghost."[75] Such is the heart of Newman's theology of salvation. The God who declares justification and renovates the soul does so by inhabiting the soul. "He justifies us by entering into us, He continues to justify us by remaining in us," Newman concludes. "*This* is really and truly our justification, not faith, not holiness, not (much less) a mere imputation; but through God's mercy, the very Presence of Christ.[76]

Newman recognizes that Scripture describes divine presence in various ways. Sometimes it is "described as God's presence or indwelling," he summarizes, "sometimes that of Father and Son; sometimes the Holy Ghost; sometimes of Christ the Incarnate Mediator; sometimes of God through the Spirit; sometimes of Christ."[77] The common thread among these appellations is divine inhabitation that results in the justified becoming an adopted son or daughter. Like Christ, who was "justified by the Spirit"[78] and "declared to be the Son of God with power,"[79] achieving sonship that "did not supersede but implied His inherent righteousness,"[80] we also, by virtue of our association with Christ, realize these salvific benefits in concert with the divine persons.[81]

Newman's emphasis comes to flower in Lecture VII, in which he develops the subject of union with Christ more fully, describing how "justification is the setting up of the Cross within us."[82] This chapter, entitled "The Characteristics of the Gift of Righteousness," explores the sanctifying capacity of justification in terms of the adherent presence of Christ, the one who brings the incarnation, sacrament, and justifying presence of God to the human soul.

E. The Christocentric Focus of Justification

Reflecting on how Newman relates the concept of mysterious union with Christ to the sanctifying capacity of justification, Morales offers a helpful summary.

75. Ibid., 144 [160].
76. Ibid., 150 [167].
77. Ibid.
78. Ibid., 77 [83]. Newman quoting 1 Tim 3:16.
79. Ibid. Newman quoting Rom 1:4.
80. Ibid.
81. Ibid., 77–78 [83–84].
82. Ibid., 173 [200].

Close consideration of these texts makes it appear that Newman in fact opts for what the theology of the sixteenth century called the doctrine of *double justification*, according to which in order to be true and complete our justice must be completed by that of Jesus Christ, which would come to make up for the deficiencies that the previous sinful condition always leaves in the justified individuals.[83]

In working out his double righteousness position, Newman traces the logical progression of redemptive history with reference to the judicial and actual dimensions of salvation, particularly as they unfold from the Gospels to Acts. For example, after developing the Old Testament metaphors of "clothing" and "temple"[84] and the significance of Adamic typology,[85] Newman explores how these motifs enrich the cruciform shape of justification.[86] He makes this argument along the parallel tracks of a forensic and real righteousness, progressing toward the *telos* of justification, which is "the fruit of our Lord's resurrection."[87] It is here, in the *shekinah* presence of God, that one is accepted and renewed on the basis of God's inward presence, which is simply to say that one is justified.

Newman applies the biblical theme of *shekinah* to the issue of justification in order to illustrate what he means by the salvific gift of God.[88] For him, this glory denotes an "attribute, property, virtue, or presence of the Divine Nature manifested visibly."[89] After establishing the meaning of this presence for salvation and for moral order, as exemplified in the experience of Moses who passed through the Sea (salvation) before arriving at Sinai (moral order), Newman considers the words of Jesus in which the Lord prayed to the Father, "The glory which Thou gavest Me, *I have given them.*"[90] Newman then asks, "What is this glory which has passed from Christ to

---

83. Morales is quite mistaken to suggest that the theology of the sixteenth century had a synoptic view on double justification. As our examination of *Cinquecento* Italy has revealed, positions differed considerably among figures such as Bucer, Calvin, Contarini, Gropper, Pole, Seripando, Valdes, and Vermigli. Morales, "Problems of Justification," 150.

84. Newman, *Jfc.*, 155–57 [176–78].

85. Ibid., 157–62 [179–85]. Newman's logic contends that since protology typifies eschatology, the progress of redemption from earthly clothing to heavenly clothing suggest that actual righteousness ought to be central in Christian salvation.

86. Ibid., 170–78 [195–207].

87. Ibid., 202 [233]. Newman's title here reads, "Christ's Resurrection: The Source of Justification."

88. Ibid., 156 [177–78].

89. Ibid., 162–63 [186].

90. Ibid., 163 [187].

us?"⁹¹ His answer points to the glory of the Father that raised Jesus from the dead.⁹² It is this same glory that justifies sinful humanity. Quoting Paul, he notes: "'All have sinned, and come short of,' or *are in need of,* 'the *glory* of God.'"⁹³

Newman proceeds along this redemptive-historical trajectory to introduce the mission of the Holy Spirit as the gift and the agent who applies the benefits of Christ's death and resurrection in the form of divine gifts, a complex of blessings that are summarized by the word "atonement."⁹⁴ These benefits include pardon, grace, reconciliation, renewal, holiness, and spiritual communion. Newman's point eventually becomes clear—the manner in which the presence of Christ inhabits the justified one is by the Spirit. Once again, Newman's idea of the activity of justification, in which the divine members cooperate, is facilitated by Newman's Trinitarian synthesis. After the Son merits salvation, the Holy Spirit applies it through personal inhabitation.

One interesting aspect of Newman's synthesis is the way he reads the Old Testament teaching on justification. Between Sinai and Pentecost, when the Mosaic Law governed God's covenant with Israel, the Jewish people enjoyed the *promise* of God's Spirit (e.g., Joel 2, Zech 12), Newman claims, but they were devoid of actual possession of his divine presence.⁹⁵ "Judaism was the time of shadows," according to Newman, "it was Judaism which contained but the profession, the appearance of great things, exciting hopes which it could not gratify."⁹⁶ Abraham and saints of old were the recipients of "righteousness or acceptableness."⁹⁷ The difference, however, between this and the blessing of the New Covenant, lies in "*what* this righteousness is under the Gospel; or *in what way* this acceptableness is conveyed, whether by a mere act of God's will or by a positive gift on His part?"⁹⁸ Newman's definition of the precise nature of this Old Covenant version of "righteousness" or "acceptableness" does not venture beyond these words in his *Lectures*. For further insight, we must look to a message that he preached three years later.

---

91. Ibid.
92. Ibid.
93. Ibid., 164 [188].
94. Ibid., 202–3 [233–35].
95. Dessain, "The Biblical Basis of Newman's Ecumenical Theology," 113.
96. Newman, *Jfc.*, 56–57 [61].
97. Ibid., 192 [223].
98. Ibid., 193 [223–24].

In a sermon from 1841, "Faith the Title for Justification,"[99] Newman begins with the question, "If all that is necessary for acceptance with God be faith in Christ, how is Church Communion, how are Sacraments, necessary?"[100] He is anxious to affirm the primacy of faith as described by the Apostle Paul, that which legitimately lays claim to justification apart from conditions, while at the same time preserving the obligatory nature of baptism as an instrumental rite. Newman's attempt to reconcile these positions is predicated on the assertion that "to have a title [i.e., faith] is not the same thing as to be in possession."[101] For Newman, the "mere act of God's will," which comes by faith, does not equate to his "positive gift," which comes through baptism. Developing the idea further, Newman continues by asserting that the one "who believes shall to a certainty at some time and by some means be justified."[102] "Faith," in this case, "is the means of gaining justification,"[103] but justification is unrealized until one undergoes baptism. In this way, Newman seeks to do business with the Pauline texts commonly marshaled on behalf of *sola fide* by reading them as a real, proleptic movement toward justification among Old Covenant believers. However, and this is a profound qualification, in Newman's argument, *the title or claim of faith does not actually obtain justification until it receives the endowment of the Spirit which is properly realized in baptism.*

As a positive example of this pattern, Newman points to the Apostle Peter who concluded his Pentecost sermon by calling his hearers to be "baptized for remission of their sins and the reception of the Holy Spirit."[104] He is also keen to point out how he observes the sacramental emphasis unfolding in later chapters of Acts, such as when the Ethiopian eunuch, Paul, and Cornelius and his household underwent baptism. Then, arguing negatively, Newman contends that, "Satan has so disordered Christendom, that numbers perhaps have faith without as yet having justification,"[105] a fact that is obvious to him in the meager progress toward sanctification, profanity, pride, despondency, and headstrong blindness to the truth on the part of Christians of his day.

Because Abraham and saints of old were deprived of the New Covenant sacrament of baptism, Newman puts them into a special class that

---

99. Newman, *PPS*, 1282–94. This sermon was published in 1842.
100. Ibid., 1282.
101. Ibid., 1287.
102. Ibid.
103. Ibid.
104. Ibid., 1290.
105. Ibid., 1294.

carries the "title" for justification, without truly *possessing* justification, a category that resembles one for whom baptism is unavailable—such as in the catechumen who dies before he is received into the Church, or the believer who undergoes baptism by martyrdom—but who is nevertheless a child of God. The novelty of this position may explain why Newman doesn't address it in detail outside of his 1841 sermon. Nevertheless, an important question to emerge from Newman's soteriological disjunction between the Old and New Covenants is the relationship of Christ and the Holy Spirit in his doctrine of justification.

F. Pneumatic, Resurrected Life

Late in 1834, still in the early stages of the Tractarian Movement, Newman preached a sermon at St. Mary's entitled, "The Indwelling Spirit." It sheds light on the way he relates Christ to the Holy Spirit in justification.

> This wonderful change from darkness to light, through the entrance of the Spirit into the soul, is called Regeneration, or the New Birth; a blessing which, before Christ's coming, not even Prophets and righteous men possessed, but which is now conveyed to all men freely through the Sacrament of Baptism.[106]

When Newman speaks of Christ's presence in the believer, he does so in terms of the Holy Spirit. This is potentially confusing since Newman is emphatic about the Trinitarian shape of divine indwelling, but, as he insists, the pneumatic and the Trinitarian Presence are entirely compatible.[107]

> Here I would observe of this part of the wonderful Economy of Redemption, that God the Son and God the Holy Ghost have so acted together in their separate Persons, as to make it difficult for us creatures always to discriminate what belongs to each respectively.[108]

Because the divine indwelling of the Holy Spirit brings the saving merits of Christ to one's soul, alien righteousness thereby resides in the believer, and thus serves as the fundamental ground of one's justification.[109] Simply

---

106. Ibid., 368.

107. For a fuller treatment of how Newman correlated the Trinity and the Spirit, see Strange, *Newman and the Gospel of Christ*, 153–55.

108. Newman, *Jfc.*, 208 [240].

109. Because Newman insists that adherent righteousness is a form of *gratia increata* that remains distinct from one's soul, some interpreters have described it as an "alien" righteousness: for example, O'Leary, "Impeded Witness," 167 and Holtzen,

put, to have the Spirit is to have Christ, which includes the forensic and operative movement of righteousness. The two are integrally linked, just as justification and sanctification are regarded by Newman as "substantially one and the same thing."[110]

Even though Newman combines justification and sanctification, he nonetheless recognizes an epistemological sequence when he states that "in logical order, or exactness of idea, Almighty God justifies before He sanctifies."[111] This follows the traditional Protestant *ordo salutis*. A couple of sentences later, Newman specifies the causal relationship of these activities: "to 'justify' *means* in itself 'counting righteous,' but includes *under* its meaning 'making righteous;' in other words, the sense of the *term* is 'counting righteous,' and the nature of the *thing* denoted by it is making righteous."[112] This explanation allowed Newman to claim subscription to the Thirty-Nine Articles while also following St. Augustine and the eastern fathers in their emphasis upon the internal work of the Spirit.[113]

One figure on whom Newman especially relied at this point was the French historian and patristic scholar of the mid-seventeenth century, Denis Pétau, SJ (1583–1652), more commonly known by his Latinized name, Dionysius Petavius, who articulated the Spirit's substantial indwelling in the human soul.[114] Thinking with eastern fathers, such as Cyril of Alexandria, Petavius promoted the notion of the Holy Spirit as the *gratia increata*.[115] In the context of a Trinitarian synthesis similar to Newman's, Petavius defined the work of the Holy Spirit in terms of a "substantial" indwelling and not a mere "accidental" indwelling.[116] In other words, it is the mission of the Spirit, and not the Father or the Son, to establish himself in the believer. In this respect, Petavius defines indwelling more narrowly than

---

"Newman's '*Via Media*' Theology of Justification," 72. Holtzen says of Newman's position, for instance, that "the *alien* righteousness of Christ exists *internally* as the proper formal cause of justification." Since Newman, like Vermigli, does not actually use the word "alien," we have avoided using the term. However, in view of the fact that Newman defines justification as nothing less than "the very Presence of Christ" (Jfc., 150 [167]), there is a sense in which this righteousness is properly "alien." Sheridan thus says of Newman's position, "Our justification, while in us, is not of us." Sheridan, *Newman on Justification*, 248.

110. Ibid., 63 [67].

111. Ibid., 65 [70].

112. Ibid.

113. Ibid., 64–65 [68–70].

114. On the use of Petavius in Bishop George Bull, see Thomas, *Newman and Heresy*, 171–73.

115. Baumgartner, *La grâce du Christ*, 190.

116. Holtzen, "Union with God and the Holy Spirit," 31.

Newman. And yet, in Petavius's vision, the Spirit also in some sense mediates the life of the Trinity to one's soul.[117]

An important implication of the Spirit's inhabitation is the primacy of *gratia increata* over any form of *gratia creata* or *habitualis*.[118] This is precisely where Petavius makes his contribution to Newman's *Lectures*. In the advertisement to the third edition (1874), Newman writes, "Moreover, Petavius speaks of another, or fifth [form of justification], viz. the substantial Presence of the Holy Ghost in the soul."[119] This presence of the Spirit mediates Christ's imputed righteousness, which is properly distinguished from one's own inchoate righteousness.[120] This distinction is not intended to denigrate personal virtue. Newman affirms that "the inherent righteousness of a true Christian, viewed as distinct from Christ's inward presence, is something real, and doubtless far higher than that of a Jew."[121] However, he does sharply distinguish "'Christ,' our propitiation, 'within us'" from one's actual righteousness.[122]

When Newman describes the believer's imperfect, inchoate righteousness he calls it "actual," for it comes *directly* from the "divinely imparted principle of righteousness."[123] While affirming that justification effectively "renews" one's soul,[124] Newman is emphatic that such renewal is *not* derived from an infusion of inherent righteousness or the cultivation of *habitus*.[125] Here he quotes Petavius, who "does not scruple to call the Holy Ghost the formal cause of the righteousness imparted to us."[126] The cause of justification is, in Newman's terms, "adherent" righteousness, "depending wholly and absolutely on the Divine Indwelling."[127] Simply stated, "Justifying righteousness consists in the coming and presence of the Holy Ghost within us."[128]

Given Newman's stress on imputed righteousness (in the form of divine indwelling), not the production of a created habit, as the proper ground

---

117. Petavius, "De Trinitate," 453–62.
118. Rondet, *The Grace of Christ*, 367.
119. Newman, *Jfc.*, xii.
120. Ibid., 349 [395].
121. Ibid., 199–200 [230].
122. Ibid., 200 [231].
123. Ibid., 351 [397].
124. Ibid., 86 [93].
125. Ibid., 348–52 [394–98].
126. Ibid., 352 [398].
127. Ibid., 187 [218].
128. Ibid., 139 [155].

of justification, one might expect for him to have a doctrine of assurance. Of course, this is where Vermigli and Reformed theology go, with their emphasis on imputation. For Newman, however, there is no forward-looking assurance since he espouses an increasing *development* of justification. How can justification by divine indwelling be increased? Newman answers, "Righteousness then, considered as the state of being God's temple, cannot be increased; but, considered as the divine glory which that state implies, it can be increased."[129] But how exactly does one's righteous state relate to the operation of righteousness? For that crucial answer we must consider the formal cause of justification in Newman's doctrine.

G. The Formal Cause of Justification

Before examining how Newman defines the formal cause of justification, we must summarize the basic contours of his position. For starters, Newman raises the topic with a valuable question concerning the believer's union with Christ.

> Again: if it be laid down that our justification consists in union with Christ, or reconciliation with God, this is an intelligible and fair answer; and then the question will arise, what is *meant* by union with Christ?[130]

For Newman, this Christological union comes to one's soul by the Holy Spirit, who properly imputes the righteousness of Christ by means of divine indwelling. This "adherent" righteousness is distinguished from an "inherent," "infused," or a "habitual" deposit of justice in that the former consists in the personal inhabitation of the Triune God. Of the three divine persons, the Holy Spirit is explicated as the proper agent of justification, as a matter of his own role (*proprium*) in the economy of salvation,[131] although strict lines of differentiation between members of the Godhead are not drawn. Thus, divine indwelling is the *gratia increata* upon which one is declared righteous. In connection with this, Newman summarizes what he considers to be the proper formal cause of justification: "This is really and truly our justification, not faith, not holiness, not (much less) a mere imputation; but through God's mercy, the very Presence of Christ."[132]

129. Ibid., 151 [168].

130. Ibid., 134 [148].

131. Newman, *PPS*, xi, 10, 1270. These sermons were published between 1834 and 1843.

132. Newman, *Jfc.*, 150 [167].

In addition to a "proper" formal cause of justification, Newman also posits an "improper" formal cause.[133] Accordingly, when the justifying merits of Christ are imparted to an individual by divine indwelling, a real, actual righteousness is simultaneously operative.[134] This inchoate or incipient righteousness belongs to the Christian and in this sense may be called "inherent." A metaphor that Newman commonly employs to convey this notion is "shekinah"—the salvific gift of God that is an "attribute, property, virtue, or presence of the Divine Nature manifested visibly."[135] It is here where Newman closely resembles Augustine, a connection that Newman himself often makes when he describes the active, fruit-bearing quality of righteousness.[136] Therefore, in view of this improper, formal cause, Newman states, "to 'justify' *means* in itself 'counting righteous,' but includes *under* its meaning 'making righteous;'" in other words, the sense of the *term* is 'counting righteous,' and the nature of the *thing* denoted by it is making righteous."[137]

One way to describe Newman's position on justification is in terms of a two-fold righteousness—imputed *and* actual—although such a distinction is intended to be logical and not temporal. The strength of this formulation, as is commonly true of *duplex iustitia*, is that it can stress a forensic action based upon righteousness while also taking seriously the need for faith to be formed by love. In Newman's words, it is the simultaneous movements of "pardon and renovation."[138] Such a construction seeks to avoid legal fiction, bringing the Protestant categories of justification and sanctification into a closer relationship. What is the precise nature of this connection?

In the original 1838 version of his *Lectures*, Newman located the formal cause of justification in the imputation of righteousness. He made this point by emphasizing forensic imputation by divine indwelling as the proper formal cause of his *via media*:[139] "Justification tends to sanctify," Newman specifies; "in logical order, or exactness of idea, Almighty God justifies before He sanctifies."[140] The Catholic Newman retained these statements in his third edition (1874), but qualified them when he shifted emphasis to the

133. Ibid., xi, 337 [386], 381–82 [423–25], 392 [425–26].
134. Ibid., 199–200 [230].
135. Ibid., 162–63 [186].
136. Ibid., 58–61, 64–65 [52–55, 68–70]. Newman usually refers to Augustine as "Saint Austin."
137. Ibid., 65 [69–70].
138. Ibid., 101 [112].
139. Newman, *Jfc.*, 1st ed., 386, 427.
140. Ibid., 95, 70.

one internal formal cause, a shift that he explicates in his "Advertisement to the Third Edition," when he clarifies, "The first of these [changes from the first edition] is the proposition that more than one formal cause can be assigned to the justified state."[141]

By the year 1874, Newman had switched the formal cause to a form of internal righteousness. "And so far as the author of these Lectures contradicts this categorical statement, he now simply withdraws what he has said in them. But he was mistaken if he supposed that it was thereby determined *what* the '*unica forma*' really was, or again that there might not be more *forms* than one (whether improper *forms*, or *forms* of the justifying justice or renovation)."[142] The reason that Newman feels free to make this alteration without revising his overall position is because he regards Trent to be ambiguous on the precise nature of the *unica forma causa*.

> Though, then, there be but one formal cause (and there never can be more than one proper form of anything), still it is not settled precisely what that form is. We are at liberty to hold that it is not the renewed state of the soul, but the Divine gift which renews it.[143]

In the "Advertisement," Newman supports his case by introducing several post-Tridentine Catholic voices on the doctrine of justification. He starts with Bellarmine, who acknowledges that it is an open question whether righteousness consists in grace or charity, and who, according to Newman, "allows that there are theologians who think otherwise."[144] Pallavicino, the second example, allowed for a mixture of grace and charity. Likewise, Vasquez posited two possible forms. Third, was Sporer, who held to two "partial" forms, an external divine act and an internal work—the former defined as *favor Dei*, the latter as *habitus iustitiae*. Bellarmine is mentioned again, as a fourth option, with regard to the Council's emphasis on *esse fidem charitate formatam*. Fifth, and most significant for its proximity to Newman's position, is Petavius who argued for the "substantial Presence of the Holy Ghost in the soul."[145] From this, Newman unfolded his argument that the formal cause of justification is the Spirit who brings the divine presence to one's soul and who in turn stimulates actual righteousness as the improper form of the soul's righteousness.

---

141. Newman, *Jfc.*, x–xi.
142. Ibid.
143. Ibid., xi.
144. Ibid.
145. Ibid., xii.

Newman's question of whether the teaching of Trent unequivocally defined the *unica formalis causa* of justification in terms of *habitus* grows out of his relative discomfort with grounding justification squarely upon created grace. His concern, once again, is that *gratia inhaerens* in terms of mere renewal suggests that justification is reduced to a matter of obedience and meritorious works, which he believes to have the pastorally disastrous effect of leading one toward unhealthy introspection.[146] "Hence," says Newman, "the charge against Romanism, not unfounded as regards its popular teaching, that it views the influence of grace, not as the operations of a living God, but as a something to bargain about, and buy, and traffic with."[147] The fact that Newman retained this sentence after becoming a Catholic underscores his continued uneasiness with building justification upon the sole ground of *gratia creata*.[148]

Newman's contention, however, goes further than the Church's "popular teaching." In the appendix of the third edition (1874) of his *Lectures*, he dedicates sixty-one pages to the question of justification's formal cause.[149] In the opening footnote of the first page, he explains,

> The purpose of this Appendix is to show that the cardinal question to be considered by Catholics and Protestants in their controversy about Justification is, What is its *formal cause*? When this is properly examined, it will be found that there is little or no difference of view between the disputants.[150]

Newman's appendix provides valuable historical background to the arguments contained in his *Lectures* (1838). For much of the appendix, Newman's analysis concentrates on the controversies of the sixteenth century, when Catholics opposed Luther's "justification by faith alone" by citing Galatians 5:6, "*fides quae per caritatem operatur*," which was then translated into Aristotelian categories as "*fides caritate formata*." This history of interpretation vis-à-vis the formal cause of justification is then traced through subsequent history, including the Caroline Divines, and eventually into his

---

146. Ibid., 190 [220].

147. Ibid., 186 [163].

148. Newman qualifies this statement in a footnote, "It requires a considerable acquaintance with the working of the Catholic system to have the right thus to speak of it." Ibid., 186.

149. The first edition of Newman's Lectures (1838), also contain an appendix entitled, "On the formal cause of Justification" [Newman, *Jfc.*, 1st ed., 391–443]. At fifty-two pages in length, there are no substantive differences from the third edition apart from explanatory notes that appear on pages 343, 348–49, and 353.

150. Newman, *Jfc.*, 343.

own day. The appendix supports the lectures with valuable historical background, but it does not advance substantive arguments beyond that which is postulated in the lectures themselves.

Sheridan rightly indicates that the two seminal chapters of the *Lectures* are found in the sixth and seventh lectures.[151] They are instructive for understanding Newman's formal cause, especially if one compares the first (1838) and third (1874) editions. In the first edition, Newman emphasizes that renewal follows as an extension from justification; in the third edition (1874) he stresses that these are identical. In the very center of these chapters—in the closing words of chapter six before starting chapter seven—Newman explains,[152] "Lastly, we may now see what the connexion really is between justification and renewal." A careful analysis of what follows reveals that Newman's mature position (the third edition) no longer regards forensic justification as possessing a logical priority over renewal; they are inextricably bound up with one another.

In summarizing the development of Newman's synthesis, Sheridan points out that "to the extent that Newman's thought developed away from Evangelicalism, his conception of grace became more ecclesial."[153] Accordingly, what started as internal renewal *derived* from divine indwelling (first edition, 1838) became a *unica forma causa* with renewal at the very center. In this sense, Newman's *via media* evolved into a *via Romana*. But did it evolve to such an extent that he can be said to have jettisoned his middle way, or is it simply that Newman moved closer to the Roman position?

What makes this question so vexing is that Newman's *Lectures* are essentially the same from his first (1838) to his third edition (1874). Most of his statements on the relationship of justification and renewal remain unchanged in the latter edition, leading one to conclude that his position is likewise unchanged. Then one reads a piece by the Catholic Newman, such as the above segment from the third edition (1874), which reflects a clear difference (leaving behind a logical sequence between justification and

---

151. "On the Gift of Righteousness," and "The Characteristics of the Gift of Righteousness." These titles are the same in both versions of the *Lectures*. See ibid., 130–54; 155–78; [143–75; 176–207].

152. Newman's first edition has a four page "Note on Lecture VI" (*Jfc.*, 1st ed., 172–75.), which examines his thesis from the *Homilies*. Drawing continuity with Anglicanism is less of a concern for the Catholic Newman.

153. Sheridan, *Newman on Justification*, 242. In context, Sheridan is concerned with illustrating the centrality of baptism. Elsewhere Sheridan makes this same point with regard to Newman's position on faith alone, "As a matter of fact, in the third edition (1874) he [Newman] simply denied it [the instrumentality of faith alone], albeit merely in a footnote. "Catholics hold that, not faith only, but faith, hope, and charity, are the 'sustaining causes of justification." Ibid., 255.

renewal to draw an essential continuity between them), and the question reasserts itself. Perhaps insight can be found by identifying other areas of development (or outright disagreement) between the Anglican and the Catholic Newman.

One subject of the *Lectures* in which Newman the Roman Catholic clearly disagreed with Newman the Anglo-Catholic was sin and the justified. In the third edition (1874), he qualifies the statement, "For we must consider that since we are *ever falling into sin and incurring God's wrath*, we are ever being justified again and again by His grace"[154] (emphasis added), with a footnote: "This is incorrect. If by 'sin' is meant grievous sin, those who are in the grace of God need not ever be falling into it; and if lighter sins are meant, these do not bring us back again under 'God's wrath.'"[155]

Similarly, Newman's third edition (1874) also retracts a statement with regard to the "perfect" state of righteousness among those who are justified:

> Lastly, we may now see what the connexion really is between justification and renewal.
>
> [The justified are "perfect"] in relation to the past, as being a simple reversal of the state of guilt, and a bringing into God's favour; but as God's favour towards us will grow as we become more holy, so as we become more holy, we may receive a higher justification. The words in the text are inconsistent with an increase of justification, which Catholics hold.[156]

Remembering that such notes were written twenty-nine years after Newman converted to Catholicism, it is not very surprising to find him conforming earlier statements to Catholic dogma.[157] Owing to the fact that he regards justification and sanctification as one, and that the latter grows in meritorious works (performed by grace), it is logical for Newman to envisage the gradual increase of justification.[158] So he asserts that the gift of righteousness "then is habitual; both permanent and increasing."[159] More specifically, he insists,

> [The] Gift which justifies us is, as we have seen, a something distinct from us and lodged in us, yet it involves in its idea its own work in us, and (as it were) takes up into itself that renovation

---

154. Newman, *Jfc.*, 101.
155. ibid.
156. Ibid., 73.
157. See chapters 7, 10–11, and 16 in Tanner, *Decrees*, 673–76; 677–78.
158. Newman, *Jfc.*, 151–52 [168–69].
159. Ibid., 164 [188].

of the soul, those holy deeds and sufferings, which are as if a radiance streaming from it.[160]

It is at this point that Jose Morales cries foul. The problem consists in the fact that Newman seeks to preserve a ground of justification that is defined by the absolute perfection of the Triune God, and, at the same time, he asserts that this righteousness becomes a human possession which grows in a real and proper sense. Expressing his contention, Morales quotes from Newman's sermon, "Righteousness, Not of Us, but in Us," (1840) in which actual righteousness is said to be "not merely given to us and imputed to us, but really implanted in us by the operation of the Blessed Spirit."[161] Morales then concludes, "The vocabulary used by Newman henceforth clearly suggests the idea of *inherent* justice, [language] which he avoided in the *Lectures*."[162] And again, from the *Discourses*, Morales quotes Newman, "When God, for Christ's sake, is about to restore any one to His favour, His first act of mercy is to impart to him a portion of His grace."[163]

Here again we see that Newman's position is basically compatible with St. Augustine's. As such, the cultivation of virtue happens actively *in nobis* and not passively *extra nos*, which then gives rise to the development of *charitas*,[164] or in Newman's terminology, "actual righteousness."[165] This is one reason why Newman was able to reissue his *Lectures* (1874) as a Catholic thirty-six years after their original publication: because his position was in fundamental agreement with Augustinian soteriology in the first place (although expressed in different terms).[166]

Morales suggests that, after 1840, Newman's "dialectic approach, which prompted the establishment of a forced symmetry between Protestantism and Romanism," began to disappear.[167] Dessain offers a similar assessment when he writes, "On becoming a Catholic, however, Newman wrote little

---

160. Ibid., 178 [207].

161. Morales, "Problems of Justification," 157.

162. Ibid.

163. Ibid.

164 Augustine, "The Spirit and the Letter," 228–29.

165. Newman, *Jfc*., 80 [86].

166. Newman writes in the appendix of the third edition, "However, a few words of explanation are called for here in relation to two propositions of the Volume, which he distinctly professed to be at variance, but (as he now believes) are not really at variance, with the doctrines held in the Roman schools of recent times on the subject of justification." Ibid., x.

167. Instead, Newman posits the diametric opposition of Protestantism and Pelagianism instead of a *via media* between Protestantism and Romanism. Morales, "Problems of Justification," 155.

on the subject of Uncreated Grace."¹⁶⁸ Sheridan recognizes that Newman's doctrine of justification moved with him to Rome, especially with regard to baptism and faith, but he does not address the question of whether this also applies to the concept of uncreated grace.¹⁶⁹ Holtzen, on the other hand, disagrees with this view, particularly with Morales's contention that "Newman increasingly dwells on created grace as the cause of justification."¹⁷⁰ Holtzen gives three reasons why he believes Newman's *via media* by uncreated grace stands, even after the third edition (1874) of his *Lectures*.

> Because: (1) he adds an appendix that asserts the Holy Spirit is the formal cause of justification after his conversion, (2) he therein asserts the Holy Spirit is the proper form of justification and actual righteousness is the improper form, (3) he explicitly rejects the notion of *habitus* that accompanies the idea of *gratia creata*.¹⁷¹

Holtzen's argument must be criticized. First, he is evidently under the wrong impression that Newman introduced his appendix in the third edition (1874), when, in fact, the appendix was present from the start.¹⁷² A look at the first edition (1838) reveals that they are essentially the same, including the title, "On the Formal Cause of Justification."¹⁷³ This makes the first of his three arguments a moot point. As for his second point, Holtzen is correct to point out that Newman continues to assert that the Holy Spirit is the proper form of justification, and actual righteousness is the improper form, however, Holtzen does not account for the above-mentioned section in the *Lectures* where Newman moves off of his *via media* script to emphasize one formal internal cause in terms of internal renewal.¹⁷⁴ Finally, while Newman

---

168. Dessain, "Cardinal Newman and the Doctrine of Uncreated Grace," 285.

169. Sheridan, *Newman on Justification*, 255.

170. Holtzen, "Union with God," 183. For a more recent treatment by Holtzen, in which he argues that Newman's theology of justification is a true *via media* between Roman Catholicism and Protestantism, see Holtzen, "Newman's 'Via Media' Theology of Justification," 64–74.

171. Holtzen, "Union with God," 178.

172. Ibid. Holtzen cites three alterations to the third edition of Newman's Lectures. In addition to a movement toward inherent righteousness and the addition of sixteen explanatory notes, he points out the "addition of an extensive sixty-one page appendix on the formal cause of justification." Holtzen's confusion is perhaps due to the initial footnote of the appendix which may give the impression that it was a subsequent addition (Newman, *Jfc.*, 343). However, it is the footnote that was added to the *Lectures*, not the appendix itself.

173. Newman, *Jfc.*, 343 [391].

174. Ibid., 154 [170–71].

disavows *habitus* as the necessary accompaniment to *gratia creata*, he comes close to embracing it when he acknowledges that infusion of an inherent righteousness is the formal ground of justification. "In this then I conceive to lie the unity of Catholic doctrine on the subject of justification," he contends, "that we are saved by Christ's imputed righteousness, and by our own inchoate righteousness at once."[175] Holtzen acknowledges this fact when he writes, "[In the third edition, Newman switched] his understanding of the formal cause of justification from the imputation of an alien righteousness to the infusion of an inherent righteousness."[176] Newman may not call this inherent righteousness "*habitus*," but what he says about it in terms of its capacity to grow, even describing it in terms of "habitual,"[177] certainly gives the impression that it is something like *habitus* that he has in mind.

H. Conclusion

If in Tract 90 (1841), the Anglican Newman overreached his claim of solidarity with Rome, it may be that, in the third edition (1874) of his *Lectures*, the Catholic Newman gives the appearance of having retained more unity with his Anglican *via media* than was actually the case. It would certainly be wrong to suggest that Newman left his Anglican position in "shreds and tatters"—Newman's words from his autobiographical memoir to describe the state of his Calvinism when he had left Evangelicalism decades earlier;[178] but it seems clear that his *via media* developed into a *via Romana*.

Whether the Catholic Newman eventually rested his doctrine of justification on the formal cause of created grace is inconclusive. If one concentrates on the majority of Newman's *Lectures*, which reach back to 1838, the answer is "no." If, however, one gives priority to the sections that the Catholic Newman added, especially in light of his wider life and ministry, as Morales contends, the answer is probably "yes." More conclusive is the fact that, by 1874, Newman's *via media* had become fully Roman, albeit an unconventional way that leveraged the semantic range of the *unica forma causa* to emphasize a real sense of imputation and also an internal righteousness, both growing out of the divine presence. This is Newman's formal cause, in his words:

---

175. Ibid., 368 [414].
176. Holtzen, "Union with God," 178.
177. Newman, *Jfc.*, 164 [188].
178. Newman, *Letters and Correspondence*, 106.

> [Justification] viewed relatively to the past is forgiveness of sin [a real imputation], for nothing more it can be; but considered as to the present and future it is more, it is renewal wrought in us by the Spirit of Him who by His merits completes what is defective in that renewal [real inherent righteousness]."[179]

In this sense, Newman's position may be called a *duplex iustitia*. In the next chapter, we shall compare and contrast this position with that of Peter Martyr Vermigli and other proponents of two-fold righteousness.

179. Newman, *Jfc.*, 36 [38].

Chapter 5: A Comparison of Newman and Vermigli on the Doctrine of Justification

A. Newman and Vermigli in Conversation

WE HAVE THUS FAR recognized a combination of similarities and differences between Newman's and Vermigli's doctrine. With regard to similarities, we have noted that despite three centuries of distance, their doctrines of justification were motivated by similar concerns, such as the danger of meritorious works, cheap grace, and a proper relationship between forensic and actual righteousness. They also possess common theological commitments, notably an Augustinian harmartology, union with Christ, the need for a forensic imputation, the internal renewal of the Holy Spirit, and *duplex iustitia*. Most interesting and significant is the fact that the Catholic Newman maintains forensic imputation and that the Protestant Vermigli upholds the Spirit's work of renewal, issuing forth in good works, under the rubric of justification. The term *duplex iustitia* has served as a way to describe these anomalies.

Furthermore, probing more deeply into their respective positions, we have also observed how Newman and Vermigli give attention to many of the same sources. They are both biblical exegetes, rock-ribbed in their commitment to the authority of Scripture. This is especially apparent in Vermigli's work, where he explores Hebrew and Greek etymology.[1] Of course, the genre of Martyr's *locus*, embedded in his commentary on Romans, encourages such analyses. But it must be acknowledged that Newman is no exegetical slouch. Even though his *Lectures* were intended to be more systematic in their scope and sequence, he does not hesitate to examine the meaning of words in their biblical context.[2]

---

1. Vermigli specifically focuses on the terms "justification" and "faith." *Romanos*, 1181–83 [87–89].

2. "I say, then, that the words of Scripture, as of every other book, have their own meaning, which must be sought in order to be found." *Jfc*, 118.

Also in the vein of similarities, Newman and Vermigli give considerable attention to non-biblical sources, particularly church fathers and councils.[3] The outstanding difference in their use of these sources largely consists of Newman's heavy reliance on the eastern fathers, his interaction with Luther, and his references to the Caroline Divines (who of course followed Vermigli by the better part of a century). While it is true that Vermigli's doctrine of *sola scriptura* leads him to use the fathers and church councils largely as a means of supporting the authority of Scripture, he is, like Newman, concerned to prove his doctrine from the broader Christian tradition, that is, so long as Scripture is assigned the priority.[4] When this order is confused, however, as Martyr perceived to be the case among his interlocutors, he objects in forceful terms. Thus, he clarifies, "We have certain adversaries who judge little or nothing at all on the basis of the Holy Scriptures, but measure all their religion by the Fathers and councils, so much that they can be called *Patrologi* instead of *Theologi*."[5] With regard to church councils, Vermigli asserts that they "should not be heard without selectivity and judgment. We ought to receive and reverence only those councils which have kept their doctrine within the rule of Holy Scriptures."[6] Newman would agree with this notion in principle, although he spends less time trying to chasten conciliar statements with the explicit teaching of Scripture.

For all of their similarities, Newman and Vermigli also have *differences* in their doctrines of justification. This is especially true concerning other sets of theological commitments and the conclusions that logically follow from them. Such commitments include the sacramental framework of justification and *sola fide*. The theological outworking of these commitments bring Newman and Vermigli to contrasting conclusions, most significantly on justification's formal cause, on *habitus*, on the doctrine of perseverance, and on merit.

---

3. In his Romans *locus*, (far more than in his Genesis and 1 Corinthians *loci*), Vermigli devotes significant attention to the fathers and church councils. This attention is concentrated at the conclusion of each of the three propositions, 1237–53 [143–60], 1297–1311 [202–18], 1316–24 [221–30].

4. Vermigli, *Romanos*, 1236–51 [143–58]. For example, to support his argument that the unregenerate cannot be justified by works, he cites Basil, Gregory of Nazianzus, Augustine, Chrysostom, Ambrose, Cyprian, and Origen.

5. Ibid., 1236 [143]: "Sed quonium quosdam habemus adversarios, qui aut parum, aut nihil a scripturis pendeant, omnem autem suam pietatem, Patribus, et Concilijs metiantur, ut magis Patrologi, quam Theologi dici possint." Those who commit this error are said to "easily obscure the truth" (Ibid.).

6 Ibid., 1245–47 [152–55]. Because Vermigli's central concern is the problem of Pelagianism, he cites councils that explicitly renounce it, namely Milevis (A.D. 416) and the Second Council of Orange (A.D. 529).

In this chapter we trace the lines of continuity and difference between Newman's and Vermigli's doctrines. We begin each section with Newman's thought as a point of departure, since his position is relatively more complex, examining the essence of his thought on a given topic, before contrasting it with Vermigli's position, followed by a brief summary. With such perspective, we will be poised to reflect on contemporary implications for dialogue at the Roman Catholic and Reformed Protestant intersection, which follows this chapter as an overall conclusion.

B. Common Concerns: Works Righteousness

Newman and Vermigli both opposed the notion of works righteousness. From Newman's perspective, Roman Catholic soteriology was vulnerable to this critique. Citing the reason for this vulnerability, Newman opines: "they do not discern, they do not believe in, anything else [besides 'obedience'] in which [justification] can consist."[7] This led Newman to criticize the Roman Catholic position for reducing the ground of justification to a "habit" of obedience.[8] Such an approach, he argues, easily makes the mistake of replacing a properly Christ-centered vision with unhealthy introspection (*incurvatus in se*).[9]

In a similar vein, Newman regarded the doctrine of *gratia inhaerens* as unwittingly reducing justification to a matter of meritorious works, a move that he considered detrimental to the development of personal faith.[10] Concern for the practical liabilities of meritorious works vis-à-vis unhealthy introspection, it turns out, was shared by Peter Martyr:

> Certainly no one understands except those who have experienced how difficult it is for a bruised heart, dejected and weary with the burden of sins to find comfort.... If we, like the Sophists, commanded a person to have regard for his own works, then he would never find comfort, would always be tormented, always in doubt of his salvation and finally, be swallowed up with desperation.[11]

In addition to cautioning against the danger of falling in "desperation" beneath the righteousness requirement of God, Vermigli and Newman

---

7. Newman, *Jfc*, 183 [160].
8. Ibid., 348–52 [394–98].
9. Ibid., 190 [220].
10. Ibid.
11. Vermigli, *Romanos*, 1208 [114].

also identified the tendency toward impersonal worship in the Catholic tradition. For instance, Newman viewed much of popular Romanism as promoting a sort of religious transaction, an exchange of "the [mere] influence of grace, not as the operations of a living God, but as something to bargain about, and buy, and traffic."[12] Peter Martyr also addressed what he regarded as the impersonal nature of the Roman Catholic system when he contrasts the ritualistic function of the Petrine "keys" with the preaching of the word, appropriated by personal faith.[13] When Christ was at dinner with the Pharisees, Vermigli argues, "he exhorted them to first purify the heart, which is inward. This is something done by faith, for it is written in Acts, 'by faith cleansing their hearts.'"[14]

Regarding the "grace of eternal life," Peter Martyr asserts, "what is given freely, excludes merit completely."[15] In contradiction to his doctrine is the "Pelagian" view of the Roman Church (as he saw it), which he understood to effectively undermine divine grace by including human merit in the ground of justification.[16] Newman does not employ the specific language of "Pelagianism" to describe the problem of works righteousness, but he shares Vermigli's fundamental concern with grounding justification in human merit.[17] However, by the time Newman wrote the third edition of his *Lectures*—twenty-nine years after converting to Catholicism—he had retreated from this concern:

> This school is elsewhere called in these Lectures ultra-Roman or extreme Romanist. Such Catholic divines as Caietan, Vasquez, and Bellarmine were intended by this title, who, by making justification consist in the habit of charity or again in good works, not in sanctifying grace as an initial and distinct gift from above, seemed to the writer to fix the mind, equally with Anglican Arminians, not on a Divine inward Presence vouchsafed to it, but on something of its own, as a ground to rest upon and take

---

12. Newman, *Jfc.*, 186–87 [216–17].

13. Vermigli, *Romanos*, 1234–35 [141–42].

14. Ibid., 1234–35 [141–42].

15. Ibid., 1290 [197]. Elsewhere, Vermigli wrote, "Therefore, we must take away all merit, not only in those who are not yet justified, but also in those who have been justified" (1288 [195]).

16. Ibid., 1248–49 [156]. As noted, Vermigli's portrayal of Trent's position vis-à-vis Pelagianism, is less than fair. Chapter eight of the Council's *Decree on Justification* explicitly states that justification comes as a "free gift," and does so on the perennial consent of the Catholic Church, on the basis of faith, "without which 'it is impossible to please God'" (Heb 11:6). *Decree on Justification*, in Tanner, *Decrees*, 2:674.

17. Newman, *Jfc.*, 147 [163–64].

satisfaction in. *Of course, such a judgment seems to him now unreal and arbitrary.*[18]

Newman and Vermigli may describe the problem of meritorious works with different language and identify its tendencies in different parts of the church, but they stand together in opposing human merit as a fundamental ground of justification.

C. Common Concerns: Cheap Grace

Since Newman interpreted the Evangelicals of his day as maintaining justification by *mere* imputation, he sought to show the integral connection of justification and renewal.[19] As we have observed, Newman's bone of contention was not with "imputation" strictly speaking, as much as a *reduction* of the doctrine of justification to imputation.[20] The reason for the Evangelicals' error, according to Newman, was the popular belief in justification by *sola fide*, which he regarded as a direct route to antinomianism.[21] Newman suggests that this tendency is evidenced in the typical Evangelical exegesis of James concerning the necessity of works in justification, a teaching that Newman finds wholly inadequate.[22]

Vermigli recognizes the possibility that justification by faith alone can become a form of cheap grace. At the beginning of his "Justification is by Faith Alone" section of his *locus*, for instance, he emphasizes:

> Further, this also is to be noted, as we have already taught, that we do not say that faith through which we are justified is in our minds without good works, though we do say that the same "only" is that which takes hold of justification and the remission of sins. The eye cannot be without a head, brains, heart, liver, and other parts of the body, and yet the eye alone apprehends color and light. Therefore, those who reason against us in this way commit the error of false argument: faith (as they say) justifies; but faith is not alone; ergo faith alone does not justify.[23]

---

18. Ibid., 190 [statement contained in Footnote 1 of the *third edition*, absent from the 1838 version]. Emphasis added.

19. Ibid., 63 [112].

20. Ibid. Newman explains his understanding of imputation at some length on pages 67–78 [72–83].

21. Sheridan, *Newman on Justification*, 26–29, 265.

22. Newman, *Jfc.*, 291–93 [331–33].

23. Vermigli, *Romanos*, 1312 [218].

Furthermore, Vermigli, like Calvin, affirms that the virtuous life (or good works) of the one who is justified in Christ is acceptable to God. He writes, "We have never denied that the works of those now justified are acceptable to God."[24] Nevertheless, for Peter Martyr, *sola fide* is not the problem; it is the solution, so long as it is rightly understood. Therefore, he goes to great lengths to argue that faith may be alone, but it must never *remain* alone.[25]

In their mutual concern to avoid "cheap grace," Newman and Vermigli stand together in the conviction that the one who is justified will most certainly live a life that bears witness to the holiness of God.

D. Common Concerns: Holding Forensic and Actual Righteousness Close Together

Following from the previous point, Newman and Vermigli are also concerned to include the production of actual righteousness in their doctrines of justification. Newman, operating from the conviction that Jesus' incarnation accomplished more than merely delivering sinners from guilt, emphasizes the sinner's fellowship and communion with the Divine,[26] a relationship that gives way to a tangible form of righteousness, or "actual righteousness."[27]

Similarly, Vermigli insists on the connection between forensic and actual righteousness in his doctrine of justification. Before describing God's activity of forensic imputation in his Romans *locus*, he pauses to state the following:

> It is important to understand that when such an act [of justification] comes from God it is accomplished in two ways. Sometime, in reality, he brings forth righteousness in men. First, he endows them with his own Spirit and renews them fully by restoring the strength of their minds and by retrieving their human faculties from the greater part of their natural corruption; this idea is first a righteousness (*iustitia*) that is within and clings to our minds by the goodness of God through Christ. Second, when he has

---

24. Ibid., 1227–28 [134]. Cf. *Institutes*, 3:17:5, 10.

25. Ibid., 1307 [212]. Quoting Jerome, Vermigli wrote: "'If love is absent, faith also departs with it.' These words clearly declare that his judgment was that true faith cannot be divided from love, something we also teach and defend, but Pighius and his colleagues scorn it and cry out against it. Yet let him growl as much as he will; it is enough for us that this doctrine agrees with both the Scriptures and the fathers."

26. Newman, *Jfc.*, 182–88 [211–18].

27. Ibid., 36 [38].

fashioned and renewed them in this way he gives right and holy works, and by their frequent and continuing use there is born in our minds a quality or (as they call it) a "habit" by which we are inclined to right and holy living. We do not deny that this type of righteousness is renewed in the hearts of the regenerate.[28]

To a greater extent than Vermigli, Newman's doctrine of justification consistently highlights God's work of sanctification: "The Voice of the Lord is mighty in *operation*."[29] Concerning the content of this activity, Newman writes, "Imputed righteousness is the coming in of actual righteousness."[30] On account of the dynamic presence of God's Spirit, such a work transcends the legal domain to include the moral renovation of one's soul, that is, sanctification.[31] Newman regards the separation of sanctification from justification, which, in his view, was so often argued by the Evangelical party of the Church of England, as "technical and unscriptural."[32] This "unreal righteousness," insists Newman, is an aberration.[33]

Peter Martyr also desires to hold forensic and actual righteousness together. Accordingly, Martyr upholds regeneration and sanctification as constituent elements of justification. For example, in his 1 Corinthians *locus*, *On Justification*, Martyr draws this connection,

> A different kind of justification follows this upright life of holiness by which we are clearly praised, approved or declared just. For although good works do not bring that first righteousness which is given freely, yet they point to it and show it is present.[34]

The upright life of holiness, according to Martyr, is supplemented by the imputation of Christ's righteousness, which restores what is lacking in our "weak and mutilated" works.[35] Even though these works ultimately fail to prevail with God, one's life of holiness nevertheless belongs to the doctrine of justification. Why? A Christian life of holiness serves to vindicate one's forensic justification, providing material proof that one is indeed regenerate. It is also accepted as pleasing to God and rewarded on the last day.[36]

28. Vermigli, *Romanos*, 1182 [87].
29. Newman, *Jfc.*, 79–80 [86].
30. Ibid., 80 [86].
31. Ibid., 80–81 [86–87].
32. Ibid., 41 [44].
33. Ibid., 57 [61].
34. Vermigli, *PMR*, 147.
35. Ibid.
36. Vermigli, *Romanos* 1288 [195], 1291 [196].

Vermigli questions whether one can actually realize eternal salvation without such a living faith.[37]

With respect to the relationship of forensic and actual righteousness, Newman and Vermigli insist that both of them deserve a place in the doctrine of justification.

E. Common Concerns: Distinguishing Forensic and Actual Righteousness

While holding forensic imputation and sanctification together, Newman and Vermigli also insist on a proper distinction. Newman, for instance, is careful to distinguish "'Christ,' our propitiation, 'within us,'" from one's actual righteousness.[38] While affirming that justification effectively "renews" one's soul,[39] Newman is emphatic that such renewal is *not* derived from an infusion of inherent righteousness or the cultivation of *habitus*.[40] Rather, it comes from an "adherent" righteousness, "depending wholly and absolutely on the Divine Indwelling."[41] Simply put, Newman's doctrine recognizes in this indwelling a clear distinction between God's forensic declaration and the cultivation of virtue, that is, "actual righteousness." While unified in a single act, the two are regarded as notionally distinct.[42]

For Vermigli, "justification," in a strict sense, is limited to a forensic activity; yet he also understands regeneration and sanctification as necessarily accompanying forensic imputation. At the outset of his Romans *locus*, he raises an important question that lays groundwork for his distinction between forensic and actual righteousness: "Are men justified by works or by faith?"[43] He answers his question by asserting that "there are two meaning of 'to justify,'" namely, in fact or in judgment or estimation.[44] Identifying which of these two options is more fundamental, he explains, "[W]hen debating the matter, Paul was influenced by the testimony of the history of Abraham in Genesis and by the authority of David; he used the verb 'to be reckoned,' and, with proper understanding, reasons in light of our present

---

37. Ibid., 1318 [224]
38. Newman, *Jfc.*, 200 [231]. When Newman describes this righteousness—that which is associated with the believer's obedience—he calls it "actual." Ibid., 351 [397]).
39. Ibid., 86 [93].
40. Ibid., 348–52 [394-98].
41. Ibid., 187 [218].
42. Ibid., 67 [71–72].
43. Ibid., 1181 [87]: "Iustificentur ne homines operibus, ab fide."
44. Ibid., 1182 [88].

concern and question."[45] Thus, Vermigli chooses imputation over spiritual renewal as the proper ground of justification.

Newman and Vermigli, while seeking to hold forensic and actual righteousness together, insist on their proper distinction.

F. Common Commitments: Augustinian Harmatology

Newman and Vermigli both follow Augustine's doctrine of sin. Along with the Bishop of Hippo, Newman underscores the initiative of divine grace, which is altogether necessary for salvation on account of our bondage to sin.[46] To deny the reality of sin, or to rely upon one's own righteousness, from Newman's point of view, is the sin of pride, a vice that he routinely opposed in the liberalism of his day.[47] For Newman, God's legal pronouncement is "a real and gracious act on God's part towards us sinners," precisely because sinners are otherwise without hope.[48]

Peter Martyr shares Newman's belief in the anthropological necessity of divinely initiated grace. On this point, Martyr refers to the transgression of Adam as described in Romans 5, where one observes "the cause of so great an evil."[49] Following from the first man's disobedience, humanity is "lost and condemned," which includes infants.[50] Later in his Romans *locus*, Vermigli asserts this point rather explicitly: "The works of unregenerate men are sins."[51] In other words, people are incapable of producing works that are acceptable to God. Therefore, the basis of justification cannot possibly rest on human ability. This sober awareness of sin is what Frank James has labeled Vermigli's "intensive Augustinianism."[52]

Martyr vehemently opposes the notion that God extends a general grace to all people in such a way that it enables them to exercise justifying faith. He labels such a view "Pelagianism" and considers it to be an affront to

---

45. Ibid.

46. Walgrave, *Newman the Theologian*, 42–44. Newman explains how divine grace overcomes the unrighteousness of original sin in Newman, *Jfc.*, 88–91 [95–96].

47. Bouyer, *Newman: His Life and Spirituality*, 19.

48. Newman, *Jfc.*, 72 [77].

49. Vermigli, *Romanos*, 1196 [101]: "Accedit adhaec, quòd tanti mali causa exprimitur."

50. Ibid., 1196 [102]: "iam inde à prima ipsa origine per primum hominem perditi sumus & damnati."

51. Ibid., 1301 [201]: ".opera hominum non renatorum esse peccata."

52. James, "The Complex of Justification," 52–53.

Scripture.[53] According to Vermigli, if redemptive grace is obtainable prior to the initial work of the Spirit that enlivens the soul, the justification that follows would be based upon human effort:[54] "They [his Roman Catholic interlocutors] hold that there is a kind of general grace accessible to all and common even to the unregenerate, who are in a sense helped to merit justification and do works which please God. But in saying this, they fall into the heresy of Pelagius."[55]

While the problem of human sin factors more significantly into Vermigli's overall doctrine of justification, Newman may be credited with the rhetorical edge when he posits,

> I observe, then, we become inwardly just or righteous in God's sight, upon our regeneration, in the same essence in which we are utterly reprobate and abominable by nature, or (to use the strong language of the Homilies) as we are since Adam's fall "corrupt and naught," "without any spark of goodness in us," "without any virtuous or godly motion," "the image of the devil," "firebrands of hell and bondslaves of the devil," "having in ourselves no one part of our former purity and cleanness;" but being "altogether spotted and defiled," and "nothing else but a lump of sin."[56]

Newman and Vermigli maintain a sober and severe estimation of sin which recognizes the paucity of human righteousness in the unregenerate. Together they insist on the necessity of God's enlivening grace, "regeneration" in Newman's terms, which leads sinners to exercise justifying faith.

G. Common Commitments: Union with Christ

Newman's doctrine of divine presence, with its emphasis on participation in the life of God, may also be described in terms of union with Christ.[57]

> Christ, in rising, raises His saints with Him to the right hand of power. They become instinct with His life, of one body with His flesh, divine sons, immortal kings, gods. He is in them, because

---

53. Vermigli, *Romanos*, 1218–19 [125].

54. Pressed through the framework of his intensive Augustinianism, Vermigli can't begin to countenance the idea that meritorious works of the unregenerate are somehow pleasing to God. Ibid., 1195 [101], 1199 [105], 1214–15 [121–22], 1235–36 [142–43], 1260–61 [168], 1288 [194], 1313–14 [219–20].

55. Ibid., 1216 [123].

56. Newman, *Jfc.*, 89 [96].

57. Dessain, "Cardinal Newman and the Eastern Tradition," 95.

He is in human nature; and He communicates to them that nature deified by becoming His, that them It may deify.[58]

We have noted how the concept of union with Christ comes to flower in Lecture VII, in which Newman develops the subject more fully, describing how "justification is the setting up of the Cross within us."[59] Newman explores the sanctifying capacity of justification in terms of the adherent presence of Christ in the human soul. But simply saying this much invites an additional question. "Again: if it be laid down that our justification consists in union with Christ, or reconciliation with God," explores Newman, "this is an intelligible and fair answer; and then the question will arise, what is *meant* by union with Christ?"[60]

For Newman, this Christological union comes to one's soul by the Holy Spirit, who properly imputes the righteousness of Christ by means of divine indwelling. Of the three divine persons, the Holy Spirit is identified as the proper agent of justification as a matter of his particular role in the economy of salvation, although not to the exclusion of the other persons.[61] "This is really and truly our justification," Newman asserts, "not faith, not holiness, not (much less) a mere imputation; but through God's mercy, the very Presence of Christ."[62]

Newman's doctrine bears a remarkable similarity to Vermigli at this point. In view of his Augustinian conviction that humanity is a *massa perditionis*,[63] Vermigli reasons, "Unless [one's heart] has been renewed by the Spirit," there can be no justifying faith.[64] He envisages this faith to grow out of the Spirit's initial work, resulting in Christological union.[65] "But now, delivered by the grace of God," Vermigli concludes, "we are joined with Christ by the Spirit, to Christ himself being raised from the dead. By this union we may bring forth fruit to God, and no more death and damnation."[66] While Vermigli hardly uses the explicit terminology of "union with Christ," the notion that one is accepted by God on account of being "joined with Christ

---

58. Newman, *An Essay on the Development of Christian Doctrine*, 140.

59. Newman, *Jfc.*, 173 [200].

60. Ibid., 134 [148].

61. Newman, *PPS*, xi, 10, 1270. These sermons were published between 1834 and 1843.

62. Newman, *Jfc.*, 150 [167].

63. Vermigli, *Romanos*, 1196 [102].

64. Ibid., 1249 [157]: "Sed animus humanus nisi innovetur spiritu."

65. Similar to John Calvin, *Institutes*, 3.16.1.

66. Vermigli, *Romanos*, 1196–97 [102].

by the Spirit" is posited as the necessary bond that liberates one from death and enables one to "bring forth fruit to God."[67]

Union with Christ is for Newman and Vermigli the state in which one realizes spiritual deliverance from judgment and the fructifying work of the Spirit.[68]

H. Common Commitments: The Need for Forensic Imputation

Newman and Vermigli are equally committed to upholding the doctrine of imputation. Newman, for example, stresses the forensic nature of justification by distinguishing the declaration from the gift that it declares. As noted, he regards them as notionally distinct even though they are unified in a single act.

> Justification is the "glorious Voice of the Lord" declaring us to be righteous. That it is a declaration not a making, is sufficiently clear from this one argument that it is the justification of a *sinner*, of one who *has been* a sinner; and the past cannot be reversed except by *accounting* it reversed.[69]

Newman emphasizes the need for an "*imputing* righteousness,"[70] an "estimation of righteousness [in Christ] vouchsafed to the past, and extending from the past to the present as far as the present is affected by the past."[71] Since the problem of human guilt is of such depth and is exhibited before the judgment seat of God, a *judicial* action is therefore required.[72] Because this imputation consists in the divine presence, its basis is on one hand understood to be distinct from one's soul, while at the same time it is considered to exist *in nobis*.[73]

Vermigli likewise recognizes the catastrophic problem of guilt, bequeathed to humanity from Adam, and the need for imputation to effectively

---

67. Ibid., 1196–97 [102–103].

68. McLelland argues that union with Christ is a key to understanding Vermigli's doctrine of justification, even though the language is not made explicit in the Romans *locus*. McLelland, *Visible Words*, 113, 142.

69. Newman, *Jfc.*, 67 [71–72].

70. Ibid., 67 [72].

71. Ibid., 68 [72–73].

72. Ibid., 72 [76–77].

73. Ibid., 187 [217]. Newman does not use the phrase *extra nos* to describe the external dimension of imputation. In keeping with his doctrine of God's adherent presence, he prefers to emphasize its interiority (cf. Ibid., 187 [218]).

deal with the legal dimensions of the problem. In this sense, Peter Martyr basically agrees with Newman by defining imputation as a judicial transference of righteousness to the sinner.[74] The difference between their views comes down to the location of imputation's formal cause. For Vermigli, it is not in the divine presence but rather in the righteousness of Christ, which God reckons to the sinner so that one is considered to be righteous *coram deo*.[75] We shall examine this difference more thoroughly later; for now, we will focus on analyzing the basic similarities in their doctrines of forensic imputation.

Like Newman, Vermigli stresses that the crediting of Christ's righteousness only happens by divine initiative. Commenting on Romans 4:1–4, Martyr explains how the concept of "imputation" is based entirely on grace: "[Paul postulates imputation] as an antithesis to merit or debt, so that he to whom something is imputed neither deserves it nor receives it as debt."[76] Furthermore, this imputation is two-fold in that the sinner receives a forensic crediting of Christ's righteousness and also the non-imputation of his own sins.[77] On this level, Vermigli and Newman are essentially of one mind.[78]

For Vermigli, imputation is also *extra nos* in that it addresses one's legal status, and is not a form of *iustitia in nobis*, which affects the soul. Contrary to medieval Roman Catholic theology, Martyr asserts that justifying righteousness, "does not adhere [*inhaere*] to our souls, but is imputed by God."[79] As noted, Martyr also articulates a reverse imputation in which the sinner's guilt is put upon Christ.[80] This much is consonant with Newman, who likewise understands imputation in terms of one's legal status before God apart from an inherent form of righteousness. Furthermore, Newman and Vermigli also agree on the result of imputation, that it entails the absolution of sin[81] and the reception of divine favor.[82] "Moreover, as to the remission of sins, a blessing promised to us," Vermigli explains, "we should remember that the chief and principal point consists in this, that we

---

74. Vermigli, *Romanos*, 1182 [87].

75. Ibid., 1201 [107], 1314 [220].

76. Ibid., 1194 [100].

77. Ibid., 1252 [159].

78. The one significant point of discontinuity is Newman's contention that actual righteousness accrues merit *coram deo*. Newman, *Jfc.*, 151–52 [168–69].

79. Ibid., 1194 [100].

80. Ibid., 1264 [172].

81. Ibid., 1182 [87]: "Deus absolvendo à peccatis."

82. Ibid., 1217 [123].

are received into favor by God and our sins forgiven us."[83] With such favor, reconciliation is established between the defendant and the judge, bringing one into a position of righteousness *coram deo*.

Agreement between Newman and Vermigli on the need for forensic imputation grows from the realization that the problem of human guilt is of profound depth and of a particularly legal nature. Therefore, God provides forgiveness and favor through a forensic transference of his own righteousness.

I. Common Commitments: The Gift of the Holy Spirit and Manifestation of "Works"

Newman and Vermigli both maintain a robust pneumatology. For Newman, the Holy Spirit is the gift *and* the agent, who applies the benefits of Christ's death and resurrection. Starting with an initial grace that enlivens the sinner's soul,[84] this work includes pardon, grace, reconciliation, renewal, holiness, and spiritual communion—a collection of benefits that Newman summarizes with the word "atonement."[85] According to Newman, this is the manner in which the presence of Christ comes to bear upon one who is justified: by the Spirit. The Son merits salvation and the Holy Spirit applies it through personal inhabitation.

Similarly, Vermigli begins his *locus* by explaining how God endows believers "with his own Spirit and renews them fully by restoring the strength of their minds."[86] As with Newman, a concern for the Spirit's renewing work is basic to Vermigli's doctrine, as demonstrated by his description of justification as "the summit of all *piety*."[87] Such piety begins with the enlivening presence of the Spirit, which in turn produces faith, resulting in justification.[88]

When Newman describes the source of the Christian's piety, he often employs the biblical concept of *shekinah* to describe the tangible work of the Spirit.[89] For Newman, this glory denotes an "attribute, property, virtue, or

---

83. Ibid., 1274 [182].

84. Jfc., 80–81 [86–87].

85. Ibid., 202–3 [233–35].

86. Vermigli, *Romanos*, 1182 [87].

87. Emphasis added. Ibid., 1191 [96]: "columen totius pietatis." Calvin uses similar language to describe justification: "*quae pietatis est totius summa*" in Calvin, *Institutes* 3:15:7. *Johannis Calvini Opera Selecta*, 4:245.

88. Ibid., 1282 [190].

89. Newman, *Jfc*, 156 [177–78].

presence of the Divine Nature manifested visibly."[90] He cites the words of Jesus in which the Lord prayed to the Father, "The glory which Thou gavest Me, *I have given them.*"[91] Newman then asks, "What is this glory which has passed from Christ to us?"[92] He answers by pointing to the *glory* of the Father which raised Jesus from the dead, a glory that Paul attributes to "the Spirit of holiness."[93]

Vermigli is also concerned with how justification leads to the development of tangible faith,[94] and, with Newman, he looks to the Spirit for the answer. Martyr posits "two inward movements" of the Holy Spirit in which God exerts influence upon one's mind and volition.[95] From this double movement, faith is "engendered."[96] Vermigli conveys this idea—that God forgives those whom he has already enlivened—in his exposition of Romans 8:1–2, in which he states that "after the Spirit has first moved the hearts of the hearers to believe, then at last the Gospel obtains its power to save."[97] For this reason, Martyr describes the Holy Spirit as the "cause" of faith.[98]

The presence of the Spirit produces virtuous "works" in and through a believer. For Newman, these works are generated by the adherent presence of God. Such works are meritorious, rooted in the merit achieved by Christ, and are essential for salvation. For Vermigli, however, works before God are always non-meritorious.[99] Their different conceptions of merit will be explored below.

Partly because of their Augustinian understanding of sin, and partly because of their concern to emphasize the need for Christian virtue, Newman and Vermigli share a pneumatological emphasis in their doctrines of justification, in which the agency of the Spirit transforms the sinner's mind and volition with a view to manifesting good works. Such works validate the reality of one's initial justification. In this way, Newman and Vermigli both affirm justification *of* works.

---

90. Ibid., 162–63 [186].
91. Ibid., 163 [187].
92. Ibid.
93. Ibid.
94. Vermigli, *Romanos*, 1182 [87], 1215–16 [122].
95. Ibid., 1249–50 [156–57].
96. Ibid., 1284 [191].
97. Ibid., 609.
98. Ibid., 1284 [191].
99. Ibid., 1288 [195].

J. Common Commitments: *Duplex Iustitia*

One way to describe the doctrines of Newman and Vermigli on justification is in terms of a "two-fold righteousness," imputed *and* actual. This commitment grows out of their desire to ground justification in a forensic righteousness while also promoting the formation of actual righteous works. In Newman's words, it is the twin movements of "pardon and renovation."[100] Such a position seeks to avoid a legal fiction, which might drive a wedge between the two, thus bringing the Protestant categories of justification and sanctification into a closer relationship.

Holtzen is correct to point out that Newman's doctrine of justification is not a *duplex iustitia* if one strictly defines the position by two *equal* formal causes:

> Despite the assertion of "two formal causes," Newman does not hold to a strict theory of a *duplex iustitia*; that is a theory of two equal formal causes of justification. Rather, when he speaks of "two formal causes" of justification he distinguishes what he calls a proper formal cause and an improper formal cause (or proper form or improper form).[101]

While Newman does not posit two equal formal causes, he does include two distinct forms of righteousness in his overall doctrine of justification, a position that has an equally legitimate claim on the term *duplex iustitia*. Along this line, it is noteworthy that, in his appendix, Newman highlights how his position "very nearly resemble[s] Bucer's, among the Protestants, and that of Pighius, Mussus, and many others of the Roman School."[102] In this context, he likens the logic of his doctrine of justification, which insists upon both "holiness and works," with the position of these outstanding exemplars of the *duplex iustitia*.[103]

When Newman speaks of "two formal causes" (one proper—the forensic imputation of Christ's righteousness, and the other improper—the actual righteousness *in* the Christian, though not "of" him, mediated by the indwelling of the Spirit), he insists that both are fundamental to justification.[104] Holding these actions together, Newman maintains that the

---

100. Newman, *Jfc.*, 101 [112].

101. Holtzen, "Union with God and the Holy Spirit," 181–82.

102. Newman, *Jfc.*, 348 [394].

103. "Mussus" is a reference to Cornelio Musso (1511–74), Bishop of Bitonto, an outspoken advocate of double justice at the sixth session of the Council of Trent. Malloy, *Engrafted into Christ*, 71.

104. Newman, *Jfc.*, xi, 361 [407], 367 [413], 381–82 [423–25].

improper (internal) is derived and dependent on the proper (external) form of righteousness. In this sense, Newman's position meaningfully resembles Vermigli's doctrine, as he indirectly indicates,

> Now it happens that this doctrine appears to have been held by Bucer as distinct from the other Reformers; it is also the doctrine of the Canons of Cologne in their Antididagma of 1544; it was held by Pighius, Seripando, and others, at the Council of Trent. . . . In this then I conceive to lie the unity of the Catholic doctrine on the subject of justification, that we are saved by Christ's imputed righteousness, and by our own inchoate righteousness at once.[105]

As we have argued, Peter Martyr's doctrine of justification, even in its most mature form, remained fundamentally consistent with that of Bucer. And with regard to the basic contours of the *duplex iustitia*, we are arguing that it resembles Newman's. Take for instance the conclusion of Newman's statement quoted above, "[W]e are saved by Christ's imputed righteousness, and by our own inchoate righteousness at once." In a similar vein, Vermigli asserts, "But now, delivered [from our sin which results in condemnation] by the grace of God, we are joined with Christ by the Spirit, to Christ himself being raised from the dead. By this union we may bring forth fruit to God, and no more death and damnation."[106] "For Vermigli, the proper understanding of the nature of justification is that it includes both the act and its consequences; its cause and effects and indeed, eternal consequences," James helpfully summarizes. "Justification is thus an event necessarily accompanied by a process."[107]

Given their commitment to imputed *and* actual righteousness, and despite significant differences in how their doctrines hang together, Newman and Vermigli maintain positions on justification that are appropriately described as *duplex iustitia*.

---

105. Ibid., 368 [414]. In this context, Newman also mentions the "Ratisbon [Regensburg] Conference" as another example of the sort of *duplex iustitia* with which he is sympathetic (369 [415]).

106. Vermigli, *Romanos*, 1196–97 [102].

107. James, "*De Iustificatione*," 346.

K. Different Commitments: Sacramental Framework of Justification

For Newman, the sacraments have instrumental value. Accordingly, "Justification comes *through* the Sacraments; is received *by* faith; *consists* in God's inward presence; and *lives* in obedience."[108] Against the low-church Evangelicals of his day, whom he understood to be denigrating the importance of the sacraments,[109] Newman contends that sacramental rites actually inculcate Christian faith.[110]

By contrast, Vermigli's *locus* on justification contains scant attention to the role of the sacraments in mediating justifying grace. He first broaches the subject in proposition one of his Romans *locus*, in which he confronts the position of his Roman Catholic opponents with regard to the role of ceremonies.[111] Martyr finds their position to be inconsistent with the New Testament for the way it ascribes "the forgiveness of sins and bestowing of grace to the sacraments, just as, in the Old Testament, they were attributed to circumcision."[112] "Indeed, we utterly deny that any sacraments bestow grace," Martyr asserts. They do offer grace, but it is by "signification."[113] "For in sacraments and words, and in the visible signs, the promises of God made through Christ are set before us."[114]

Operating with the above conviction, Vermigli repudiates the Roman Catholic doctrine of baptismal regeneration.[115] He asserts that as Abraham was justified by faith before receiving the sign of circumcision, the Christian experience of justification is antecedent to the experience of baptism.[116] For Vermigli, the sacrament of baptism has no more power to justify than do the virtues of love and hope.[117] To insist on the mediation of baptism for justification, according to Peter Martyr, is to teach a position of meritorious works. "So great is the opposition between grace and works," Martyr

108. Newman, *Jfc.*, 278 [318].
109. Ibid., v.
110. Ibid., 280–82 [320–22].
111. Ibid., 1208–9 [115–16].
112. Ibid., 1212 [118–19].
113. McLelland, *The Visible Words of God*, 130–35.
114. Vermigli, *Romanos*, 1212 [119]. Later in his *locus*, in proposition three, Martyr makes a similar point: "As to the sacraments, we have often taught how justification is to be attributed to them, for they stand in relation to justification as does the preaching of the Gospel and the promise of Christ offered to us for salvation." Ibid., 1318 [224].
115. Ibid., 1251 [158].
116. Ibid., 1251 [159]. See also 1315 [221].
117. Ibid., 1315 [221–22].

concludes, "that Paul says, 'If of grace then it is not now of works, and if of works, then it is not of grace.'"[118]

Important differences exist between Newman and Vermigli on the sacraments, differences that are seemingly rooted in their respective backgrounds. In Newman's case, the denigration of the sacraments, which he ascribed to the Evangelicals of his day, contradicted his articulation of their centrality.[119] For Vermigli, after forty-two years as a Catholic priest, the notion of the sacraments functioning as instruments of grace beyond "signification" (i.e., functioning as the efficacious means by which one is enlivened by the Spirit) was tantamount to works righteousness.[120]

L. Different Commitments: Faith Alone

In a certain sense, Newman and Vermigli both affirm *sola fide*.[121] In the first edition of his *Lectures*, Newman, writing as an Anglican, used the language of "faith only" as a "lively mode of speech [figurative] for saying that we are justified neither by faith nor by works, but by God only." However, it is clear that Newman's interpretation of *sola fide* differs vastly from Vermigli's, who regards faith as the sole instrument. For Newman, faith is "the sole *internal* instrument, not the sole instrument of any kind."[122] Such a distinction is a critical component of Newman's doctrine:

> There would be nothing inconsistent, then, in Faith being the sole instrument of justification, and yet Baptism also the sole instrument, and that at the same time, because in distinct senses; an inward instrument in no way interfering with an outward instrument. Baptism might be the hand of the giver, and Faith the hand of the receiver. However, this is not the exact relation of Faith to baptism, as is plain for this reason—that Baptism

---

118. Ibid., 1316 [222].

119. As Newman put it in his advertisement, "The present Volume originated in the following way: It was brought home to the writer from various quarters, that a prejudice existed in many serious minds against certain essential Christian truths, such as Baptismal Regeneration and the Apostolical Ministry, in consequence of a belief that they fostered notions of human merit, were dangerous to the inward life of religion, and incompatible with the doctrine of justifying faith." Newman, *Jfc.*, v.

120. Ibid., 1316 [222]. McLelland, *Visible Words of God*, 130–35.

121. Newman, *Jfc.*, 244 [279]. Although in the third edition (1874) of his *Lectures*, the Catholic Newman retreated from faith alone in a brief footnote: "Catholics hold that, not faith only, but faith, hope, and charity, are the 'sustaining causes of justification.'" Ibid., 255.

122. Ibid., 226 [259].

occurs but once, whereas justification is a state, and Faith "abides." Justification, then, needs a perpetual instrument, such as faith can be, and Baptism cannot. Each, then, has its own office in the work of justification; Baptism at the time when it is administered, and faith ever after.[123]

In Newman's vision, the means by which one grasps Christ includes more than faith; it also consists in baptism.[124] Faith, Newman argues, represents a series of activities that include the sacraments, love, and obedience.

While then we reserve to Baptism our new birth, and to the Eucharist the ultimate springs of the new life, and to Love what may be called its plastic power, and to Obedience its being the atmosphere in which faith breathes, still the divinity appointed or (in other words) the mysterious virtue of Faith remains. It alone coalesces with the Sacraments, brings them into effect, dissolves (as it were) their outward case, and through them unites the soul to God.[125]

Newman and Vermigli both countenance Hebrews 11:1 in their definition of faith: "the substance of things hoped for, the evidence of things not seen."[126] For Newman, this "substance" of faith, because it is "unseen," remains undefined until it grasps its proper object, which, for the Christian, is the living Christ.[127] With this exegesis, Newman understands the object of faith to be the presence of Christ.[128] Thus, faith is not merely assent of the mind (*assensus*); nor is it simply trust (*fiducia*)—it is, for Newman, essentially union with Christ.[129] As we have noted, the closest Newman comes to offering a positive definition of faith alone is in the following words: "Salvation by faith only is but another way of saying salvation by grace only."[130]

By contrast, Vermigli uses Hebrews 11 to insist that faith is the instrument by which one first appropriates justification, and, furthermore, continues to lay hold of it:[131] "But nothing else is meant by those words [of Hebrews

---

123. Ibid.

124. Newman explicitly rejects the notion, attributed to Luther, that faith is the "primary instrument" of justification. Ibid., 244 [279].

125. Ibid., 236–7 [271].

126. Ibid., 252 [288].

127. Ibid., 253–54 [289–90].

128. Ibid., 266–73 [304–13].

129. Ibid.

130. Ibid., 283 [324].

131. Vermigli, *Romanos*, 1253 [160], 1261 [169], 1283 [190], 1292 [198], 1321 [227].

11] than that the things we hope for are strengthened and confirmed in our minds by faith."[132] In the context of expositing this passage, Martyr offers a cogent definition of how he understands *faith*. It is, he explains, "a firm and assured assent of the mind to the words of God, an assent inspired by the Holy Spirit to the salvation of believers."[133] Looking at the larger context of Martyr's Romans *locus*, he moves from the proposition that justification is "not by works" to the proposition that forgiveness is properly "received by faith." Here he concentrates on Romans 4, stressing Paul's statement, "To one who does not work but trusts him who justifies the ungodly, faith is reckoned to him as righteousness."[134] Thus, the believer "takes hold and receives" the promise of forgiveness.[135] It is "never alone but always draws along with it various motions of the mind," particularly "confidence, hope, and similar affections."[136] The manifestation of righteous qualities verifies that the believer truly possesses justifying faith.[137]

Newman's overall vision of Christian faith, with its emphasis on virtue, is not far from Vermigli's concern to fortify post-conversion faith with qualities such as hope and affection. Again, in Vermigli's words, "Christ requires more of us than faith, for who doubts that he wants those who are justified to live uprightly and to practice virtue of all kinds."[138] Thus, one might say that, for Peter Martyr, the *nature* of faith is active and holy. But if we were to ask Vermigli about the *function* of faith with regard to justification, he would instinctively answer with *sola fide*, arguing that one's good works have no role whatsoever in causing justification.[139] "And when we say that one is justified by faith alone," Vermigli specifies, "we obviously say nothing else than that one is justified only by the mercy of God and by the merit of Christ, which we cannot grasp by any other instrument than faith alone.[140]

---

132. Ibid., 1278–79 [186].

133. Ibid., 1184 [90]. Martyr uses Hebrews 11 as a touchstone in his definition of faith from pages 1184 to 1187 [90 to 92].

134. Ibid., 1254–55 [161–62]. Martyr also considers Ephesians, Philippians, Hebrews, 1 Peter, 1 John, the Gospels, Acts, and the Old Testament. Ibid., 1258–64 [165–72].

135. Ibid., 1262 [170]: "apprehendimus promissiones Dei."

136. Ibid., 1183 [89].

137. Ibid., 1183 [89].

138. Ibid., 1318 [224].

139. Ibid.

140. Ibid., 1321 [227].

M. Different Conclusions: Formal Cause

An interesting way to compare Newman and Vermigli with regard to the formal cause of justification is with reference to Andreas Osiander. It has been observed that John Henry Newman and Osiander share a similar conception of justification by divine indwelling; furthermore, Newman and Vermigli both comment on Osiander's position.[141] Richard Laurence, Archbishop of Cashel, pointed out in 1839 that Newman assigned "a particular sense to the word Justification which with exception of Osiander no Protestant ever affixed before him."[142] Newman himself also hints of this connection in the appendix of his *Lectures*,[143] in which he comments that Osiander's doctrine concerning the essential righteousness of Christ is "not very different from the doctrine of Petavius."[144] Therefore, consideration of Osiander's formulation offers insight into the way that Vermigli may have assessed Newman's doctrine.

Osiander held that the essential righteousness of Christ's divine nature (apart from his human nature) was the sole cause of justification. The deity of Christ justifies because it alone is essentially righteous.[145] Such righteousness, according to Osiander, is not forensically attributed to the sinner in an alien righteousness (*iustitia aliena*); rather it consists in the substantial indwelling of Christ's righteousness (*iustitia Dei inhabitans*). In other words, according to Osiander's hypothesis, justification is not the forgiveness of sins; rather, it consists in this essential indwelling, which renews one's soul.[146] "Therefore, we are justified with his essential righteousness," Osiander explains, "as it is written, 'One will call him YHWH, who is our

---

141. After Andreas Osiander (1498-1552) moved from Nuremburg to the University of Königsberg, as professor of theology, he published his controversial book, *De Iustificatione* (1550), in which he proposed an alternative Lutheran view of justification. Osiander, "Eine Disuptation von der Rechtfertigung," 427-47. For more on the Osiandrian controversy, see Billings, *Calvin, Participation, and the Gift*, 53-63; Seeberg, *Textbook of the History of Doctrines* trans. Charles E. Hay, vol. 2, 369-74; Garcia, *Life in Christ*, 43-45, 197-99, 201-18, 239-52; Steinmetz, *Reformers in the Wings*, 91-99; cf. Alister McGrath, *ID*, 241-43.

142. Toon, *Evangelical Theology, 1833-1856*, 155.

143. Newman, *Jfc.* 387-89 [426-28]. Newman admits that he was unable to obtain Osiander's writings first hand: "His *Confessio de Justificatione* was published in Latin and German, but neither it nor any of his other works have fallen in my way" (387 [426-27]).

144. Ibid., 388 [427].

145. This is a fundamental difference between Osiander and Newman, as the latter makes no such distinction between the natures of Christ's indwelling presence.

146. Seeberg, *Textbook of the History of Doctrines*, 370.

righteousness.'"[147] Simply put, justifying righteousness is located in Christ who abides in the believer.[148]

It is interesting to consider the central motivation behind Osiander's position,[149] which he conveys in his *De Justificatione*, reacting to the forensic emphasis of Melanchthon and his followers:[150] "They teach [doctrines] colder than ice, that we are accounted righteous only on account of the remission of sins, and not also on account of the righteousness of Christ dwelling in us by faith. God is indeed so unjust as to regard him as righteous in whom there is really nothing of true righteousness."[151] In response to this statement, Seeberg concludes, "This citation reveals [Osiander's] aim. Justification as connected solely with imputation is to his mind an irreligious conception."[152]

Osiander's concern to avoid reducing justification to a legal fiction is noteworthy because it is shared by both Newman and Vermigli. As we have seen, this concern is part of what drove Newman to join forensic imputation and internal renewal in the adherent presence of God. It was also a motivating force behind Vermigli's insistence that justification must, in a meaningful way (although not as the fundamental ground), include regeneration

---

147. Osiander, "Eine Disuptation von der Rechtfertigung," 439.

148. Steinmetz summarizes the basic logic of Osiander's hypothesis, "As the flesh of Jesus was the bearer of the Logos, so now the spoken word of the preacher is the bearer of the divine word which is received by faith alone. When the word is grasped by faith, it indwells man and unites with him. Where the word is present it transforms man and renews him in the image of God. Man is justified not because his works are now holy, but because Christ indwells him. The indwelling Christ is the basis of man's acceptance, and not the renewal as such, though where Christ is present man is renewed in the image of God." Steinmetz, *Reformers in the Wings*, 96.

149. Undergirding Osiander's hypothesis is a redemptive historical understanding of Adam which regards his prelapsarian state to be originally righteous on account of having been made in God's image. This image was thought to consist in the divine Logos, which constituted Adam's righteousness before God. At the fall, Adam lost the indwelling presence of the Logos and thus lost his original righteousness. In the unfolding of salvation history, however, it was through the incarnation of Jesus Christ that the effects of the fall were ostensibly reversed. When Christ, the "inner Word," is brought to the soul of the believer through the preaching of the gospel, one is made essentially righteous through the indwelling of Christ, the divine Logos. On this basis one is justified. Seeberg, *Textbook of the History of Doctrines* 371; Steinmetz, *Reformers in the Wings*, 96–97.

150. McGrath points out how Melanchthon's doctrine of justification employed images and categories from the sphere of human law, while Luther drew from the thought world of personal relationships (i.e., human marriage). McGrath, *ID*, 238–39.

151. Osiander, *De Justificatione*, 73, cited in Seeberg, *Texbook of the History of Doctrines*, 369–70.

152. Ibid.

and sanctification. In each of these proposals, including Osiander's, the need to identify justification's formal cause—and, by extension, the question of how to properly relate forensic imputation and internal renewal—calls for attention.

In addition to Philipp Melanchthon[153] and John Calvin,[154] Peter Martyr expressed opposition to Osiander's position in his letter to the "Polish Lords and Ministers" in 1556:

> We reject as foreign and alien to the Scriptures the 'essential justice' which Osiander has invented. We do not recognize any other basis for justification than that which Paul in Romans and Galatians teaches us[,] . . . how righteousness is imputed to us by faith. . . . Moreover, if the just live by faith, as Habakkuk has testified, and our justification is our life, we do not now have an essential justification but one imputed by faith, as the apostolic letters have handed down.[155]

It is noteworthy that Vermigli's assessment of Osiander's position does not mention the problem of Osiander driving a wedge between the natures of Christ when he singles out the divine nature as the basis of justification. Nor does Martyr specifically address the matter of how to properly define the nature of our union with Christ, as Calvin does with his *mystica unio*.[156] Of course, there is every reason to believe that Martyr would have vehemently opposed Osiander on these points.[157] However, what we do observe is Vermigli addressing his critique to Osiander's decision to ground

---

153. Melanchthon, *Melanchthon on Christian Doctrine*, 168-69.

154. Calvin refutes Osiander in the final edition of his *Institutes*, 3.11.5-12.

155. The letter is written from Strasbourg, 14 February 1556, and is found in *Loci Communes*, 1114. A recent English translation is found in Donnelly, *Life Letters and Sermons*, 153.

156. So Calvin writes, "We do not, therefore, contemplate [Christ] outside ourselves from afar in order that his righteousness may be imputed to us but because we put on Christ and are engrafted into his body—in short, because he deigns to make us one with him." Calvin, *Institutes*, 3.11.10. For Calvin, solidarity with Christ is always the work of the Holy Spirit who unifies us to Christ.

157. Vermigli makes it clear that union with Christ is by the Spirit. *Romanos*, 1196-97 [102]. With reference to the person and natures of Christ, Vermigli does not have a specific volume, but he did engage the subject in a letter written to address a dispute in Poland in 1560, when the Italian theologian Francesco Stancaro (1501-74) was teaching that Christ is mediator only in his human nature. After the death of Martyr's friend, John a Lasco (1499-1560, also called Jan Łaski), Martyr replaced him in the role of opposing Stancaro, by writing to the church in Poland on behalf of the ministers in Zürich (dated May 27, 1560). Martyr asserts in good Chalcedonian fashion that "Christ Jesus is one person in whom the two natures subsist in a way that they are joined with each other so that they cannot in any way be pulled apart from each other." *PMR*, 127-31.

justification in something other than forensic imputation. In raising this objection, not only does Vermigli reveal the central concern of his doctrine, he also offers a clue to how he may have responded to Newman's position.

It is also significant that Vermigli's response to Osiander begins and ends with reference to the way in which justification by essential righteousness violates the teaching of Scripture. This is what one might expect, since, in his *locus*, Vermigli is principally concerned with demonstrating from the Bible the inadequacy of works and the futility of basing justification on anything other than the forensic imputation of divine righteousness.[158] Similar to Calvin, who also critiqued Osiander on this point,[159] Vermigli insists that justification cannot be based upon any sort of inherent righteousness but rather on the forensically imputed righteousness of Christ alone.

What do the above observations suggest about the way Vermigli may have responded to Newman? To begin with, it is very possible that Vermigli would have affirmed aspects of Newman's doctrine.[160] They share a common concern to avoid the reduction of justification to a legal fiction and for giving due attention to the Spirit's ongoing work of renewal in making Christians righteous. They also agree on the need to affirm forensic imputation as the formal cause by which one is declared righteous and thus made acceptable to God. That is to say, unlike Osiander, Vermigli and Newman maintain that a man may only attain forgiveness through a crediting of righteousness. Real and significant as these commonalities are, however, there remains a fundamental element of Newman's position to which Vermigli would fervently protest: Newman's inclusion of internal renewal along with forensic imputation in the formal cause of justification. For Vermigli, this inclusion represents a category confusion that effectively undermines what he regards as the biblical foundation of justification. Because the *sine qua non* of Martyr's doctrine is the reckoning of divine righteousness as the sole

---

158. With regard to the ultimate meaning of justification, Vermigli asserts, "Then 'to justify' means that through judgment, words, witness, or assertion one counts the person just" (1182 [88]). This conviction is also illustrated by the overall structure of Martyr's *locus*, that justification is "Not by Works," "It Is by Faith," and "Faith Alone."

159. So Calvin writes: "When it comes to Scripture, Osiander completely corrupts every passage he cites. In Paul's statement that 'faith is reckoned as righteousness' not for the 'one who works' but for the 'one who believes in him who justifies the ungodly' [Rom 4:4–5], Osiander explains 'justify' as 'to make righteous.'" Calvin, *Institutes*, 3.11.6.

160. Given the state of sixteenth-century polemics, it is hard to imagine Vermigli saying too many flattering things in response to the Catholic Newman. But if Calvin could affirm a bit of Osiander in the midst of his invectives, it is conceivable that Vermigli could do the same. (Calvin says, for example, "[Osiander] says that we are one with Christ. We agree." Calvin, *Institutes*, 3.11.5.)

fundamental cause of one's forgiveness, Newman's doctrine, in the final analysis, would be unacceptable.

What would Newman have said about Vermigli? In the absence of any such comment, we do not know for sure. But it is probable that he would have likened Vermigli's position to that of Calvin and Bucer, which Newman describes in his appendix as being quite close to his own.[161] The key difference, according to Newman, concerns the role of faith, which Bucer upholds as "the interposing and acceptable principle between us and God."[162] While it is likely that Martyr's forceful assertion of *sola fide* would have been off-putting to Newman, reminding him perhaps of those one-dimensional Evangelicals to whom he was reacting,[163] he would have recognized an affinity between Vermigli's and Bucer's positions, and, therefore, a certain compatibility with his own.

Despite the fact that they both include the forensic imputation of Christ's righteousness in their doctrines of justification, along with a desire to meaningfully connect justification to the work of the Spirit in producing virtue, Vermigli and Newman differ on the precise nature of justification's formal cause. For Vermigli, this cause is strictly the forensic imputation of Christ's righteousness accessed by faith alone. For Newman, it is the divine presence of God, which includes both imputation and internal renewal. Newman could have recognized an affinity with Vermigli, due to Vermigli's position that justification entails a two-fold righteousness. However, Peter Martyr would have been unable to reciprocate. As he puts it concerning the basis of justification, it "is not to be looked for from works; it should be enough for us, that the good works we do after justification are sacrifices of thanksgiving (*eucharistika*). Let us not make them propitiatory sacrifices, by which we would do great injury to Christ."[164]

N. Different Conclusions: *Habitus*

While this point is perhaps minor compared to the others, it is worth considering. As we have observed, Newman disavows *habitus* as the internal

---

161. Newman, *Jfc.*, 348 [394]. Elsewhere in his appendix, Newman claims that a two-fold righteousness position on justification is more commonly held than one might at first realize. In various places one finds support, says Newman, in such people as Hooker, Mr. Alexander Knox, Calvin, Baxter, and Barrow. Ibid., 378–84 [420–26].

162. Ibid., 348 [426]. In fact it would have been more accurate for Newman to say that Bucer's position posits *imputation* as the interposing principle, accessed through the *instrumentation of faith*.

163. Ibid., 291–93 [331–33].

164. Vermigli, *Romanos*, 1205 [111].

form of righteousness by which one is justified. He does, however, come close to affirming the idea in the third edition of his *Lectures* when he acknowledges that the infusion of an inherent righteousness is the formal ground of justification: "In this then I conceive to lie the unity of Catholic doctrine on the subject of justification, that we are saved by Christ's imputed righteousness, and by our own inchoate righteousness at once."[165] As we noted, this was one of the more significant developments of Newman's doctrine after his conversion to Catholicism. The basis of his formal cause of justification moved from the forensic imputation of righteousness to the impartation of an inherent righteousness.[166] Even as a Catholic, Newman did not explicitly call this inherent righteousness "*habitus*." However, his description of its capacity to grow, even describing it as "habitual,"[167] suggests that this internal disposition of righteousness is essentially *habitus*.

By contrast, Peter Martyr readily affirms the progressive development of holiness in terms of a "habit" of righteousness.[168] Because men and women in Christ are having their minds and wills renovated by the renewing work of the Holy Spirit, they "cooperate with the power of God."[169] Such cooperation grows in time and actually becomes a form of *iustitia inhaerens* which leads to further acts of piety.[170] This, in Vermigli's words, is the "inherent righteousness which is rooted in us, which we obtain and confirm by leading a continually upright life."[171]

In the final analysis, the question of whether Newman and Vermigli agree on this point depends on how one understands the development of Newman's doctrine from the first to the third editions of his *Lectures*. Those who recognize continuity between these works will argue that Newman maintains his rejection of *habitus*. For those who think Newman altered his position in a more Catholic direction, Newman came to embrace *habitus*, even without the specific term. The latter of these positions seems more probable.

---

165. Newman, *Jfc.*, 368 [414].

166. As Holtzen notes in his dissertation: Holtzen, "Union with God and the Holy Spirit," 178.

167. Newman, *Jfc.*, 164 [188].

168. Vermigli, *Romanos*, 1182 [87].

169. Ibid., 1250 [158]: "et gratia, atque spiritu instauratus cum divina virtute una cooperatur."

170. Vermigli quotes Augustine with approval "with regard to the righteousness that adheres in us." (*Augustinum sensisse de iustitia inhaerente*) Ibid., 1320 [226].

171. Ibid., 1299 [205]: "sed de illa intrinseca nobis inhaerente, quam recte vivendo perpetuo acquirimus, et confirmamus."

O. Different Conclusions: Perseverance

Given Newman's insistence on efficacious grace that leads to divine indwelling, one might expect him to have a place for perseverance. Such an expectation is potentially reinforced when Newman makes statements such as the following: "Righteousness then, considered as the state of being God's temple, cannot be increased; but, considered as the divine glory which that state implies, it can be increased."[172] But for Newman there is no guarantee of perseverance. Because the glory of the Spirit in and through a Christian fluctuates in growth, justification itself is also thought to grow (or decline). In like manner, this pneumatic state of being also admits the possibility that one may fall from grace, that is, lose one's justification. In other words, just as possessing the Spirit amounts to justification, losing the Spirit means that one has jeopardized justification. So Newman insists the following in one of his *Parochial and Plain Sermons*:

> There is no such person under the Gospel as a "justified sinner," to use a phrase which is sometimes to be heard. If he is justified and accepted, he has ceased to be a sinner. The Gospel only knows of justified saints; if a saint sins, he ceases to be justified, and becomes a *condemned* sinner. Some persons, I repeat, speak as if men might go on sinning ever so grossly, yet without falling from grace, without the necessity of taking direct and formal means to get back again. They *can* get back, praised be God, but still they *have* to get back, and the error I am speaking of is forgetfulness that they *have* fallen, and *have* to return.[173]

By contrast, Vermigli upholds a doctrine of perseverance.[174] In keeping with the conviction that man is unable to secure divine favor by performing good works, Peter Martyr asserts that one who is truly regenerate can do nothing to forfeit his justification.

> In general, it may be stated that faith cannot be completely extinguished because serious sins are committed by the justified and those destined to salvation. In such cases, faith is lulled to sleep and lies hidden and does not burst forth into action unless awakened again by the Holy Spirit. In such fallen ones, the seed of God remains, although for a time it produces no fruit.[175]

---

172. Newman, *Jfc.*, 151 [168].
173. Newman, *PPS*, 5.13, 1079.
174. Ibid., 1253–54 [160–61], 1292–93 [198–200], 1315–16 [221–22].
175. Vermigli, *Romanos*, 1278 [186].

Vermigli believes that when a regenerate person falls into sin—even sin of a serious nature—his/her justification remains secure ("the seed of God remains"). Martyr acknowledges that "true faith," sometimes "slips" or is "lulled to sleep," but is not lost.[176] Given his emphasis on the gratuitous and persevering nature of salvation, it is easy for Martyr to say that "those who seek God, to be justified by him through faith, as the apostle teaches, attain what they desire; but those who would be justified by works fall away from justification."[177] The doctrine of perseverance reveals that for all of their similarities, the variation between Newman and Vermigli is significant.

P. Different Conclusions: Merit

Earlier we considered how, in Newman's schema, the gift of the Spirit produces virtuous "works" in and through a believer. We noted that for Newman these works are meritorious, rooted in the merit achieved by Christ and essential for salvation: "we are absolutely saved by obedience," he argues, ". . . by *what we are* . . . [and] we are absolutely saved by faith, or by *what Christ is*."[178] In a footnote to this statement, added in Newman's third edition, he adds the following:

> Catholics hold that our good works, as proceeding from the grace of the Holy Ghost, cannot be worthless, but have a real and proper value; on the other hand, that the great reward of eternal life is due to them only in consequence of the promise of God. Good works have on this ground a claim on God's faithfulness to His promises, and there a claim on His justice, for it would be unjust to promise and not fulfill.[179]

Newman's *via media* is sufficiently elastic to accommodate the Catholic emphasis on the meritorious character of good works. Because, in Newman's view, Christians possess two-fold righteousness (forensically imputed and also inchoate, that is, the incipient form of righteousness that resides in the believer) it is natural for him to maintain that the former consists of Christ's merits while the latter involves merit that belongs to the Christian. This *et . . . et* approach allows him to say that "the inherent righteousness of a true Christian, viewed as distinct from Christ's inward presence, is

---

176. Ibid., 1302 [208]: "amitti . . . aut ita consopiri ut suum."
177. Ibid., 1288 [194].
178. Newman, *Jfc.*, 2 [2].
179. Ibid.

something real."[180] Part and parcel of this real righteousness is the Christian's real works which accrue real merit before God. Such meritorious works can increase as one's apprehension of justification itself increases (by a greater manifestation of the Spirit).[181] Simply put, since justification and sanctification are united in Newman's doctrine, and grow together in proportion to God's manifest presence, the believer's meritorious works likewise grow.[182]

Vermigli is absolutely emphatic that works can in no way merit justification.[183] However, because he includes regeneration and sanctification in the broader confines of justification, the production of (non-meritorious) works is a necessary component of justification. This broader view of justification, which Martyr calls "a different kind of justification," anticipates the final judgment when men and women are finally justified.[184] We have noted that in this sense Vermigli can be said to maintain *duplex iustificatio*,[185] not that he understands justification to have a double formal cause (what McGrath suggests is the standard form of *duplex iustificatio*) as was true during the Tridentine proceedings.[186] If there is one thing that Martyr's *locus* makes clear, it is, once again, that "works" in no way cause justification ("in reality good works are effects of righteousness, and not causes").[187] Therefore, justification is never "by" works when we talk about the formal cause. As does his colleague, Martin Bucer, Vermigli understands God to accept[188] and reward[189] works as a necessary constituent of final justification. The regenerates' works are central to sanctification,[190] which for Vermigli belongs to the doctrine of justification.

On the basis of the above considerations, we can conclude that, for Vermigli, the production of good works by the regenerate indicates that

---

180. Ibid. 199–200 [230]. Newman usually describes this inherent righteousness in terms of "actual righteousness" in order to support his doctrine of uncreated grace and avoid the notion of *habitus* (80).

181. Ibid., 151–52 [168–69].

182. Ibid.

183. "Therefore, we must take away all merit, not only in those who are not yet justified, but also in those who have been justified." Vermigli, *Romanos*, 1288 [195].

184. Vermigli, *Corinthios Commentarii*, 19 [147]. Cf. *Romanos*, 1182 [88].

185. Ibid.

186. Alister E. McGrath, *ID*, 313.

187. Vermigli, *Romanos*, 1228, [135].

188. Ibid., 1227–28 [134]; cf. *Corinthios Commentarii*, 19 [147].

189. Ibid., 1288 [195].

190. Martyr writes, "I answer that such [non-meritorious] works are profitable to the regenerate, for by living uprightly and orderly they are renewed and made perfect." Ibid., 1291 [196].

they have received the imputation of Christ's righteousness.[191] The warp and woof of Martyr's *locus* is dedicated to arguing against justification by works in the sense of a prior formal cause. But when we broaden the focus of our question beyond the formal cause to consider the place of works in the future judgment, when God justifies someone "in fact" and not simply in "estimation," accepting and rewarding such works because they are performed in Christ, there is a sense in which Vermigli affirms justification *by* works.

In short, for Newman works are meritorious since those who are justified manifest an incipient form of righteousness by their obedience, animated by the adherent presence of God. For Vermigli, works are never meritorious; they constitute the effect (or fruit) of forensic imputation, which is recognized as the proper cause (or root). But since the believer's works are supplemented by the forensic righteousness of Christ,[192] they are accepted and rewarded by God.

Q. Conclusion

This chapter has compared and contrasted salient elements of Newman's and Vermigli's doctrine of justification. In view of their common concerns (i.e., the danger of meritorious works, cheap grace, and a proper relationship between forensic and actual righteousness) and common theological commitments (an Augustinian harmatology, union with Christ, the need for a forensic imputation, the internal renewal of the Holy Spirit, and *duplex iustitia*), the notion of *duplex iustitia* has served as a heuristic lens for understanding the catalysts of their respective doctrines. Following from these concerns, two-fold righteousness also sheds light on the reasons and methods by which these doctrines are constructed, illustrating how a commitment to upholding both forensic *and* operative righteousness encourages theological decisions that are shared by Roman Catholics and Reformed Protestants.

These commonalties have implications for interaction at the Roman Catholic and Reformed Protestant intersection. On a practical level, for example, a shared concern for the danger of meritorious works and cheap grace will lead both traditions to carefully articulate and qualify their doctrines

---

191. Ibid., 1228–29 [135]. "And Christ would want everyone to understand that none except the just are received into the kingdom of heaven. Therefore, he considers these external works so that it might be clearly understood by them that righteousness is imputed to men by faith."

192. Vermigli, *PMR*, 147.

of justification in order to avoid these errors. Common theological commitments such as an Augustinian view of sin, union with Christ, and the dynamic work of the Holy Spirit are also points of agreement. At the very least, this recognition of commonalities has the power to ameliorate the unfortunate tendency of reacting to the other tradition by retreating from elements that truly belong to a doctrine of justification, such as when Protestants categorically deny the fructifying role of the Spirit or when Catholics refuse to recognize the possibility of forensic imputation.

We have also noted, however, that just because two theologians agree on *duplex iustitia* in the context of justification, it does not mean that they will agree fully. Newman and Vermigli illustrate this in spades. Despite the aforementioned affinity between Newman's and Vermigli's doctrine, they maintain fundamentally different commitments on key points (i.e., the sacramental framework of justification and *sola fide*) which naturally drive them toward divergent conclusions, particularly with reference to justification's formal cause, the existence of a disposition [*habitus*], and the doctrine of perseverance. In the concluding, we will reflect on the implications of these differences, and our similarities, for contemporary Roman Catholic and Reformed Protestant dialogue.

Chapter 6: Justification in Contemporary Roman Catholic and Reformed Theology

A. Justification in Contemporary Ecumenical Focus

IN HER CHAPTER, "JUSTIFICATION," in *The Oxford Handbook of Systematic Theology*, Dawn DeVries suggests, "There has been something of a renaissance of interest in the doctrine of justification at the turn of the twenty-first century."[1] DeVries notes four developments from the preceding decades that have exemplified this movement: Hans Küng's landmark book, *Justification: The Doctrine of Karl Barth and a Catholic Reflection*, the "New Perspective on Paul," the new Finnish interpretation of Luther as expressed by Tuomo Mannermaa et al., and the *Joint Declaration on the Doctrine of Justification*. Interestingly, each of these examples have found a way of bringing forensic and transformative approaches to justification into a closer relationship.[2] To gain perspective on the ecumenical promise of this renaissance, we will examine six issues that have emerged from our study of Newman and Vermigli—human powerlessness and divine initiative; justification's formal cause; concupiscence and sin; faith alone and works; assurance of faith; and the role of merit.

Before examining these issues, we must say a word about the ecumenical moment in which we live. As DeVries suggests, discussions between Roman Catholics and Protestants have moved beyond stereotypical approaches. The most significant example is arguably the *Joint Declaration on the Doctrine of Justification* (*JD*) between the Lutheran World Federation and the Roman Catholic Church, signed in Augsburg on October 31, 1999 in commemoration of Luther's Ninety-five Theses. Especially indebted to previous statements—particularly the American report entitled *Justification*

---

1. DeVries, "Justification," 197–211 (209).

2. DeVries uses the language of "double grace" or "two graces" instead of *duplex iustitia*, but it is the same concept that she has in view. Ibid., 198, 201.

by Faith (1983) and, from Germany, *The Condemnations of the Reformation Era: Do They Still Divide?*[3]—the *JD* is the culmination of earlier discussions on justification.[4]

The task of enlisting support for the *JD* in wider Catholic and Lutheran communities was initially a significant challenge. Toward this end, a draft was distributed in 1995, and feedback was solicited from church leaders in both communities. The first iteration of the *JD* was then published in 1997, followed by a period of conversation. The disagreement that ensued on both sides of the ecclesial fence has been well documented.[5] Such debate culminated in the Vatican's "Official Response" on June 25, 1998, which seemed to undermine prospects of a joint signing. Before discussions deteriorated, however, a propitiatory annex addressing critical points of ambiguity was added, thus allowing both sides to sign the "Official Common Statement." This "Annex to the Official Common Statement" officially belongs to the *JD*.

The text of the *JD* is remarkably brief compared to previous documents (for example, *Justification by Faith*, 1983).[6] Nevertheless, having been formally accepted by the Roman Catholic Church at the highest level, it is recognized as "the most significant report" on justification.[7] The *JD* is also significant for its stated goal of officially rescinding the mutual anathemas of the sixteenth century—for those who understand justification in the

---

3. *JD*, 1–3.

4. *JD*, 6.

5. Lane, *Justification by Faith*, 120–22; Blocher, "The Lutheran-Catholic Declaration," 198–99; Radano, *Lutheran & Catholic Reconciliation*, 146–65.

6. The *JD* consists of a Preamble (1–7) providing historical prologue, the "Biblical Message of Justification (8–12), followed by a brief section entitled, "The Doctrine of Justification as Ecumenical Problem," which addresses the application of the sixteenth century condemnations (13). Thirdly, "The Common Understanding of Justification" identifies mutual commitments (14–18), followed by the largest section, "Explicating the Common Understanding of Justification (19–39), which analyses seven key issues: "Human Powerlessness and Sin in Relation to Justification" (4.1), "Justification as Forgiveness of Sins and Making Righteous" (4.2), "Justification by Faith through Grace" (4.3), "The Justified as Sinner" (4.4), "Law and Gospel" (4.5), "Assurance of Salvation" (4.6), "The Good Works of the Justified" (4.7). The fifth section, "The Significance and Scope of the Consensus Reached" (40–44), is quite brief, and it is followed by the "Sources for the *Joint Declaration on the Doctrine of Justification*," a sampling of materials from previous dialogues that support conclusions drawn in the *JD*. Finally, following the "Official Common Statement," is the "Annex" which seeks to address issues concerning which the preceding had failed to produce sufficient consensus.

7. Lane, *Justification by Faith*, 124.

way "presented in this *Declaration*."⁸ Nevertheless, the sixteenth-century condemnations are to be taken seriously as "salutary warnings."⁹

Despite the consensus it represents, the *JD* also acknowledges ongoing differences between Lutherans and Catholics on seven key issues connected to the doctrine of justification.¹⁰ However, it describes them not as bona fide doctrinal differences, but as discrepancies "of language, theological elaboration, and emphasis," proceeding to proclaim them "acceptable" (rather than targets of anathematizing canons).¹¹ Dulles regards the term "acceptable" as poorly chosen and would have preferred the word "tolerable."¹² But even with such shortcomings, the *JD* is recognized as offering the most current and authoritative statement on justification among many Catholics and Protestants.¹³

Finally, it is important to note that conversation between Catholics and Protestants is in some measure asymmetrical because while the Catholic Church possesses a magisterial authority binding upon the faithful (as summarized in the *Catechism of the Catholic Church*),¹⁴ Protestants (even within the Reformed tradition) have no such referee outside of Scripture itself.¹⁵ Therefore, it is important to clarify that our analysis will concentrate, for the Catholic side, on the Council of Trent's *Decree on Justification* (1547), the *Catechism of the Catholic Church* (1994), and the *Joint Declaration on*

---

8. *JD*, 41–44.

9. Ibid., 42.

10. Therefore, it is called the "Joint Declaration" (*Gemeinsame Erklärung*) and not the "Common Confession of Our Faith."

11. *JD*, 40.

12. Dulles notes that the English text differs from the German, in which the word "*tragbar*" (tolerable) is used instead of "*annehmbar*" (acceptable). Dulles, "Justification and the Unity of the Church," 127.

13. The World Methodist Council officially associated with the *JD* in Seoul (South Korea), on July 23, 2006. For a Reformed perspective on the *JD* in the context of assessing contemporary Lutheran and Reformed approaches to justification, see Fackre, "Affirmations and Admonitions: Lutheran and Reformed," 1–26.

14. Concerning the nature and purpose of the *Catechism*, it says of itself: "This catechism aims at presenting an organic synthesis of the essential and fundamental contents of Catholic doctrine, as regards both faith and morals, in the light of the Second Vatican Council and the whole of the Church's Tradition. Its principal sources are the Sacred Scriptures, the Fathers of the Church, the liturgy, and the Church's Magisterium. It is intended to serve "as a point of reference for the catechisms or compendia that are composed in the various countries." *CCC*, para. 11.

15. Confessions such as The Belgic Confession (1561), The Heidelberg Confession (1563), and The Westminster Confession of Faith (1647), have enduring value, but there is no single Reformed confession that has a binding nature quite like the *CCC*.

the *Doctrine of Justification* (1999);[16] Peter Martyr Vermigli will represent a Reformed Protestant approach (readers can decide for themselves the extent to which Peter Martyr is a suitable representative of Reformed Protestantism). Finally, we will also note points where John Henry Newman's doctrine of justification indicates fresh opportunities for rapprochement.

B. Human Powerlessness and Divine Initiative

The Council of Trent was quite clear in its *Decree on Original Sin* that the damage done by humanity in Adam—that is, in original sin—could not be repaired by efforts of human nature or by any other means besides the merit of Christ.[17] In the same paragraph, it also emphasizes the sacrament of baptism as responsible for mediating this merit, bringing forgiveness and new life. These two convictions—that humans are naturally guilty before God, and that God comes to their rescue through Christ in the sacrament of baptism—lay essential groundwork for understanding the Catholic doctrine of justification.

The Council of Trent's *Decree on Justification* begins by revisiting the portrait of humanity's "unclean" condition as described by the *Decree on Original Sin*. Neither the forces of nature nor the law of Moses, it states, can provide liberation from the corrupting and condemning power of sin. Human assets are simply insufficient. It is only by God's grace given through the passion of Christ that anyone acquires the ability to move in the direction of righteousness.[18] This "predisposing grace," which God imparts, is the initial step in an individual's conversion (when he is transferred from sin to forgiveness), and, by the empowerment of the Holy Spirit, it enables him to "freely assent to and cooperate with this same grace."[19] Thus, God empowers the one so endowed to freely repent, believe, hope, love and keep the commandments.[20]

We have observed how Peter Martyr vigorously repudiates the idea that anyone can dispose himself for justification through willful co-operation (despite the fact that it is on the basis of God's empowering grace). Since Vermigli regards human nature as corrupt (unlike the Catholic position

---

16. The Second Vatican Council offered little explicit attention to the doctrine of justification; however, it indirectly addresses the subject in its teaching on such themes as grace, faith, salvation, and the ministrations of the church.

17. "Decree on Original Sin," Tanner, vol. 2, 665-67; *CCC*, 1849-50, 1871-73.

18. "Decree on Justification," Tanner, *Decrees*, 2:671.

19. Ibid., 672.

20. Ibid.

which regards nature as working in concert with a predisposing grace), he also necessarily hold it to be impossible for any human to move toward God prior to regeneration.[21] After making this point against Trent, Martyr then quips, "What else would Pelagius say if he were now alive?"[22] For Vermigli, it is not a "predisposing grace" empowering one's volition that results in justifying faith; it is the complete renewal of the heart from stone to flesh that "fully persuades, bends, and changes the will."[23] He thus concludes, "Our men of Trent do indeed grant that God renews the heart of man by illumination of the Holy Spirit. However, so that a man himself should do something, they add that the man who admits such inspiration may also reject it." For Vermigli, the Tridentine understanding of human volition is guilty of "works" righteousness and thus amounts to Pelagianism.[24]

As Vermigli illustrates, to the extent that the Catholic position grants human will a contribution to the ground of justification, Reformed Protestantism will dissent from it. This dissension, however, should not prevent Reformed Protestants from recognizing their agreement with Catholics on the basic conviction that God's intervening grace in some way enables a person to believe (call it "prevenient grace" if you like).[25] Accordingly, the most significant differences between Vermigli and Rome are two-fold: the ultimate basis of acceptance (the formal cause) and the delivery system—the instrumental means by which the Holy Spirit and his gifts are imparted

---

21. Trent teaches that adults are required to prepare themselves for justification by co-operating with "the light of the Holy spirit" prior to baptism. *Decree on Justification*, ch. 5.

22. Vermigli, *Romanos*, 1249–50 [156–57].

23. Ibid.

24. Ibid. Vermigli conveys this same concern are found in *Romanos*, 1216 [123], 1218–20 [125–26]. Vermigli grants and approves other kinds of preparation, that is, experiences that lead to faith. However, he is emphatic that salvation should not be ascribed to such experiences. "Indeed," he writes, "they are instead enemies of our salvation." 1219–20 [126].

25. Contra the medieval notion of congruent merit, the Council of Trent asserted the idea that anything preceding justification is incapable of meriting the impartation of justifying grace (*Decree on Justification*, chs. 5, 6, and 8; Tanner, ed., *Decrees*, 2:671–72). In chapter eight, it states that nothing prior "*promeretur*" to justification can merit the grace of justification. Certain Franciscans of the period argued that using "*promeretur*" rather than "*meretur*" excludes meriting justification by condign merit, but not by congruous merit (this argument is predicated on the belief that *mereri* and *promereri* equate to congruous and condign merit). However, in light of chapters 5 and 6 of Trent's *Decree on Justification*, which underscores the need for a divinely imparted predisposing grace, such an interpretation seems highly unlikely. Heiko Oberman offers a detailed examination of the history of interpretation surrounding *promeretur* in his volume, *The Dawn of the Reformation*, 222–33. In the words of the *CCC*, "God brings to completion in us what he has begun." *CCC*, 2001.

(the sacraments compared to *sola fide*). We shall consider these differences in due course; but for the moment we are interested in recognizing the common commitment to upholding divine initiative in justification. In the words of Trent, chapter seven:

> For though no one can be just unless the merits of the passion of our Lord Jesus Christ are communicated to him; nevertheless, in the justification of a sinner this in fact takes place when, by the merit of the same most holy passion, the love of God is poured out by the agency of the holy Spirit in the hearts of those who are being justified, and abides in them. Consequently, in this process of justification, together with the forgiveness of sins a person received, through Jesus Christ into whom he is grafted, all these infused at the same time: faith, hope and charity.[26]

The same note is hit by the *Catechism of the Catholic Church*:

> The first work of the grace of the Holy Spirit is conversion, effecting justification in accordance with Jesus' proclamation at the beginning of the Gospel: "Repent, for the kingdom of heaven is at hand." Moved by grace, man turns toward God and away from sin, thus accepting forgiveness and righteousness from on high. "Justification is not only the remission of sins, but also the sanctification and renewal of the interior man."[27]

Finally, the *JD* also safeguards divine initiative when it asserts that every salutary act directed at salvation relies on divine grace, and no action prior to justification is strictly meritorious:

> We confess together that all persons depend completely on the saving grace of God for their salvation. The freedom they possess in relation to persons and the things of this world is no freedom in relation to salvation, for as sinners they stand under God's judgment and are incapable of turning by themselves to God to seek deliverance, of meriting their justification before God, or of attaining salvation by their own abilities. Justification takes place solely by God's grace.[28]

---

26. "Decree on Justification," Tanner, *Decrees*, 2:673–74.

27. *CCC*, 1989. This point is also made in 1987 and 1988. Along this line, *Lumen Gentium* 14 asserts that, "All the sons of the Church should remember that their exalted status is to be attributed not to their own merits but to the special grace of Christ."

28. *JD*, 19, see also 17: "[The New Testament] tells us that because we are sinners our new life is solely due to the forgiving and renewing mercy that God imparts as a gift and we receive in faith, and never can merit in any way."

C. Justification's Formal Cause

If contemporary Catholicism were to embrace Newman's notion of justification by divine indwelling, agreement at the Catholic/Protestant intersection would go significantly deeper.[29] To this point, the critical question is whether Newman's theology of union with Christ by the adherent presence of God is consistent with Trent's single formal cause. As we noted, in his advertisement of his third edition (1874), the Catholic Newman exploits the ambiguous nature of the *unica forma causa*, pointing to other post-Tridentine Catholic authors who likewise propose an option other than a habitual or actual form of inherent righteousness. Newman is convinced that because Trent's *Decree* simply states that justification's formal cause is "the righteous of God . . . by which he makes us righteous," without explicating its precise nature, his position on justification by divine indwelling is a plausible option. If Rome were to accept Newman's proposal on this point, a greater amount of agreement could be reached with Protestants on their most fundamental point of disputation with Catholicism: justification's formal cause.

If, as Newman argues, justification consists in the indwelling presence of God, Catholics would have the freedom to recognize justification's formal cause to be every bit as forensic as it is operative.[30] And because this position admits the simultaneous reception of sanctifying righteousness, the Catholic concern for justification to feed and manifest itself in ethics (i.e., faith, hope, and love) is ameliorated. Thus, the debate would no longer turn on whether justification is strictly forensic or operative. According to Newman, it is both. A more significant dividing line, in this case, is whether justification is simply a forensic declaration of Christ's righteousness (as some forms of Protestantism would contend, such as the traditional Lutheran view)[31] or the reception of Christ's righteousness by the indwelling Spirit (which Vermigli affirms).

---

29. This is assuming that the Catholic Newman's doctrine of justification vis-à-vis *gratia increata* (as expressed in the third edition of his *Lectures* from 1874) remained consistent with the *via media* of the original 1838 version.

30. Concerning the forensic nature of this work, we have noted Newman's assertion that justification is the "glorious Voice of the Lord' declaring us to be righteous. That it is a declaration not a making, is sufficiently clear from this one argument that it is the justification of a *sinner*, of one who *has been* a sinner; and the past cannot be reversed except by *accounting* it reversed." Newman, *Jfc.* 67 [71–72]).

31. So Luther writes about the righteousness of justification, "It is a great thing so to lift oneself up and to walk in a foreign [literally "alien"] righteousness, one that lies outside yourself, one you neither see nor understand but hear in the Word alone." Plass, *What Luther Says, An Anthology*, vol. 3, 1229.

In favor of Newman's emphasis on this divine indwelling, we read the following statements in the Catholic *Catechism*:

> Grace is a *participation in the life of God*. Grace is *favor*, the *free and underserved help* that God gives us to respond to his call to become children of God, adoptive sons, partakers of the divine nature and of eternal life.[32]
>
> The grace of Christ is the gratuitous gift that God makes to us of his own life, included by the Holy Spirit into our soul to heal it of sin and to sanctify it. It is the *sanctifying* or *deifying grace* received in Baptism. It is in us the source of the work of sanctification.[33]
>
> Filial adoption, in making us partakers by grace in the divine nature, can bestow true merit on us as a result of God's gratuitous justice.[34]

These quotations demonstrate that contemporary Catholic teaching recognizes and affirms a considerable amount of Newman's central thesis: that justification is by grace on account of divine indwelling. But do Trent and the *Catechism* actually permit such a position in what they say elsewhere? In other words, is the adherent presence of God completely sufficient for justification or does an individual also need to manifest an inherent righteousness (either habitual or in works)?

At the very least, Newman's argument appears to be in accord with the requirement of *initial* justification; however, it is not so clear whether divine indwelling is entirely sufficient for justification beyond this point. For example, in the context of defining justification's formal cause, chapter seven of Trent's *Decree* says justification is that by which God "makes us just and endowed with which we are renewed in the spirit of our mind ... according to the measure which the holy Spirit apportions to each one as he wills, and in view of each one's dispositions and co-operations."[35] This language sounds a lot like the sort of habit of righteousness that Newman disavows. The Catholic *Catechism* conveys the same idea:

> Sanctifying grace is an habitual gift, a stable and supernatural disposition that perfects the soul itself to enable it to live with God, to act by his love. *Habitual grace*, the permanent disposition to live and act in keeping with God's call, is distinguished from actual graces which refer to God's interventions, whether

---

32. *CCC*, 1997.
33. *CCC*, 1999.
34. *CCC*, 2009.
35. "Decree on Justification," Tanner, *Decrees*, 2:673–74

at the beginning of conversion or in the course of the works of sanctification.[36]

Nevertheless, there are reasons why Catholics may still find Newman's formulation tenable. Even though he maintains *gratia increata* as the ground of forgiveness, we have observed how he seeks to also include internal renewal as part of that ground.

> [The] Gift which justifies us is, as we have seen, a something distinct from us and lodged in us, yet it involves in its idea its own work in us, and (as it were) takes up into itself that renovation of the soul, those holy deeds and sufferings, which are as if a radiance streaming from it.[37]

Some would accuse Newman of slicing the onion a little too thin at this point.[38] He is arguing for the causality of uncreated grace over *habitus*—which suggests disagreement with the Catholic position—but, at the same time, he insists that this presence includes under its meaning the act of "making righteous."[39] Is this claim to internal renewal genuine enough to carry the transformational freight demanded by Trent and the *Catechism*? One is tempted to categorically reply in the negative, since Newman posits a notional distinction between the (forensically) justifying word and the (actual) renewal by the Spirit.[40] But this is where it gets complicated. The reader will recall that, in his 1874 edition (writing as a Catholic), Newman retracted this distinction (that "justification is perfectly distinct from renewal")[41] in order to suggest that sanctification and justification are simultaneous.[42] If this is in fact Newman's position, there appears to be greater compatibility with Roman Catholic doctrine. Unfortunately, while Newman removes the wedge in the above-mentioned statement, he fails to do so in the appendix of his third edition, in which he asserts that "incipient righteousness, which is the improper form [of justification], is but the necessary attendant on the Divine Presence, which is the proper."[43] Therefore, as we concluded in chapter four, faced with this ambiguity, readers will have to decide for themselves which of these two positions more accurately reflects the Catholic Newman.

36. *CCC*, 2000.
37. Newman, *Jfc.*, 178 [207].
38. Morales, "Newman and the Problems of Justification," 143–64.
39. Newman, *Jfc.*, 65 [70].
40. Newman, *Jfc.*, [170–71].
41. Newman, *Jfc.* first edition, (1838) [170–71].
42. Newman, *Jfc.*, (1874), 154.
43. Newman, *Jfc.* (1874), 381–82.

In addition to considering whether Newman's formal cause developed in a Rome-ward direction, we need to also consider whether Rome has moved any closer to the *duplex iustitia* positions represented by Vermigli and Newman. Lane reminds us that the Council of Trent's position on justification was formulated "in response to what it then understood the Reformers to be saying."[44] Therefore, as Lane continues to explain, we must listen carefully to contemporary Catholic theology to understand the nuances of its current position, especially as it relates to Protestantism. In this regard, there is an interesting statement in the Catholic *Catechism* that might be understood as a tacit approval of imputation, at least to the extent that those who have already been justified have an ongoing need for Christ's righteousness as superior to their own. At the conclusion of the section on the role of merit in justification, at which point it takes up the matter of the charity of Christ as the source in us of all merit before God, there is the following quotation from Thérèse of Lisieux (Catholic ecumenists can decide whether this emphasis opens the door widely enough to admit any of Newman's doctrine):

> After earth's exile, I hope to go and enjoy you in the fatherland, but I do not want to lay up merits for heaven. I want to work for your *love alone*. . . . In the evening of this life, I shall appear before you with empty hands, for I do not ask you, Lord, to count my works. All our justice is blemished in your eyes. I wish, then, to be clothed in your own *justice* and to receive from your love the eternal possession of *yourself*.[45]

Dulles explains that with regard to the question of whether righteousness is imputed or inherent, twentieth-century Catholic theology emphasized the notion of *gratia increata*. Accordingly, "the righteousness of the creature," says Dulles, "always remains a gift; it is a participation in the righteousness of God, given in Christ."[46] While Catholics do not employ the language of "imputation" in the same way as Reformed Protestants to describe the reckoning of Christ's righteousness as the sole ground of one's forgiveness, they are nevertheless keen to underscore the fact that our righteousness is derived from our participation in Christ. Thus, Dulles concludes, "In that sense, the Reformation categories of *iustitia aliena* and "imputed righteousness" convey an important truth that Catholics do not wish to ignore."[47]

44. Lane, *Justification by Faith*, 85.
45. *CCC*, 2011.
46. Dulles, "Contemporary Catholic Theology," 258.
47. Ibid.

The *JD* does not use the term "impute" to identify the basis on which the converted Christian is accepted by God.[48] The closest it comes to providing an answer is in the fifteenth paragraph, which says that by "grace alone, in faith in Christ's saving work and not because of any merit on our part, we are accepted by God and received the Holy Spirit, who renews our hearts." While acceptance and renewal both appear in this statement, it is possible to understand the latter to follow from the former.[49] It is of course also possible for this pattern to be limited to initial justification (and not one's ongoing status), in which case the *JD* is simply reiterating the teaching of Trent. Unfortunately, the *JD* is ambiguous on this particular point.

When Vermigli directed his critiques toward Trent, the major target was what he perceived to be the heresy of "Pelagianism."[50] We noted that this was not entirely fair since Trent, unlike Pelagius, insisted that justification comes as a "free gift" because it is impossible for man to naturally please God.[51] Nevertheless, Peter Martyr goes to great lengths to oppose the notion of grounding justification in the Spirit's work *in nobis*, arguing instead for Christ's imputed righteousness *pro nobis* as the fundamental basis of justification: "Therefore, we say that justification cannot consist in that righteousness and renewal by which we are created anew by God. For it is imperfect because of our corruption, so that we are not able to stand before the judgment of Christ."[52] For Peter Martyr, sinners are accounted righteous because Christ's righteousness is forensically reckoned to them.[53]

In short, our study has illustrated that the fundamental difference between the Roman Catholic and Reformed Protestant doctrines of justification comes down to the "formal cause." Even if Newman's concept of God's adherent presence is applied, Reformed Protestants still oppose the combination of forensic imputation and internal renewal as the proper cause of justification, since doing so fails to produce the perfect righteousness that is required to meet the demands of divine holiness.[54]

---

48. The verb "to impute" only appears in 22 ("God no longer imputes to them their sin") regarding the non-imputation of guilt. The word "reckoned" appears in 10. A "declaration of forgiveness" is mentioned in 23, in summarizing the Lutheran position.

49. Lane makes this point in *Justification by Faith*, 167.

50. Vermigli, *Romanos*, 1248–49 [156].

51. Chapter eight of the Council's *Decree on Justification* explicitly states that justification comes as a "free gift," and does so on the perennial consent of the Catholic Church, on the basis of faith, "without which 'it is impossible to please God'" (Heb 11:6). Tanner ed., *Decrees*, 2:674.

52. Vermigli, *Romanos*, 1252 [159].

53. Ibid., 1182 [88]; 1251–52 [159].

54. Ibid., 1182 [88]; 1252 [159].

D. Concupiscence or Sin

Peter Martyr agrees with Rome on the fact that those who have been justified continue to have concupiscence, that is, Christians still possess an inclination toward evil despite the indwelling presence of the Spirit.[55] His opposition to Rome on this point centers on the question of the status of concupiscence. Is concupiscence simply an inclination to sin, or does the inclination itself constitute sin? Vermigli chooses the latter, recognizing sin as an ongoing obstacle to fellowship with God, which only the imputation of Christ's righteousness can remedy.[56] By contrast, the Council of Trent, in its "Decree on Original Sin," unequivocally opted for the former.[57] In the words of the Catholic *Catechism*,

> Conversion to Christ, the new birth of Baptism, the gift of the Holy Spirit and the Body and Blood of Christ received as food have made us "holy and without blemish," just as the Church herself, the Bride of Christ, is "holy and without blemish." Nevertheless the new life received in Christian initiation has not abolished the frailty and weakness of human nature, nor the inclination to sin that tradition calls concupiscence, which remains in the baptized such that with the help of the grace of Christ they may prove themselves in the struggle of Christian life. This is the struggle of conversion directed toward holiness and eternal life to which the Lord never ceases to call us.[58]

It is interesting to note that this is another place where the Catholic Newman revised his position in conformity to the teaching of Rome. Accordingly, in his third edition (1874), he qualifies his original statement that "since we are ever falling into sin and incurring God's wrath,"[59] by noting that, "If by 'sin' is meant grievous sin, those who are in the grace of God

---

55. For instance, Martyr makes this point from the Lord's Prayer, "Moreover, the Son of God commanded believers to say in their prayers, 'Forgive us our trespasses.' This shows that the faithful also need forgiveness for the things they do, for our works are not perfect nor are they able to satisfy." Ibid., 1207 [113].

56. From the beginning of his *locus*, Martyr asserts that "'to justify' comes by way of judging or accounting, to ascribe righteousness to someone and not make him just in reality." Vermigli, *Romanos*, 1183 [88-89]. More explicitly, he states "justification cannot consist in that righteousness and renewal by which we are created anew by God. For it is imperfect because of our corruption, so that we are not able to stand before the judgment of Christ." Ibid., 1252 [159].

57. "Decree on Original Sin," Tanner (ed.), *Decrees*, 2:665-67

58. *CCC*, 1426.

59. Newman, *Jfc.*, 101.

need not ever be falling into it; and if lighter sins are meant, these do not bring us back again under 'God's wrath.'"[60]

The question of the status of concupiscence continues to be a point of contention between contemporary Catholics and Protestants. Dulles explains why this is the case.

> Trent unequivocally taught the reality of the transition from unrighteousness to righteousness that occurs in justification. It denied that grace consists merely in God's favor or in the non-imputation of sins.... For this reason Catholics remain to this day somewhat nervous about the formula, *simul iustus et peccator*, which might suggest that we are justified only in hope or in a purely nominalistic way that leaves us internally untouched.[61]

This study has not ascribed the doctrine of *simul iustus et peccator* to Peter Martyr's teaching, since he does not actually employ the phrase. However, we agree with James who makes a compelling case that, despite Martyr's reticence in explicating the formula, the concept is alive and well in his theology.[62] In light of this, the anthropology of the *JD*, in keeping with Trent, differs from Martyr and the Reformed tradition insofar as it regards concupiscence as not strictly sin in the "proper sense" and not meriting "the punishment of eternal death."[63] At the same time, the *JD* upholds the Lutheran *simul* in a way that affirms that we are "totally sinners" according to the law, while also recognizing that a Christian's inclination to sin is also ruled by Christ to the extent that "Christians can in part lead a just life."[64] Disagreement on this subject became a point of contention that resulted in continued clarification in the annex, in which a mutually agreeable balance was sought. This balance highlighted the reality of spiritual renewal (2 Cor 5:17) while simultaneously requiring Christians to pray "God, be merciful to me, a sinner" (Luke 18:13).[65] To this extent, at least, Catholics and Protestants have a synoptic view.

---

60. Ibid.
61. Dulles, "In Contemporary Catholic Theology," 269.
62. James, "The Complex of Justification," 51–52.
63. *JD*, 30.
64. *JD*, 29.
65. *JD*, Annex, 2.A.

E. Faith Alone and Works

Disagreement over the status of concupiscence is related to another genuine and ongoing difference between Catholics and Protestants, namely the instrumental cause or means by which one is justified. Whereas Rome teaches baptismal regeneration, Peter Martyr asserts that justification is accessed by faith alone. Since Rome maintains that in baptism one receives "the forgiveness of all sins and the gift of new life,"[66] it is in her view impossible for two contradictory states to simultaneously co-exist in a baptized person: the righteousness of God and mortal sin. For Vermigli, however, baptism is simply a covenantal sign similar, in its status and function, to circumcision for Israel.[67] The only way to appropriate the remission of sin, in this view, is by means of faith.

Concerning the relationship of faith and baptism in Newman's *Lectures*, we noted the extraordinarily creative way in which he distinguished the "internal" from the "external" instruments of justification.[68] In this formulation, Newman wins points for his novelty, but it appears that this position is largely motivated by his *via media* project; his desire to maintain subscription to the Book of Common Prayer's eleventh article, which asserted that "we are justified by *Faith only*," while also retaining his commitment to the efficacious and necessary nature of baptismal regeneration.[69] It is noteworthy that the Catholic Newman does not articulate this particular understanding of faith and baptism outside of his re-issued *Lectures*.

Vermigli illustrates the central importance of faith alone to Reformed Protestantism, a position that he enthusiastically champions. His conviction is born out of the belief that one's good works have no role whatsoever in *causing* justification.[70] However, adamant as he is, Vermigli also insists that good works must necessarily attend and vindicate one's justification. As noted, this emphasis has led some interpreters to label Martyr a *Reformkatholic*. But this reading fails to appreciate the way Reformed theology seeks to hold sanctification in dynamic tension with justification. The *Reformkatholic* charge is akin to Steven Ozment's suggestion that Calvin's emphasis upon good works (in the context of his social ethics) had the effect of "re-catholicizing" Protestant theology on the doctrine of justification by faith.[71]

---

66. CCC, 1427.
67. Vermigli, *Romanos*, 1251 [158].
68. Newman, *Jfc.*, 226 [259].
69. Ibid.
70. Vermigli, *Romanos*, 1321 [227].
71. Ozment, *The Age of Reform*, 374.

It should be pointed out that contemporary Catholicism, as seen in the annex to the *JD*, has occasionally expressed a willingness to use the *sola fide* formula in order to emphasize that God is to be relied upon for salvation over self.[72] But this should not be understood as fully equivalent to the position for which Vermigli and his fellow Reformers contended. With Trent, modern Catholicism is keen to uphold the need for *fides formata caritate* in a sacramental framework, beginning with baptism. Hence, the Catholic *Catechism* asserts, "The grace of the Holy Spirit confers upon us the righteousness of God. Uniting us by faith and Baptism to the Passion and Resurrection of Christ, the Spirit makes us sharers in his life."[73] For Rome, therefore, faith is "alone" over against relying upon one's human resources, but it is nevertheless always embedded in charity in the context of the sacramental life.

Part of the controversy between Catholics and Protestants on the subject of *sola fide* has grown out of the different understanding of the word "faith." The Tridentine fathers, employing the term in keeping with the medieval scholastic sense of giving mental assent, insisted that this faith is "'the beginning of human salvation,' the foundation and root of all justification, 'without which it is impossible to please God.'"[74] This faith, although necessary for justification, must be augmented by the infusion of charity by the Holy Spirit. "For faith, unless hope and charity be added to it," Trent insists, "neither unites one perfectly with Christ, nor makes one a living member of his body."[75] Hence, to be complete, faith must be a *fides formata caritate*.

---

72. This is true in Catholic biblical studies and theology alike. Joseph A. Fitzmyer, for instance, argues in his exegesis of Romans 3:28 that "in this context Paul means [to teach justification] 'by faith alone.'" Fitzmyer also provides support for *sola fide* from patristic and medieval interpreters. Fitzmyer, *Romans*, 360–63. Then in Pope Benedict's sermon on justification in Saint Peter's Square on November 19, 2008 he said, "Being just simply means being with Christ and in Christ. And this suffices. Further observances are no longer necessary. For this reason Luther's phrase: 'faith alone' is true, if it is not opposed to faith in charity in love." Pope Benedict XVI, *Saint Paul*, 82. A week later, on November 26 in the Paul VI Audience Hall, the pontiff continued this emphasis: "Following Saint Paul, we have seen that man is unable to 'justify' himself with his own actions, but can only truly become 'just' before God because God confers his 'justice' upon him, uniting him to Christ his Son. And man obtains this union through faith. In this sense, Saint Paul tells us: not our deeds, but rather faith renders us 'just'" (84). Finally, there is the annex (2.C.) to the *JD*, which states that "Justification takes place 'by grace alone' . . . by faith alone; the person is justified 'apart from works.'" *JD*, 45.

73. *CCC*, 2017.

74. "Decree on Justification," Tanner, *Decrees*, 2:674

75. Ibid.

For Reformers such as Vermigli, on the other hand, the essence of faith is more than mental assent.[76] Vermigli understands faith as that which actively "takes hold and receives" the promise of forgiveness.[77] As we have noted, he sharply distinguishes this "most sure and certain" faith from a "dead faith," a "historical faith," a "human faith," a "temporary faith," and a "naked" faith.[78] Such faith, argues Vermigli, is "never alone but always draws along with it various motions of the mind," particularly "confidence, hope, and similar affections."[79] We can only imagine how the Tridentine fathers might have responded differently to Protestantism had they grasped this emphasis in the Reformers' teaching. Thankfully, developments in Catholic thought since Trent have broadened the official Catholic understanding of faith to include the possibility that faith might include the giving of one's whole self to God, mind and volition.[80]

With respect to the development of a faith formed by love, or in Newman's terms "actual righteousness," it is interesting to note that Vermigli includes the category of *habitus* in his doctrine of justification, whereas Newman strictly excludes it.[81] In this way, Vermigli more closely resembles the language of the Catholic position, insisting upon the development of *iustitia inhaerente*, which leads to further acts of piety.[82] Does this position imply for Vermigli a *partim-partim* view of justification? The answer is "no" concerning the basis or formal cause of justification; likewise, it is "no" in regard to the accumulation of merit *coram deo*, which Martyr categorically disavows.[83] But the answer is "yes" when justification is broadly conceived, as Martyr insists that the tangible manifestation of righteousness among

---

76. It was in his Romans commentary that Vermigli started to feature faith as *fiducia* (trust).Vermigli, *Romanos*, 1183 [89]. In this development, Martyr did not jettison *assensus*, but simply broadened his definition to include the volitional nature of justifying faith. Ibid., 1188 [94].

77. Ibid., 1262 [170]: "apprehendimus promissiones Dei."

78. Ibid., 1183 [89], 1187 [93], 1285-86 [192], 1271 [179], 1188 [93], 1266 [174].

79. Ibid., 1183 [89]: "id est, ut nunquam sit nuda, sed trahat secum semper multos ac varios animi motus."

80. *Dei Verbum* 5 describes faith as one "by which man entrusts his whole self freely to God offering 'the full submission of intellect and will to God who reveals' [Vatican I] and freely assenting to the truth revealed by Him."

81. Instead, Newman prefers to speak of the personal inhabitation of the Spirit as the agent of actual righteousness (i.e., good works).

82. Vermigli quotes Augustine with approval regarding "the righteousness that adheres in us" (Augustinum sensisse de iustitia inhaerente). Vermigli, *Romanos*, 1320 [226]; *CCC*, 2000.

83. Vermigli, *Romanos*, 1289 [195].

those who are justified is *not* accessed by faith alone, but rather is produced by spiritual discipline.[84]

Despite their difference over the existence of *habitus*, Vermigli and Newman both stress the necessity of personal holiness, holding forensic and actual righteousness together. As the apprehension of righteousness grows, so does one's capacity to perform good works, which are implicated in the final judgment as necessary constituents of faith. Such works are accepted and rewarded by God as a requirement of final justification, a conviction that Newman and Vermigli share with twenty-first-century Catholic teaching on the subject.[85]

F. Assurance of Faith

Another crucial difference between the Catholic and Protestant positions concerns the assurance of faith. Apart from the possibility of receiving insight through special revelation, the council fathers deny that a believer can know that he will persevere to the end.[86] According to Trent, it is only with the special help of God that anyone can indeed persevere,[87] always attended by the possibility of falling away from grace.[88] This notion is reiterated in the *Catechism of the Catholic Church*:

> *Mortal sin* destroys charity in the heart of man by a grave violation of God's law; it turns man away from God, who is his ultimate end and his beatitude, by preferring an inferior good to him.[89]

In contrast to the Catholic position, Peter Martyr argued that one who is justified will most assuredly persevere to the end.

---

84. Ibid., 1318 [224]: "[W]e grant that Christ requires more of us than faith, for who doubts that he wants those who are justified to live uprightly and to practice virtue of all kinds."

85. According to Vermigli, the future "not yet" dimension of justification requires believers to pursue a greater apprehension of love. Vermigli, *Romanos*, 1305–7 [210–12]. Quoting Augustine, Martyr asserts that by producing virtuous works, justified ones fulfill the law by the grace of the gospel. Ibid., 1239 [146]. Such works are required by the final judgment. Ibid., 1228–29 [135]; *CCC*, 1821, 2006, 2024.

86. "Decree on Justification," Tanner, *Decrees*, 2:676; see also "Canon 15," Tanner, *Decrees*, 2:680.

87. Ibid., Canon 22.

88. Ibid., Canon 23.

89. *CCC*, 1855. For Newman there was also no perseverance. Just as possessing the Spirit amounts to justification, losing the Spirit means that one has jeopardized justification. Newman, *Jfc.*, 151 [168].

In general, it may be stated that faith cannot be completely extinguished because serious sins are committed by the justified and those destined to salvation. In such cases, faith is lulled to sleep and lies hidden and does not burst forth into action unless awakened again by the Holy Spirit. In such fallen ones, the seed of God remains, although for a time it produces no fruit.[90]

In the "Assurance of Salvation" section of the *JD*, which Lane describes as "fairly bland,"[91] both sides affirm that the faithful can "rely on the mercy and promises of God" in spite of their weaknesses.[92] In the thirty-sixth paragraph, the Catholic position conveys what initially sounds like a robust statement on assurance, sharing the "concern of the Reformers to ground faith in the objective reality of Christ's promise, to look away from one's own experience, and to trust in Christ's forgiving word alone."[93] But this is quickly counterbalanced with the Catholic reminder that "every person, however, may be concerned about his salvation when he looks upon his own weaknesses and shortcomings."[94] Thus, the substance of Trent's position has not been changed significantly, although it is now conveyed in a way that recognizes validity in the Protestant claim to assurance of God's saving intention.[95]

G. The Role of Merit

Related to this question is the matter of whether justification admits a meritorious increase. According to Newman, meritorious works can indeed increase as one's apprehension of justification itself (by a greater manifestation of the Spirit) increases.[96] On this subject, it is interesting to see that in the first edition of his *Lectures*, Newman affirmed what he considered to be the perfection of adherent righteousness among those who are justified; but he retracted his statement in his third edition:

90. Vermigli, *Romanos*, 1278 [186].
91. Lane, *Justification by Faith*, 215.
92. *JD*, 34.
93. *JD*, 36.
94. Ibid.
95. Thus, the closing sentence of the Catholic position says, "Recognizing [the justified person's] own failures, however, the believer may yet be certain that God intends his salvation," Ibid.
96. Newman, *Jfc.*, 151–52 [168–69]. Because justification and sanctification are united in Newman's doctrine and grow together in proportion to God's manifest presence, the believer's meritorious works likewise grow.

[The justified are "perfect"] in relation to the past, as being a simple reversal of the state of guilt, and a bringing into God's favour; but as God's favour towards us will grow as we become more holy, so as we become more holy, we may receive a higher justification. The words in the text are inconsistent with an increase of justification, which Catholics hold.[97]

For Trent, justification is on account of the merits of Christ being poured into the hearts of those who are justified.[98] In this case, as with Newman's position, the *process* of justification entails an ongoing appropriation of divine righteousness by which one is increasingly justified. As the Catholic *Catechism* puts it, "Moved by the Holy Spirit, we can merit for ourselves and for others all the graces needed to attain eternal life."[99]

For Vermigli, the notion that one can merit for himself divine favor is unacceptable. He asserts, "Therefore, we must take away all merit, not only in those who are not yet justified, but also in those who have been justified." It is only by the merit of Christ (*solus Christi merito*) that one is justified. In this way, justification admits no increase with regard to the ground of our acceptance. However, although Martyr rejects the category of human merit, he affirms that God accepts and rewards Christian works as a necessary constituent of final justification. In this sense, one's works possess real value and prevail *coram deo*.[100]

The *JD*, in keeping with Trent, asserts that initial justification is unmerited.[101] Having been justified, the faithful are then expected to produce virtuous fruit and "bring forth the works of love."[102] The Catholic statement readily affirms that, firstly, such works are made possible "by grace and the working of the Holy Spirit,"[103] and, secondly, that its usage of the word "meritorious" intends to account for the fact that one's works are rewarded in heaven. In other words, the intention behind the doctrine of meritorious works is a desire "to emphasize the responsibility of persons for the action, not to contest the character of those works as gifts, or far less to deny that justification always remains the unmerited gift of grace."[104] While

---

97. Ibid., 73.
98. "Decree on Justification," Tanner, *Decrees*, 2:673–74.
99. *CCC*, 2027.
100. Vermigli, *Romanos*, 1289 [195], 1321 [227], 1274 [182], 1227–28 [134], 1288 [195].
101. *JD*, 25, 27.
102. *JD*, 37.
103. *JD*, 38.
104. *JD*, 38. See also Annex 2.E: "Any reward is a reward of grace, on which we

Reformed Protestants would prefer to describe virtuous works as the "fruit" of justification,[105] and not our own "merits," it is in fundamental agreement with the Augustinian logic of the Catholic position—that our merits are in fact God's gifts.

H. Conclusion

Breaking with their medieval past at significant points, the magisterial Reformers forged a specific understanding of the doctrine of justification. They distinguished justification from sanctification, stressing an initial forensic declaration that changes the sinner's relationship to God, and specified its formal cause as an imputed form of righteousness. With this, clear blue water flowed between the Roman Catholic and Reformed Protestant positions—or at least that seemed to be the case. Despite these differences, Roman Catholics and Reformed Protestants share more common ground than is ordinarily recognized. We find, for example, a common commitment to union with Christ by the Holy Spirit, a union that imparts the remission of sins *and* internal renewal by divine initiative. This righteousness grows in an internal disposition of grace, producing virtue as it reaches toward holiness. Such works are a necessary part of justification, which pleases God and receives his favor in the form of rewards.

Such commonalities have implications for ecumenical dialogue. For starters, they help us to recognize the inadequacy of popular conceptions that caricature the Roman Catholic and Reformed Protestant doctrines as diametric opposites. As we have observed, both traditions consider justification to comprise the forgiveness of sins *and* righteous transformation (a *duplex iustitia*)—God's work *pro nobis* and *in nobis*—albeit in different ways. Yes, Reformed Protestants continue to differentiate justifying righteousness from sanctifying righteousness, but since the Christian possesses a union with Christ by the Spirit, these two forms of righteousness are inseparably connected, and, if one follows Vermigli, may in some sense be held together beneath the banner of "justification."[106]

---

have no claim."

105. So the Lutheran position in *JD*, 39.

106. Robert Ives sheds light on this duality (without respect to Vermigli) when he raises the helpful question: "Is justification the forensic action of being made right with God or is the whole salvation process involved?" The answer, according to a *duplex iustitia* understanding, is "yes." Both activities belong to justification. The challenge, as we have observed, is to precisely define how these movements function in relation to one another and to other elements of soteriology. Ives, "An Early Effort toward Protestant-Catholic Conciliation," 99–110 (99).

A second implication concerns common ground for conversations between Roman Catholics and Reformed Protestants. In view of the above, there is good reason to begin ecumenical discussion with a pneumatological focus, recognizing humanity's need for the Holy Spirit to address original sin and for the Spirit's impartation of spiritual life (what is often called regeneration)—a focus that we observed in Newman and Vermigli. In both of their doctrines, the Spirit functions as the active agent who initiates faith by simultaneously liberating sinners from condemnation and unifying them to the living Christ. Therefore, just as the work of the Spirit is the beginning of the actual reception of justification according to the Roman Catholic and Reformed Protestant positions, the doctrine of the Spirit is a promising starting point in ecumenical dialogue.

Closely related to a focus upon the Spirit's indwelling is the activity of the Triune God in justification, since the Father who pronounces judgment imparts the Spirit, as does the Son. Moreover, the Spirit unites a man to Christ and enables him to find favor with the Father. Such interconnections are but a sample of the Trinitarian commitments that Catholics and Reformed Protestants share. Therefore, instead of starting conversation with the Protestant view of forensic imputation or the Catholic doctrine of infused righteousness, an examination of the Trinitarian economy in justification offers a broader context in which to observe a range of commonalities (and also see more clearly the reasons why we differ).[107] An example of how this approach potentially narrows the gap between Catholics and Protestants is found in Dulles's reflection on the validity of uncreated grace in justification.

> The "uncreated grace" whereby we are justified, because it consists primarily in God's personal self-communication, relates us to each of the divine persons. As Son, Christ communicates to his members the filial and servant character of his own existence. Because we are mystically identified with the second person of the Holy Trinity we become, in the memorable phrase of Emile Mersch, "sons in the Son" (*filii in Filio*). In relation to the Father we become adopted sons and daughters. The Holy Spirit, as the subsistent love uniting the Father and the Son, inwardly attunes us so that we are able to accept in loving freedom the self-communication of the Father in his incarnate Son.[108]

---

107. In the words of the *JD*, "In faith we together hold the conviction that justification is the work of the triune God. . . . Justification thus means that Christ himself is our righteousness, in which we share through the Holy Spirit in accord with the will of the Father." *JD*, 15.

108. Dulles, "Justification in Contemporary Catholic Theology," 260–61.

In addition to ecumenical implications, the above conclusions illumine the significance of the doctrine of justification for Christian ministry, providing impetus to move beyond a passive experience of faith (to which Protestants are susceptible with the doctrine of *sola fide*) or an ultra-ecclesial focus (which may occur for Catholics who overemphasize the reception of sacramental grace). In Oswald Bayer's words, "The new human is no grotesque caricature who spends his life in a darkened room, reciting with closed eyes, "I am justified by faith alone, I am justified by faith alone."[109] Rather, in this moment in history—with all its hopelessness and despair—we are called to actively reach out to the world by embodying and proclaiming the good news of justifying grace. Such grace provides motivation for the task of preaching even as it is the leading edge of our message.

The Church not only proclaims the good news of justification to the world, she also embraces it for herself as a stimulus for her own sanctification. After all, we are debtors of grace before we are dispensers of grace, and we remain debtors throughout our lives. The justifying word shines the light of grace into the darkness of condemnation. As Caroline J. Simon poignantly states: "The gospel of justification in Christ rests on the alchemy of grace—the power of grace to transform enemies into friend, to take the ungodly and put them on the road to godliness."[110] Such is the power that we invoke in the doctrine of justification.

Finally, an informed perspective on common commitments puts Roman Catholics and Reformed Protestants in a position to recognize the valuable gifts that our traditions offer one another, gifts that (ought to) extend to the parish level. In the face of what some have labeled "Catholic guilt," the Protestant notion of a forensic declaration may not lead Catholics to embrace a doctrine of imputation, but it should help them to recognize that their standing before God is predicated on their participation in Christ, a participation that follows from divine grace.[111] Likewise, Reformed Protestants should find in the Catholic teaching on internal righteousness a healthy reminder that Scripture envisions a real manifestation of righteousness, and not simply a forensic declaration. Such works may not be the ultimate ground of one's acceptance, but they are crucial nonetheless.

Just as areas of agreement have implications for ecumenical dialogue, we also find practical significance in our differences, starting with the most significant of all: the disagreement over justification's formal cause. In light

---

109. Bayer, *Living by Faith*, trans. Bromiley, 27.

110. Simon, "The Alchemy of Grace," 160–65.

111. Two excellent examples of this Christological participation from Catholic writers are the above quotation by Dulles on uncreated grace, and the previously cited prayer of Thérèse of Lisieux in the Catholic *Catechism. CCC,* 2011.

of this difference—whether divine forgiveness is fundamentally rooted in an internal work of the Spirit or on the basis of Christ's forensically imputed righteousness—it is likely that Catholics will continue to find the extrinsic character of the Reformed Protestant position ultimately unsatisfying. Insistence upon the works of a believer as part of the ground of one's acceptance, such that one volitionally participates in justification, will continue to be the Catholic vision.[112] On the other hand, Reformed Protestants will find the Catholic insistence upon meritorious works off-putting, even if "merit" is a Catholic (Augustinian) way of emphasizing that such works merit divine reward. These differences will always keep the door ajar for Protestant suspicions that the Catholic tradition is overly indebted to human volition and a Catholic impression that Reformed Protestants are tolerant of cheap grace.

The Roman Catholic and Reformed Protestant difference over justification's formal cause has direct bearing upon the way these traditions view eternal security. For the Reformed, perseverance of faith is a logical deduction from locating full acceptance in efficacious divine grace. Since the volition of the regenerate contributes nothing to acceptance, volition can do nothing to jeopardize that acceptance. From a Catholic point of view, however, this position is not only questionable, it is troubling. The problem is not so much with the logic, but with the assumption on which it stands, namely, the notion that acceptance is exclusively based on divine activity without human co-operation. It is precisely at this point that Catholics insist that the believer has more active participation in justification. To argue for eternal security, from a Catholic point of view, is to minimize the importance of virtue, which not only departs from the Church's teaching on justification, but also runs aground on the Christian's calling to manifest a life of moral substance. These concerns are not likely to go away anytime soon.

No, the Reformation is not over. But thankfully the conversation on justification has progressed in a direction that encourages honest dialogue. Indeed, more than simply listening to the other side, we have proven that such conversation can produce declarations of mutual understanding, which did not previously exist. So although the Council of Trent rejected the phrase "faith alone" a total of five times in her *Decree on Justification* (eleven times overall),[113] the *JD* affirms that there is a legitimate use of the formula. Roman Catholic teaching may not "change" in the sense of

---

112. As the *CCC* states, "Moved by the Holy Spirit, we can merit for ourselves and for other all the graces needed to attain eternal life, as well as necessary temporal goods." *CCC*, 2027.

113. Trent's repudiation of *sola fide* occurs five times in Session Six, four times in Session Seven, one time in Session 13 and once in Session 14.

revoking previously established dogma, but it obviously has the ability to adapt to new circumstances. This reality should encourage further dialogue.

With these conclusions, our research makes no pretense to the reconciliation of the Roman Catholic and Reformed Protestant positions; much less have we eliminated the *crux theologorum* associated with interpreting the biblical teaching of Paul and James on the subject. But we have hopefully offered insight into places where lines of similarity and difference fall, so that the challenge is a little less burdensome.

Bibliography

Allison, C. FitzSimons. *The Rise of Moralism: The Proclamation of the Gospel from Hooker to Baxter*. New York: Seabury, 1966.
Althaus, Paul. *The Theology of Martin Luther*. Philadelphia: Fortress, 1966.
Altholz, Josef Lewis. "The Mind and Art of Victorian Orthodoxy: Anglican Responses to 'Essays and Reviews,' 1860–1864." *Church History* 51 (1982) 186–97.
Anderson, George H., T. Austin Murphy, and Joseph A. Burgess, eds. *Justification by Faith: Lutherans and Catholics in Dialogue VII*. Minneapolis: Augsburg, 1985.
Anderson, Marvin W. "Biblical Humanism and Roman Catholic Reform 1444–1563: A Study of Renaissance Philology and New Testament Criticism from Laurentius Valla to Pietro Martyre Vermigli." PhD diss., University of Aberdeen, 1964.
———. "Peter Martyr on Romans." *Scottish Journal of Theology* 26 (1973) 401–20.
———. *Peter Martyr, a Reformer in Exile (1542–1562): A Chronology of Biblical Writings in England & Europe*. Nieuwkoop: De Graaf, 1975.
———. "Rhetoric and Reality: Peter Martyr and the English Reformation." *Sixteenth Century Journal* 19/3 (1988) 451–69.
———. "Word and Spirit in Exile (1542–1562): The Biblical Writings of Peter Martyr Vermigli." *Journal of Ecumenical Studies* 21 (1970) 193–201.
Armstrong, Brian G. *Calvinism and the Amyraut Heresy: Protestant Scholasticism and Humanism in Seventeenth-Century France*. Madison, WI: University of Wisconsin Press, 1969.
Aristotle, *Physics* 2.3. Translated by Philip H. Wicksteed and Francis M. Cornford. Loeb Classical Library. Cambridge: Harvard University Press, 1968.
Ashton, J. W. "Peter Martyr on the Function and Character of Literature." *Philological Quarterly* 18 (1939) 311–14.
Augustine. "The Spirit and the Letter." Edited by John Burnaby. Augustine: Later Works, 26:45. London: SCM, 1955.
Balleine, G. R. *A History of Evangelical Party in the Church of England*. London: Longmans, 1908.
Balserak, Jon. "1 Corinthians Commentary: Exegetical Tradition." In *A Companion to Peter Martyr Vermigli*, edited by W. J. Torrance Kirby, Emidio Campi, and Frank A. James III, 283–304. Leiden: Brill, 2009.
Baschera, Luca. "Aristotle and Scholasticism." In *A Companion to Peter Martyr Vermigli*, edited by W. J. Torrance Kirby, Emidio Campi, and Frank A. James III, 133–60. Leiden: Brill, 2009.
Baumann, Michael. "Albert Pighius." In *Oxford Encyclopedia of the Reformation*, edited by Hans Hillerbrand, Vol. 3, 459–65. Oxford: Oxford University Press, 1984.

———. "Josias Simler's Hagiography." In *A Companion to Peter Martyr Vermigli*, edited by W. J. Torrance Kirby, Emidio Campi, and Frank A. James III, 459–65. Leiden: Brill, 2009.

Bäumer, Remigius. "Albert Pigge." In *Katholische Theologen der Reformationszeit*, edited by Erwin Iserloh, 98–106. Münster: Aschendorff, 1984.

Baumgartner, Charles. *La grâce du Christ*. Mystère Chrétien: Théologie Dogmatique 10. Tournai: Desclée, 1963.

Bayer, Oswald. *Living by Faith: Justification and Sanctification*. Translated by Geoffrey W. Bromiley. Grand Rapids: Eerdmans, 2003.

Bebbington, D. W. *Evangelicalism in Modern Britain: A History from the 1730s to the 1980s*. London: Unwin Hyman, 1989.

Bellarmino, Roberto. "Disputationum de controversiis Christianae fidei tomus tertius." In *Disputationum Roberti Bellarmini Politiani Societatis Iesu, de controversiis Christianae fidei, adversus huius temporis haereticos, 1268-1269*. Ingolstadt: Davidis Sartorii, 1593.

Benrath, Karl. *Bernardino Ochino, of Siena: A Contribution towards the History of the Reformation*. Translated by Helen Zimmern. New York: Robert Carter, 1877.

Beveridge, William. *Private Thoughts upon Religion Digested into Twelve Articles, with Practical Resolutions Form'd Thereupon*. London: R. Smith, 1709.

Beza, Theodore. *Beza's "Icones."* Translated by Charles Greig McCrie. Contemporary Portraits of Reformers of Religion and Letters. London: The Religious Tract Society, 1909.

———. *Icones, id est Verae imagines virorum doctrina simul et pietate illustrium*. Geneva: C. Froschauer, 1580.

Biemer, Günter. *Newman on Tradition*. Translated by Kevin Smyth. New York: Herder and Herder, 1967.

Billings, Todd. *Calvin, Participation, and the Gift: The Activity of Believers in Union with Christ*. Changing Paradigms in Historical Theology. New York: Oxford University Press, 2007.

Blehl, Vincent Ferrer. "Early Criticism of the Apologia." In *Newman's Apologia: A Classic Reconsidered*, edited by Vincent Ferrer Blehl, 46–63. New York: Harcourt, Brace and World, 1964.

———. *John Henry Newman: A Bibliographical Catalogue of His Writings*. Charlottesville, VA: University Press of Virginia, 1978.

———. *Pilgrim Journey: John Henry Newman 1801-1845*. London: Burns & Oates, 2001.

Blocher, Henri A. "The Lutheran-Catholic Declaration on Justification." In *Justification in Perspective: Historical Developments and Contemporary Challenges*, edited by Bruce L. McCormack, 197–218. Grand Rapids: Baker Academic, 2006.

Boekraad, Adrian J. *The Personal Conquest of Truth According to J. H. Newman*. Louvain: Nauwelaerts, 1955.

Borsch, Frederick H. "Ye Shall Be Holy: Reflections on the Spirituality of the Early Years of the Oxford Movement." *Anglican Theological Review* 66/4 (1984) 347–59.

Boughton, Lynne Courter. "Supralapsarianism and the Role of Metaphysics in Sixteenth-century Reformed Theology." *The Westminster Theological Journal*, no. 48 (1986) 63–96.

Bouwsma, William J. *Venice and the Defense of Republican Liberty*. Los Angeles: University of California Press, 1984.

Bouyer, Louis. *Newman: His Life and Spirituality*. San Francisco: Ignatius, 2011.

———. *Newman: sa vie, sa spiritualité*. Paris: Cerf, 1952.

Bowd, Stephen D. *Reform before the Reformation: Vincenzo Querini and the Religious Renaissance in Italy*. Studies in Medieval and Reformation Thought, 87. Leiden: Brill, 2002.

Bozza, Tommaso. *Nuovi studi sulla Riforma in Italia, I: Il Beneficio di Cristo*. Uomini e dottrine. Rome: Edizioni di storia e letteratura, 1976.

Bremond, Henri. *Newman: Essai de biographie psychologique*. Paris: Librairie Bloud & Cie, 1906.

———. *The Mystery of Newman*. Translated by H. C. Corrance. London: Williams & Norgate, 1907.

Brilioth, Yngve. *The Anglican Revival: Studies in the Oxford Movement*. London: Longmans, 1925.

———. *Three Lectures on Evangelicalism and the Oxford Movement: Together with a Lecture on the Theological Aspect of the Oxford Movement and a Sermon Preached in Fairford Church on 11 July 1933*. London: Oxford University Press, 1934.

Brown, David. *Newman: A Man for Our Time*. London: SPCK, 1990.

Brundin, Abigail, and Matthew Treherne, eds. *Forms of Faith in Sixteenth-century Italy*. Aldershot, UK: Ashgate, 2009.

Bryant, William Douglas. "Bishop George Bull's Doctrine of Justification." PhD diss., Southern Baptist Theological Seminary, 2011.

Bucer, Martin. *Acta colloquii in commitiis Imperii Ratisponae habiti, hoc est articuli de religione conciliati, & non conciliati omnes, ut ab Imperatore ordinibus Imperii ad iudicandum, & deliberandum propositi sunt. Consulta & deliberata de his actis Imperatoris singulorum ordinum Imperii & legati Romani*. Strasbourg: Wendelin Rihel, 1541.

———. *Enarrationes perpetua in sacra quatuor Evangelia*. Strasbourg: Georgium Vlricherum Andlanum, 1530.

———. *Metaphrasis et enarratio in epist. d. Pauli apostoli ad Romanos, in quibus singulatim apostoli omnia, cum argumenta, tum sententiae & verba, ad autoritatem divinae scripturae, fidemque ecclesiae Catholicae tam priscae quàm praesentis, religiosè ac paulò fusius excutiuntur*. Basel: Apud Petrum Pernam, 1562.

———. *Sacrorum psalmorum libri quinque*. Strasbourg: Georgium Vlricherum Andlanum, 1529.

Bull, George. *Harmonia Apostolica: or, Two Dissertations: in the Former of Which the Doctrine of St. James on Justification by Works is Explained and Defended: in the Latter, the Agreement of St. Paul with St. James is Clearly Shown*. Library of Anglo-Catholic Theology. Oxford: Parker, 1842.

Burke, Peter. *Culture and Society in Renaissance Italy, 1420–1540*. Studies in Cultural History. London: Batsford, 1972.

Büsser, Fritz. "Vermigli in Zurich." In *Peter Martyr Vermigli: Humanism, Republicanism, Reformation*, edited by Emidio Campi, Frank A. James III, and Peter Opitz, 203–12. Geneva: Librairie Droz, 2002.

Butler, Joseph. *The Analogy of Religion, Natural and Revealed, to the Constitution and Course of Nature*. London: John and Paul Knapton, 1736.

Calkin, Arthur Burton. "John Henry Newman on Conscience and the Magisterium." *Downside Review* 87 (1969) 358–69.

Calvin, Jean. *De aeterna Dei praedestinatione, qua in salutem alios ex hominibus elegit, alios suo exitio reliquit; item de providentia qua res humanas gubernat, Consensus pastorum Genevensis ecclesiae, a Io. Calvino expositus*. Geneva: Jean Crispin, 1552.

———. *Defensio sanae et orthodoxae doctrinae de servitute et liberatione humani arbitrii adversus calumnias Alberti Pighii Campensis*. Geneva: Jean Crispin, 1543.

———. *Defensio sanae et orthodoxae doctrinae de servitute et liberatione humani arbitrii adversus calumnias Alberti Pighii Campensis. Ioannis Calvini Noviodunensis opera omnia: in novem tomos digesta.* Amsterdam: Apud viduam Ioannis Iacobi Schipperi, 1671.

———. *Ioannis Calvini, magni theologi, Institutionum Christianae religionis libri quatuor. Ioannis Calvini Noviodunensis opera omnia, in novem tomos digesta.* Amsterdam: Apud viduam Ioannis Iacobi Schipperi, 1671.

———. *Ioannis Calvini opera quae supersunt omnia.* Edited by Guilielmus Baum, Eduardus Cunitz, and Eduardus Reuss. Vol. 11. Corpus Reformatorum 39. Brunsviga: Schwetschke, 1873.

Calvin, John. *The Bondage and Liberation of the Will: A Defence of the Orthodox Doctrine of Human Choice against Pighius.* Edited by A. N. S. Lane. Translated by G. I. Davies. Texts and Studies in Reformation and Post-reformation Thought 2. Grand Rapids: Baker, 1996.

———. *Institutes of the Christian Religion.* Edited by John T. McNeill. Translated by Ford Lewis Battles. Philadelphia: Westminster, 1960.

———. *Letters of John Calvin.* Translated and edited by Jules Bonnet. 4 vols. Vol. 1. Philadelphia: Presbyterian Board of Publication, 1858.

———. *Selected Works of John Calvin: Tracts and Letters.* Edited by Henry Beveridge and Jules Bonnet. Grand Rapids: Baker, 1983.

Campi, Emidio. "Genesis Commentary: Interpreting Creation." In *A Companion to Peter Martyr Vermigli*, edited by W. J. Torrance Kirby, Emidio Campi, and Frank A. James III, 209–29. Leiden: Brill, 2009.

Campi, Emidio, Frank A. James III, and Peter Opitz, eds. *Peter Martyr Vermigli: Humanism, Republicanism, Reformation.* Geneva: Librairie Droz, 2002.

Cantimori, Delio. *Eretici italiani del Cinquecento: Ricerche storiche.* Biblioteca storica Sansoni. Florence: Sansoni, 1939.

———. *Prospettive di storia ereticale italiana del Cinquecento.* Bari: Editori Laterza, 1960.

Caponetto, Salvatore. *The Protestant Reformation in Sixteenth-century Italy.* Translated by Anne Tedeschi and John A. Tedeschi. Kirksville, MO: Thomas Jefferson University Press, 1999.

Cargnoni, Costanzo, Antonio Gentili, Mauro Regazzoni, and Pietro Zovatto. *Storia della spiritualità italiana.* Edited by Pietro Zovatto. Rome: Città Nuova Editrice, 2002.

Catechism of the Catholic Church. 2nd ed. Citta del vatticano: Libreria Editrice Vaticana, 1997.

The Catechism of the Council of Trent. Translated by Rev. J. Donovan. London: Keating and Brown, 1829.

Carter, Lindberg. *The European Reformations.* 2nd ed. Malden, MA: Wiley-Blackwell, 2010.

Chadwick, Henry. "The Lectures on Justification." In *Newman After a Hundred Years*, edited by Ian Ker, 287–308. Oxford: Oxford University Press, 1990.

Chadwick, Owen. *From Bossuet to Newman.* 2nd ed. Cambridge: Cambridge University Press, 1987.

———. *The Mind of the Oxford Movement.* London: Black, 1960.

———. *Newman.* Oxford: Oxford University Press, 1983.

———. *The Spirit of the Oxford Movement: Tractarian Essays.* Cambridge: Cambridge University Press, 1990.

———. *The Victorian Church: An Ecclesiastical History of England*. 2 vols. New York: Oxford University Press, 1966, 1970.
Chisnall, Peter M. *John Henry Cardinal Newman: A Man of Courage, Conflict and Conviction*. London: St. Paul's, 2001.
Church, Frederic Corss. *The Italian Reformers, 1534–1564*. 1932. Reprint. New York: Columbia University Press, 1974.
Church of England. "Articles of Religion, XI." In *The Book of Common Prayer, and Administration of the Sacraments, and Other Rites and Ceremonies of the Church*. London: Reeves, 1801.
Church, Richard William. *The Oxford Movement: Twelve Years, 1833–1845*. 3rd. ed. London: Macmillan, 1892.
Collett, Barry. *Italian Benedictine Scholars and the Reformation: The Congregation of Santa Giustina of Padua*. Oxford Historical Monographs. Oxford: Clarendon, 1985.
Contarini, Gasparo. "Cardinal Gasparao Contarini, Bishop of Belluno, Gegenreformatorische Shriften (1530c.–1542)." Edited by Friedrich Hünermann. Corpus Catholicorum 7. Münster in Westfalen, 1923.
Corda, Salvatore. *Veritas Sacramenti: A Study in Vermigli's Doctrine of the Lord's Supper*. Zürcher Beiträge zur Reformationsgeschichte. Zürich: Theologischer Verlag, 1975.
Coulson, John. *Newman and the Common Tradition: A Study in the Language of Church and Society*. Oxford: Clarendon, 1970.
Cox, G. V. *Recollections of Oxford*. London: Macmillan, 1868.
Crews, Daniel A. *Twilight of the Renaissance: The Life of Juan de Valdés*. Toronto: University of Toronto Press, 2008.
Cross, Claire. "Oxford and the Tudor State 1509–1558." In *The History of the University of Oxford. Vol. 3: The Collegiate University*, edited by James McConica, 133–40. Oxford: Oxford University Press, 1986.
Cunliffe-Jones, H. "Newman on Justification." *The Clergy Review* 54 (1969) 17–24.
Daley, Brian E. "The Church Fathers." In *The Cambridge Companion to John Henry Newman*, edited by Ian Ker and Terrance Merrigan, 29–46. Cambridge: Cambridge University Press, 2009.
Dall'Asta, G. "Pietro Martire Vermigli (1499–1562). La sua teologia eucaristica." *La scuola cattolica* 91 (1983) 275–303.
Davies, C. Martin. "The Doctrine of Justification According to J. H. Newman, Martin Luther and the Council of Trent." MPhil thesis, University of Leeds, 1970.
Davies, H. F. "Newman and Thomism." *Newman-Studien* 3 (1957) 157–69.
Dawson, Christopher. *The Spirit of the Oxford Movement*. London: Sheed & Ward, 1933.
Dessain, Charles Stephen. "The Biblical Basis of Newman's Ecumenical Theology." In *The Rediscovery of Newman: An Oxford symposium*, edited by John Coulson and A. M. Allchin, 100–122. London: Sheed & Ward, 1967.
———. "Cardinal Newman and the Doctrine of Uncreated Grace." *The Clergy Review* 47 (1962) 207–29; 269–88.
———. "Cardinal Newman and the Eastern Tradition." *Downside Review* 94 (1976) 83–98.
———. *John Henry Newman*. London: Nelson, 1966.
———. *The Spirituality of John Henry Newman*. Minneapolis: Winston, 1980.
DeVries, Dawn, "Justification." In *The Oxford Handbook of Systematic Theology*, edited by John Webster, Kathryn Tanner, and Iain Torrance, 197–211. New York: Oxford University Press, 2007.

Di Gangi, Mariano. *Peter Martyr Vermigli, 1499–1562: Renaissance Man, Reformation Master*. Lanham, MD: University Press of America, 1993.

———. "Pietro Martire Vermigli (1500–1562): An Italian Calvinist." BD thesis, Presbyterian College, Montreal, Canada, 1949.

Dickens, A. G. *The Counter Reformation*. Library of European Civilization. London: Thames and Hudson, 1968.

Dickens, Charles. *A Tale of Two Cities*. London: James Nisbet & Co., 1902.

Dionysii, Petavii. *De Trinitate. Theologica Dogmata*, vol. 2. Edited by F. A. Zacharia. Paris: 1865.

Dittrich, Franz. *Gasparo Contarini, 1483–1542: Eine Monographie*. Braunsberg: Verlag der Ermländischen Zeitungs und Verlagsdruckerei, 1885.

Donnelly, John Patrick. *Calvinism and Scholasticism in Vermigli's Doctrine of Man and Grace*. Studies in Medieval and Reformation Thought 18. Leiden: Brill, 1976.

———. "Calvinist Thomism." *Viator* 7 (1976) 441–55.

———. "Peter Martyr on Fallen Man: A Protestant Scholastic View." PhD diss., University of Wisconsin, Madison, 1971.

———. "Peter Martyr Vermigli's Political Ethics." In *Peter Martyr Vermigli: Humanism, Republicanism, Reformation*, edited by Emidio Campi, Frank A. James III, and Peter Opitz, 59–66. Geneva: Librairie Droz, 2002.

Dulles, Avery Cardinal. *John Henry Newman*. London: Continuum, 2011.

———. "Justification and the Unity of the Church." In *The Gospel of Justification in Christ: Where Does the Church Stand Today?*, edited by Wayne C. Sturm, 125–40. Grand Rapids: Eerdmans, 2006.

———. "Justification in Contemporary Theology." In *Justification by Faith: Lutherans and Catholics in Dialogue VII*, edited by H. George Anderson, et al., 256–77. Minneapolis: Augsburg, 1985.

Duncan, G. D. "Public Lectures and Professional Chairs." In *The Collegiate University. Vol. 3: The History of the University of Oxford*, edited by James McConica, 335–61. Oxford: Oxford University Press, 1986.

Durand, Elie. *Vie de Pierre Martyr Vermigli*. Toulouse: Imprimerie A. Chauvin et Fils, 1868.

Edgecombe, Rodney Stenning. *Two Poets of the Oxford Movement: John Keble and John Henry Newman*. London: Fairleigh Dickinson University Press, 1996.

Eells, Hastings. "The Origin of the Regensburg Book." *The Princeton Theological Review* 26, no. 3 (1928) 355–72.

Egan, Keith J. "The Spirituality of the Carmelites." In *Christian Spirituality: High Middle Ages and Reformation*, edited by Jill Raitt, Bernard McGinn, and John Meyendorff, 50–62. London: Routledge, 1987.

Elowsky, Joel. "Bridging the Gap." In *Theosis: Deification in Christian Theology*, edited by Vladimir Kharlamov, 146–81. Eugene, OR: Pickwick, 2012.

Erasmus Roterodamus, Desiderius. *Enchiridion militis christiani*. Leiden: Ex Officinâ Ioannis Maire, 1641.

———. *Inquisitio de Fide: A Colloquy by Desiderius Erasmus Roterodamus, 1524*. 2nd ed. Edited by Craig R. Thompson. Hamden, CT: Archon, 1975.

Faber, G. C. *Oxford Apostles: A Character Study of the Oxford Movement*. London: Faber and Faber, 1933.

Faber, George Stanley. *The Primitive Doctrine of Justification Investigated: Relatively to the Several Definitions of the Church of Rome and the Church of England and a Special Reference to the Opinions of the Late Mr. Knox, as Published in his Remains*. London: Seeley and Burnside, 1837.

Fackre, Gabriel. "Affirmations and Admonitions: Lutheran and Reformed." In *The Gospel of Justification in Christ: Where Does the Church Stand Today?*, edited by Wayne C. Sturm, 1-26. Grand Rapids: Eerdmans, 2006.

Feiner, Johann. "Die Erbsündenlehre Albert Pigges: ein Beitrag zur Erforschung der kath. Kontroverstheologie." PhD diss., Pontificia Universitas Gregoriana, 1940.

Fenlon, Dermot. *Heresy and Obedience in Tridentine Italy: Cardinal Pole and the Counter Reformation*. Cambridge: Cambridge University Press, 1972.

Fink, David C. "The Doers of the Law Will Be Justified: The Exegetical Origins of Martin Bucer's Triplex Iustificatio." *Journal of Theological Studies* 58 (2007) 485-524.

———. "Was There a Reformation Doctrine of Justification" *Harvard Theological Review* 103 (2010) 205-35.

Firpo, Massimo. "The Italian Reformation and Juan de Valdés." Translated by John A. Tedeschi. *Sixteenth Century Journal* 27 (1996) 353-64.

Fitzmyer, Joseph. *Romans*. New York: Doubleday, 1993.

Flanagan, Philip. *Newman. Faith and the Believer*. Westminster, MD: Newman Bookshop, 1946.

Foister, Susan. *Cardinal Newman 1801-90: A Centenary Exhibition*. London: National Portrait Gallery, 1990.

Forcellino, Antonio. *Michelangelo: A Tormented Life*. Translated by Allan Cameron. Cambridge: Polity, 2009.

Foxe, John. *Actes and Monuments*. London: John Day, 1563.

Fuller, Donald. "Sacrifice and Sacrament: Another Eucharistic Contribution from Peter Martyr Vermigli." In *Peter Martyr Vermigli and the European Reformations: Semper Reformanda*, edited by Frank A. James III, 215-37. Leiden: Brill, 2004.

Froude, Richard Hurrell. *Remains of the Late Reverend Richard Hurrell Froude*. Edited by John Henry Newman and John Keble. 2 vols. London: Rivington, 1838.

Garcia, Mark A. *Life in Christ: Union with Christ and Twofold Grace in Calvin's Theology*. Studies in Christian History and Thought. Milton Keynes, UK: Paternoster, 2008.

Gardy, Frédéric. "Les Livres de Pierre Martyr Vermigli conservé à la Bibliothèque de Genève." *Anzeiger für Schweizerische Geschichte* 50 (1919) 1-6.

Gibbs, Lee W. "Richard Hooker's *Via Media* Doctrine of Justification." *Harvard Theological Review* 74, no. 2 (1981) 211-20.

Gilbert, Felix. *History: Choice and Commitment*. Cambridge: Belknap Press of Harvard University Press, 1977.

Gilley, Sheridan. "Life and Writings." In *The Cambridge Companion to John Henry Newman*, edited by Ian Ker and Terrance Merrigan, 1-28. Cambridge: Cambridge University Press, 2009.

———. *Newman and His Age*. Westminster, UK: Christian Classics, 1991.

Gilly, Carlos. "Juan de Valdés: Übersetzer und Bearbeiter von Luthers Schriften in seinem Diálogo de Doctrina." *Archiv für Reformationsgeschichte* 74 (1983) 257-305.

Ginzburg, Carlo, and Adriano Prosperi. "Le due redazioni del 'Beneficio di Cristo.'" In *Eresia e riforma nell'Italia del Cinquecento: Miscellanea I*, 135-204. Florence: Sansoni, 1974.

Gleason, Elisabeth. *Gasparo Contarini: Venice, Rome, and Reform*. Berkeley: University of California Press, 1993.

———. "On the Nature of Sixteenth-century Italian Evangelism: Scholarship, 1953-1978." *Sixteenth Century Journal* 9, no. 3 (1978) 3-25.

———. "Sixteenth-century Italian Interpretations of Luther." *Archiv für Reformationsgeschichte* 60 (1969) 160-73.

Gorham, George Cornelius. *Gleanings of a Few Scattered Ears, during the Period of the Reformation in England and of the Times Succeeding A.D. 1533 to A.D. 1589.* London: Bell and Daldy, 1857.

Gorman, Michael J. *Inhabiting the Cruciform God: Kenosis, Justification, and Theosis in Paul's Narrative Soteriology.* Grand Rapids: Eerdmans, 2009.

Greenslade, S. L. "The Faculty of Theology." In *The History of the University of Oxford. Vol. 3: The Collegiate University*, edited by James McConica, 295–334. Oxford: Oxford University Press, 1986.

Gregory, Brad S. *Salvation at Stake: Christian Martyrdom in Early Modern Europe.* Cambridge: Harvard University Press, 1999.

Grendler, Paul F. "Religious Restlessness in Sixteenth-century Italy." *The Canadian Catholic Historical Association* 33 (1966) 25–38.

Greschat, Martin. *Martin Bucer: A Reformer and His Times.* Louisville, KY: Westminster John Knox, 2004.

Guyer, Benjamin. *The Beauty of Holiness: The Caroline Divines and Their Writings.* London: Canterbury Press Norwich, 2012.

Hamm, Berndt. "What Was the Reformation Doctrine of Justification?" In *The Reformation of Faith in the Context of Late Medieval Theology and Piety: Essays by Berndt Hamm*, edited by Robert J. Bast, 179–216. Leiden: Brill, 2004.

Hall, Basil. "The Colloquy between Catholics and Protestants, 1539–41." *Studies in Church History* 7 (1971) 235–66.

Harland, Marion. *William Cowper.* New York: Putnam's Sons, 1899.

Harper, Francis Whaley. *A Few Observations on the Teaching of Dr. Pusey and Mr. Newman, concerning Justification.* Cambridge: Grant, 1842.

Harrold, Charles Frederick. *John Henry Newman: An Expository and Critical Study of His Mind, Thought and Art.* London: Longmans, 1945.

Heurtley, Charles A. *Justification: Eight Sermons Preached before the University of Oxford in the year 1845.* [S.I.]. Oxford: John Henry Parker, 1846.

Holloway, John. *The Victorian Sage: Studies in Argument.* London: Macmillan, 1953.

Holtzen, Thomas L. "Newman's 'Via Media' Theology of Justification." *Newman Studies Journal* 4, no. 2 (2007) 64–74.

———. "Union with God and the Holy Spirit: A New Paradigm of Justification." PhD diss., Marquette University, 2002.

Hooker, Richard. *Tractates and Sermons.* Edited by W. Speed Hill, Laetitia Yeandle, and Egil Grislis. 7 vols. The Folger Library Edition of the Works of Richard Hooker 5. Cambridge: Belknap Press of Harvard University Press, 1990.

———. *The Works of the Learned and Judicious Divine Mr. Richard Hooker with an Account of His Life and Death by Isaac Walton.* Edited by the Rev. John Keble. Vol. II. New York: Appleton, 1844.

Huelin, Gordon. "Peter Martyr and the English Reformation." PhD diss., University of London, 1954.

Hugelshofer, Walter. "Zum Porträt des Petrus Martyr Vermilius." *Zwingliana* 3 (1930) 127–29.

Hughes, Philip Edgcumbe, ed. *Faith and Works: Cranmer and Hooker on Justification.* Wilton, UK: Morehouse-Barlow, 1982.

Huizinga, Johan. *Erasmus and the Age of Reformation.* New York: Harper and Row, 1957.

Hutton, Richard Holt. *Cardinal Newman.* 2nd ed. London: Methuen, 1891.

Imbart de La Tour, Pierre. *Les Origines de la Réforme: L' Evangélisme.* Vol. 3. Paris: Hachette, 1914.

Ives, Robert. "An Early Effort toward Protestant-Catholic Conciliation: The Doctrine of Double Justification in the Sixteenth Century." *Gordon Review* 11 (1968–70) 99–110.

James, Frank A., III. "The Bullinger/Vermigli Axis: Collaborators in Toleration and Reformation." In *Heinrich Bullinger: Life-Thought-Influence: Zurich. International Congress Heinrich Bullinger (1504–1575)*, Vol. 1, edited by Emidio Campi and Peter Opitz, 165–76. Zürich: Theologischer Verlag Zürich, 2007.

———. "The Complex of Justification: Peter Martyr Vermigli Versus Albert Pighius." In *Peter Martyr Vermigli: Humanism, Republicanism, Reformation*, edited by Emidio Campi, Frank A. James III, and Peter Opitz, 45–58. Geneva: Librairie Droz, 2002.

———. "*De Iustificatione*: The Evolution of Peter Martyr Vermigli's Doctrine of Justification." PhD diss., Westminster Theological Seminary, 2000.

———. "Juan de Valdés Before and After Peter Martyr Vermigli: The Reception of Gemina Praedestinatio in Valdés Later Thought." *Archiv für Reformationsgeschichte* 83 (1992) 180–208.

———. "A Late Medieval Parallel in Reformation Thought: Gemina Praedestinatio in Gregory of Rimini and Peter Martyr Vermigli." In *Via Augustini: Augustine in the Later Middle Ages, Renaissance, and Reformation; Essays in Honor of Damasus Trapp*, edited by Frank A. James III and Heiko A. Oberman. 157–88. Leiden: Brill, 1991.

———. "Neglected Sources of the Reformed Doctrine of Predestination: Ulrich Zwingli and Peter Martyr Vermigli." *Modern Reformation* 7 (1998) 18–22.

———. "*Nunc Peregrinus Oberrat*: Peter Martyr in Context." In *Peter Martyr Vermigli and the European Reformations: Semper Reformanda*, edited by Frank A. James III, xiii–xxv. Leiden: Brill, 2004.

———. "Peter Martyr in Bucer's Strasbourg: The Early Formulations of His Doctrine of Justification." *Perichoresis* 1, no. 2 (2003) 5–33.

———. "Peter Martyr Vermigli: At the Crossroads of Late Medieval Scholasticism, Christian Humanism, and Resurgent Augustinianism." In *Protestant Scholasticism: Essays in Reassessment*, edited by Carl R. Trueman and R. Scott Clark, 62–78. Carlisle, UK: Paternoster, 1999.

———. "Peter Martyr Vermigli." In *Historical Handbook of Major Biblical Interpreters*, edited by Donald K. McKim, 239–45. Downers Grove, IL: IVP, 1998.

———. "Peter Martyr Vermigli: Probing his Puritan Influence." In *The Practical Calvinist: An Introduction to the Presbyterian & Reformed Heritage; In Honor of Dr. D. Clair Davis*, edited by Peter A. Lillback and D. Clair Davis, 149–60. Fearn, UK: Christian Focus, 2002.

———. *Peter Martyr Vermigli and Predestination: The Augustinian Inheritance of an Italian Reformer.* Oxford: Clarendon, 1998.

———. "*Praedestinatio Dei*: The Intellectual Origins of Peter Martyr Vermigli's Doctrine of Double Predestination." DPhil diss., Oxford University, 1993.

———. *The Religion of the Heart: Anglican Evangelicalism and the Nineteenth-Century Novel.* Oxford: Clarendon, 1979.

———. "Romans Commentary: Justification and Sanctification." In *A Companion to Peter Martyr Vermigli*, edited by W. J. Torrance Kirby, Emidio Campi, and Frank A. James III, 305–17. Leiden: Brill, 2009.

Jay, Elisabeth. *The Evangelical and Oxford Movements.* Cambridge: Cambridge University Press, 1983.

Jedin, Hubert. *A History of the Council of Trent.* Vol. 2. Translated by Ernest Graf. London: Nelson, 1961.

———. "Contarini und Camaldoli." *Archivo Italiano per la Storia della Pieta* 2 (1959) 59–118.

———. *Studien über die schriftstellertätigkeit Albert Pigges.* Reformationsgeschichtliche Studien und Texte, vol. 55. Münster: Aschendorff, 1931.

Jenkins, Gary. "Peter Martyr and the Church of England after 1558." In *Peter Martyr Vermigli and the European Reformations: Semper Reformanda,* edited by Frank A. James III, 47–69. Leiden: Brill, 2004.

Jewel, John. *The Works of John Jewel, Bishop of Salisbury.* Edited by John Ayre. Vol. 3. Cambridge: Cambridge University Press, 1848.

———. *The Works of John Jewel, Bishop of Salisbury.* Edited by John Ayre. Vol. 4. Cambridge: Cambridge University Press, 1848.

Johnson, G. "Newman on the Doctrine of Justification." PhD diss., Pontificia Universita Urbaniana University of Rome, 1946.

Jost, Walter. *Rhetorical Thought in John Henry Newman.* Columbia, SC: University of South Carolina Press, 1989.

Jung, Eva-Maria. "On the Nature of Evangelism in Sixteenth-century Italy." *Journal of the History of Ideas* 14 (1953) 511–27.

Ker, Ian T. *John Henry Newman: A Biography.* Oxford: Clarendon, 1988.

———. *John Henry Newman: A Biography.* Oxford: Oxford University Press, 2009.

———. *Newman on Being a Christian.* Notre Dame, IN: University of Notre Dame Press, 1990.

———. *Newman on Being a Christian.* Edinburgh: Clark, 1997.

———. *Newman the Theologian: A Reader.* London: Collins, 1990.

Ker, Ian T., and Catholic Society (Great Britain). *Newman: His Life and Legacy.* London: Catholic Truth Society, 2010.

Ker, Ian T., and Alan G. Hill. *Newman After a Hundred Years.* Oxford: Clarendon, 1990.

Ker, Ian T., and Terrence Merrigan. *The Cambridge Companion to John Henry Newman.* Cambridge: Cambridge University Press, 2009.

King, Benjamin John. *Newman and the Alexandrian Fathers: Shaping Doctrine in Nineteenth-Century England.* Oxford: Oxford University Press, 2009.

Kingdon, Robert M. *The Political Thought of Peter Martyr Vermigli: Selected Texts and Commentary.* Travaux d'humanisme et Renaissance, 178. Geneva: Librairie Droz, 1980.

Knox, Alexander. *Remains of Alexander Knox.* Edited by James John Hornby. 4 vols. London: Duncan, 1834.

Kristeller, Paul Oskar. *Renaissance Thought: The Classic, Scholastic and Humanist Strains.* New York: Harper & Row, 1961.

Lane, Anthony N. S. "Calvin and Article 5 of the Regensburg Colloquy." In *Calvinus Praeceptor Ecclesiae: Papers of the International Congress on Calvin Research,* edited by Herman J. Selderhuis, 233–63. Geneva: Librairie Droz, 2004.

———. "Cardinal Contarini and Article 5 of the Regensburg Colloquy (1541)." In *Grenzgänge der Theologie,* edited by Otmar Meuffels and Jürgen Bründl, 163–90. Münster: Lit Verlag, 2004.

———. *Justification by Faith in Catholic-Protestant Dialogue: An Evangelical Assessment*. London: T. & T. Clark, 2002.

———. *John Calvin: Student of the Church Fathers*. Edinburgh: T. & T. Clark, 1999.

———. "A Tale of Two Imperial Cities: Justification at Regensburg (1541) and Trent (1546-1547)." In *Justification in Perspective: Historical Developments and Contemporary Challenges*, edited by Bruce L. McCormack, 119-45. Grand Rapids: Baker Academic, 2006.

Latourette, Kenneth Scott. *A History of Christianity. Vol. 2: A.D. 1500-A.D. 1975*. Rev. ed. San Francisco: Harper, 1975.

Lawrenz, Carl J. "On Justification, Osiander's Doctrine of the Indwelling Christ." In *No Other Gospel: Essays in Commemoration of the 400th Anniversary of the Formula of Concord 1580-1980*, edited by Arnold J. Koelpin, 149-74. Milwaukee: Northwestern, 1980.

Lehmann, Karl, Michael Root, and William G. Rusch. "Can the Sixteenth Century Condemnations on Justification be Declared Nonapplicable? An Introduction." In *Justification by Faith: Do the Sixteenth-Century Condemnations Still Apply?*, edited by Karl Lehmann, Michael Root, and William G. Rusch 1-90. New York: Continuum, 1997.

Lillback, Peter A. "The Early Reformed Covenant Paradigm: Vermigli in the Context of Bullinger, Luther, and Calvin." In *Peter Martyr Vermigli and the European Reformations: Semper Reformanda*, edited by Frank A. James III, 70-96. Leiden: Brill, 2004.

Löwe, J. Andreas. *Richard Smyth and the Language of Orthodoxy: Re-imagining Tudor Catholic Polemicism*. Studies in Medieval and Reformation Thought. Leiden: Brill, 2003.

Lugioyo, Brian. *Martin Bucer's Doctrine of Justification: Reformation Theology and Early Modern Irenicism*. Oxford Studies in Historical Theology. Oxford: Oxford University Press, 2010.

Luther, Martin. *What Luther Says, An Anthology*, vol. 3, edited by Ewald M. Plass. St. Louis, MO: Concordia, 1959.

The Lutheran World Federation and the Roman Catholic Church, *Joint Declaration on the Doctrine of Justification*. Grand Rapids: Eerdmans, 2000.

MacCulloch, Diarmaid. "Peter Martyr and Thomas Cranmer." In *Peter Martyr Vermigli: Humanism, Republicanism, Reformation*, edited by Emidio Campi, Frank A. James III, and Peter Opitz, 173-201. Geneva: Librairie Droz, 2002.

———. *The Reformation*. New York: Viking, 2003.

———. *Thomas Cranmer: A Life*. New Haven: Yale University Press, 1996.

Mackensen, Heinz. "Contarini's Theological Role at Ratisbon in 1541." *Archiv für Reformationsgeschichte* 51 (1960) 36-57.

Malloy, Christopher J. *Engrafted into Christ: A Critique of the Joint Declaration 233*. New York: Lang, 2005.

Mant, Richard. *An Appeal to the Gospel, or An Inquiry into the Justice of the Charge, Alleged by Methodists and Other Objectors, that the Gospel is Not Preached by the National Clergy*. Oxford: Oxford University Press, 1812.

Mantova, Benedetto da. *Il Beneficio di Cristo con le versioni del secolo XVI, documenti e testimonianze*. Edited by Salvatore Caponetto. Corpus Reformatorum Italicorum. Florence: Sansoni, 1972.

Martin, Brian. *John Henry Newman: His Life and Work*. London: Chatto & Windus, 1982.

Martin, Greschat. *Martin Bucer: A Reformer and His Times*. Louisville, KY: Westminster John Knox, 2004.

Martin, John. "Salvation and Society in Sixteenth-century Venice: Popular Evangelism in a Renaissance City." *Journal of Modern History* 60 (1988) 205–33.

———. *Venice's Hidden Enemies: Italian Heretics in a Renaissance City*. Studies on the History of Society and Culture, vol. 16. Berkeley: University of California Press, 1993.

Matheson, Peter. *Cardinal Contarini at Regensburg*. Oxford: Clarendon, 1972.

———. *English Church Reform 1815–1840*. London: Longmans, 1923.

———. "Martin Bucer and the Old Church." In *Martin Bucer: Reforming Church and Community*, edited by David F. Wright, 5–16. Cambridge: Cambridge University Press, 1994.

Mathieson, William Law. *England in Transition, 1789–1832: A Study of Movements*. London: Longmans, 1920.

———. *English Church Reform 1815–1840*. London: Longmans, 1923.

McConica, James. "The Rise of the Undergraduate College." In *The Collegiate University. Vol 3: The History of the University of Oxford*, edited by James McConica, 32–42. Oxford: Oxford University Press, 1986.

McGrath, Alister E. "Forerunners of the Reformation? A Critical Examination of the Evidence for Precursors of the Reformation Doctrines of Justification." *Harvard Theological Review* 75 (1982) 219–42.

———. "Humanist Elements in the Early Reformed Doctrine of Justification." *Archiv für Reformationsgeschichte* 73 (1982) 5–20.

———. *Iustitia Dei: A History of the Christian Doctrine of Justification*. 3rd ed. Cambridge: Cambridge University Press, 2005.

———. "Newman on Justification: An Evangelical Anglican Evaluation." In *Newman and the Word*, edited by Terrence Merrigan and Ian Ker, 91–108. Louvain: Peeters, 2000.

———. *Reformation Thought: An Introduction*. 4th ed. Chichester, UK: Wiley-Blackwell, 2012.

McIlvaine, Charles Pettit. *Oxford Divinity Compared with That of the Romish and Anglican Churches: With a Special View of the Doctrine of Justification by Faith*. London: Seeley and Burnside 1841.

McLelland, Joseph C. "A Literary History of the *Loci Communes*." In *A Companion to Peter Martyr Vermigli*, edited by W. J. Torrance Kirby, Emidio Campi, and Frank A. James III, 479–94. Leiden: Brill, 2009.

———. "Peter Martyr Vermigli: Scholastic or Humanist?" In *Peter Martyr Vermigli and Italian Reform*, edited by Joseph C. McLelland, 142–52. Waterloo, Ontario: Wilfrid Laurier University Press, 1980.

———. "The Reformed Doctrine of Predestination According to Peter Martyr." *Scottish Journal of Theology* 8 (1955) 255–71.

———. "Valdés and Vermigli: Spirituality and the Degrees of Reform." In *Peter Martyr Vermigli and the European Reformations: Semper Reformanda*, edited by Frank A. James III, 238–50. Leiden: Brill, 2004.

———. *The Visible Words of God: An Exposition of the Sacramental Theology of Peter Martyr Vermigli, A.D. 1500–1562*. Edinburgh: Oliver & Boyd, 1957.

McLelland, Joseph C., trans. and ed. *The Oxford Treatise and Disputation on the Eucharist, 1549*. The Peter Martyr Library, vol. 7. Kirksville, MO: Truman State University Press, 2000.

———, ed. *Peter Martyr Vermigli and Italian Reform*. Waterloo, Ontario: Wilfred Laurier University Press, 1980.

McNair, Philip M. J. "Benedetto da Mantova, Marcantonio Flaminio, and the 'Beneficio di Cristo': A Developing Twentieth-century Debate Reviewed." *Modern Language Review* 82, no. 3 (1987) 614–24.

———. "Biographical Introduction." *Early Writings: Creed, Scripture and Church*, by Peter Martyr Vermigli. Translated by Mariano Di Gangi and Joseph C. McLelland. Edited by Joseph C. McLelland. The Peter Martyr Library, vol. 1, 3–14. Kirksville: Sixteenth Century Journal Publishers, 1994.

———. "New Light on Ochino." *Bibliothèque d'humanisme et Renaissance: Travaux et documents* 35 (1973) 289–301.

———. "Peter Martyr in England." In *Peter Martyr Vermigli and Italian Reform*, edited by Joseph C. McLelland, 85–106. Waterloo, Ontario: Wilfred Laurier University Press, 1980.

———. *Peter Martyr in Italy: An Anatomy of Apostasy*. Oxford: Clarendon, 1967.

———. *Pietro Martire Vermigli in Italia: Un'anatomia di un'apostasia*. Translated by Edoardo Labanchi. Naples: Centro biblico, 1971.

Medley, Mark. "Participation in God: The Appropriation of Theosis by Contemporary Baptist Theologians." In *Theosis: Deification in Christian Theology*, edited by Vladimir Kharlamov, 205–46. Eugene, OR: Pickwick, 2011.

Melanchthon, Philipp. *Melanchthon on Christian Doctrine: Loci Communes 1555*. Translated and edited by Clyde L. Manschreck. Oxford: Oxford University Press, 1965.

Merrigan, Terrence. "Newman's Progress Towards Rome: A Psychological Consideration of His Conversion to Catholicism." *Downside Review* 104 (1986) 95–112.

———. "Numquam Minus Solus, Quam Cum Solus - Newman's First Conversion: Its Significance for His Life and Thought." *Downside Review* 103 (1985) 99–116.

Middleton, R. D. *Newman at Oxford: His Religious Development*. London: Oxford University Press, 1950.

Miller, Edward Jeremy. *John Henry Newman on the Idea of Church*. Shepherdstown, WV: Patmos, 1987.

Milner, Joseph. *The History of the Church of Christ*. London: Merrill, 1794.

Moeller, Charles, and Gérard Philips. *The Theology of Grace and the Oecumenical Movement*. Translated by R. A. Wilson. London: Mowbray, 1961.

Moleski, Martin X. *Personal Catholicism: The Theological Epistemologies of John Henry Newman and Michael Polanyi*. Washington, DC: Catholic University of America Press, 2000.

Morales, Jose. "Newman and the Problems of Justification." In *Newman Today: Papers Presented at a Conference on John Henry Cardinal Newman*, edited by Stanley L. Jaki, 143–64. San Francisco: Ignatius, 1989.

Moule, H. C. G. *The Evangelical School in the Church of England: Its Men and Its Work in the Nineteenth Century*. London: Nisbet, 1901.

Mozley, Thomas. *Reminiscences: Chiefly of Oriel College and the Oxford Movement*. 2 vols. London: Longmans, 1882.

Muller, Richard A. *Christ and the Decree: Christology and Predestination in Reformed Theology from Calvin to Perkins.* Durham, NC: Labyrinth, 1986.

———. *Post-Reformation Reformed Dogmatics.* 2 vols. Grand Rapids: Baker Academic, 1987.

Muller, Richard, ed. *Dictionary of Latin and Greek Theological Terms.* Grand Rapids: Baker, 1985.

Mullett, Michael A. *The Catholic Reformation.* London: Routledge, 1999.

Murray, Scott. "Luther in Newman's Lectures on Justification." *Concordia Theological Quarterly* 54 (1990) 155–78.

Neill, Stephen. *A History of Christian Missions.* 2nd ed. Harmondsworth, UK: Penguin, 1986.

Neuhaus, Richard John. "Newman, Luther, and the Unity of Christians" *Pro Ecclesia* 6, no. 3 (1997) 153–93.

Newman, Francis William. *Contributions Chiefly to the Early History of the Late Cardinal Newman: With Comments.* London: Paul, Trench, 1891.

Newman, John Henry. *Apologia Pro Vita Sua: Being a History of His Religious Opinions.* London: Longmans, 1882.

———. *The Arians of the Fourth Century: Their Doctrine, Temper, and Conduct, Chiefly as Exhibited in the Councils of the Church, between A.D. 325, & A.D. 381.* London: C. J. G. & F. Rivington, 1833.

———. *Autobiographical Writings.* Edited by Henry Tristram. London Sheed and Ward, 1956.

———. *Callista: A Sketch of the Third Century.* New York: D. & J. Sadlier & Co., 1856.

———. *Cardinal Newman and William Froude, F. R. S.: A Correspondence.* Baltimore: Johns Hopkins Press, 1933.

———. *Catholic Sermons of Cardinal Newman, Published for the First Time from the Cardinal's Autograph Manuscripts.* Edited by Birmingham Oratory. London: Burns & Oates, 1957.

———. *Certain Difficulties Felt by Anglicans in Catholic Teaching Considered.* 2 vols. London: Longmans, 1908–14.

———. *An Essay in Aid of a Grammar of Assent.* Edited by Charles Fredrick Harrold. New ed. London: Longmans, 1947.

———. *An Essay on the Development of Christian Doctrine.* 6th ed. Notre Dame, IN: University of Notre Dame Press, 1989.

———. *Lectures on the Doctrine of Justification.* 3rd ed. London: Rivingtons, 1874.

———. *Lectures on Justification.* London: Rivington & Parker, 1838.

———. *Lectures on the Prophetical Office of the Church: Viewed Relatively to Romanism and Popular Protestantism.* 2nd ed. London: C. J. G. & F. Rivington, 1838.

———. *Letters and Correspondence of John Henry Newman During His Life in the English Church: With a Brief Autobiography.* Edited by Anne Mozley. New ed. 2 vols. London: Longmans, 1903.

———. *Letters and Diaries of John Henry Newman.* 4 vols. Edited by Charles Stephen Dessain, et al. London: Nelson, 1961–77.

———. *Loss and Gain: The Story of a Convert.* London: Longmans, 1898.

———. *On Consulting the Faithful in Matters of Doctrine.* Edited by John Coulson. London: Chapman, 1961.

———. *On the Inspiration of Scripture.* Edited by J. Derek Holmes and Robert Murray. Dublin: Chapman, 1967.

———. *Parochial and Plain Sermons*. Vol. 1. San Francisco: Ignatius, 1997.
———. *The Theological Papers of John Henry Newman on Faith and Certainty*. Edited by J. Derek Holmes and Hugo M. De Achaval. Oxford: Clarendon, 1976.
———. *The Via Media of the Anglican Church*. London: Pickering, 1877.
———. *Verses on Various Occasions*. New ed. London: Longmans, 1893.
Newsome, David. *The Convert Cardinals: John Henry Newman and Henry Edward Manning*. London: Murray, 1993.
———. "Justification and Sanctification: Newman and the Evangelicals." *Journal of Theological Studies* 15 (1964) 32–53.
———. *The Parting of Friends: The Wilberforces and Henry Manning*. London: Eerdmans, 1966.
Newton, Bishop Thomas. *Dissertations on the Prophecies, Which Have Remarkably Been Fulfilled, and at This Time are Fulfilling in the World*. London: Tonson and Draper, 1754.
Newton, John, and Richard Cecil. *Out of the Depths, Being the Autobiography of John Newton*. 2nd ed. London: Thynne & Jarvis, 1925.
Nieto, José C. "The Changing Image of Valdés." In *Valdés' Two Catechisms: The Dialogue on Christian Doctrine and the Christian Instruction for Children*, edited by José C. Nieto, translated by William B. Jones and Carol D. Jones, 51–125. Lawrence, KS: Coronado, 1993.
———. *Juan de Valdés and the Origins of the Spanish and Italian Reformation*. Travaux d'humanisme et Renaissance, vol. 108. Geneva: Librairie Droz, 1970.
Nockles, Peter Benedict. *The Oxford Movement in Context: Anglican High Churchmanship, 1760–1857*. Cambridge: Cambridge University Press, 1994.
Oberman, Heiko A. *The Dawn of the Reformation. Essays in Late Medieval and Early Reformation Thought*. Grand Rapids: Eerdmans, 1986.
O'Callaghan, Paul. *Fides Christi: The Justification Debate*. Dublin: Four Courts, 1997.
Ochino, Bernardino. *Fouretene Sermons of Barnardine Ochyne, Concernying the Predestinacion and Eleccion of God: Very Expediente to the Settynge Forth of Hys Glorye among Hys Creatures*. Translated by Anne Cooke Bacon. London: John Day & Wylliam Seres, 1550.
O'Leary, Joseph S. "Impeded Witness: Newman against Luther on Justification." In *John Henry Newman: Reason, Rhetoric and Romanticism*, edited by David Nicholls and Fergus Kerr, 153–93. Bristol: Bristol Press, 1991.
Olin, John C. *Catholic Reform from Cardinal Ximenes to the Council of Trent 1495–1563: An Essay with Illustrative Documents and a Brief Study of St. Ignatius Loyola*. New York: Fordham University Press, 1990.
———. *The Catholic Reformation: Savonarola to Ignatius Loyola; Reform in the Church 1495–1540*. New York: Harper & Row, 1969.
O'Malley, John W. *The First Jesuits*. Cambridge: Harvard University Press, 1993.
———. *Trent: What Happened at the Council*. Cambridge: Belknap Press of Harvard University Press, 2013.
Ortolani, Oddone. *Pietro Carnesecchi: Con estratti dagli atti del processo del Santo officio*. Florence: Le Monnier, 1963.
———. "The Hopes of the Italian Reformers in Roman Action." In *Italian Reformation Studies in Honor of Laelius Socinus*, edited by John A. Tedeschi, 11–20. Florence: Le Monnier, 1965.

Osiander, Andreas D. A. "Eine Disuptation von der Rechtfertigung." In *Gesamtausgabe*, vol. 9, edited by Gerhard Müller and Gottfried Seebaß, 427–47. Gütersloh: Gütersloher, 1994.
Overell, M. Anne. *Italian Reform and English Reformations, c.1535–c.1585*. Catholic Christendom, 1300-1700. Aldershot, UK: Ashgate, 2008.
———. "Peter Martyr in England 1547–1553: An Alternative View." *Sixteenth Century Journal* 15, no. 1 (1984) 87–104.
Overton, John Henry. *The English Church in the Nineteenth Century*. London: Longmans, 1894.
———. *The Evangelical Revival in the Eighteenth Century*. London: Longmans, 1886.
Ozment, Steven E. *The Age of Reform, 1250–1550: An Intellectual and Religious History of Late Medieval and Reformation Europe*. New Haven: Yale University Press, 1980.
Paist, Benjamin F., Jr. "Peter Martyr and the Colloquy of Poissy." *Princeton Theological Review* 20, no. 3 (1922) 418–47.
Paoletti, John T., and Gary M. Radke. *Art in Renaissance Italy*. New York: Abrams, 1997.
Pastor, Ludwig. *The History of the Popes, from the Close of the Middle Ages: Drawn from the Secret Archives of the Vatican and Other Original Sources*. Translated by Ralph Francis Kerr. Vol. 11. London: Kegan Paul, Trench, Trübner, & Co., 1923.
Paulus, Nikoloaus. "Die Stellung der protestantischen Professoren Zanchi und Vermigli zur Gewissensfreiheit." *Katholik* 71 (1891) 201–28.
Perry, John F. "Newman's Treatment of Luther in the Lectures on Justification." *Journal of Ecumenical Studies* 36 (1999) 303–17.
Peyronel Rambaldi, Susanna. "Ancora sull'evangelismo italiano: Categoria o invenzione storiografica?" *Società e storia* 5, no. 18 (1982) 935–67.
Pfeifer, Ludwig. *Ursprung der katholischen Kirche und Zugehörigkeit zur Kirche nach Albert Pigge*. Würzburg: Rita Verlag, 1938.
Pickering, W. S. F. *Anglo-Catholicism: A Study in Religious Ambiguity*. London: Routledge, 1989.
Pighius, Albertus. *Controversiarum praecipuarum in Comitiis Ratisponensibus . . . tractarum et quibus nunc...exagitatur Christi fides et religio religio, diligens, et luculenta explication*. Paris: Apud Viuantium Gaulterot, 1549.
———. *De libero hominis arbitrio & divina gratia, libri decem, nunc primum in lucem editi*. Cologne: Melchioris Novensiani, 1542.
Pope Benedict XVI. *Saint Paul*. San Francisco: Ignatius, 2009.
Popov, Ivan. "The Idea of Deification in the Early Eastern Church." In *Theosis: Deification in Christian Theology*, edited by Vladimir Kharlamov, 42–82. Eugene, OR: Pickwick, 2011.
Prelowski, Ruth. "The Beneficio di Cristo, Translated with an Introduction." In *Italian Reformation Studies in Honor of Laelius Socinus (1562-1962)*, edited by John A. Tedeschi, 21–102. Florence: Le Monnier, 1965.
Prosperi, Adriano. *Tra evangelismo e controriforma: G. M. Giberti (1495-1543)*. Uomini e dottrine, 16. Rome: Edizioni di storia e letteratura, 1969.
Pusey, E. B. *A Letter to the Right Rev. Father in God, Richard Lord Bishop of Oxford, on the Tendency to Romanism Imputed to Doctrines Held of Old, as Now, in the English Church*. 2nd ed. Oxford: Parker, 1839.
Rambo, Lewis R. *Understanding Religious Conversion*. New Haven: Yale University Press, 1993.

Rando, John A. *Lutheran & Catholic Reconciliation on Justification.* Grand Rapids; Eerdmans, 2009.
Reynolds, J. S. *The Evangelicals at Oxford, 1735-1871: A Record of an Unchronicled Movement with the Record Extended to 1905.* Oxford: Marcham Manor, 1975.
Richgels, Robert W. "The Pattern of Controversy in a Counter-reformation Classic: The Controversies of Robert Bellarmine." *Sixteenth Century Journal* 11, no. 2 (1980) 3-15.
Robbins, William. *The Newman Brothers: An Essay in Comparative Intellectual Biography.* Cambridge: Harvard University Press, 1966.
Rondet, Henri. *The Grace of Christ: A Brief History of the Theology of Grace.* Westminster, MD: Newman, 1967.
Ross, James Bruce. "The Emergence of Gasparo Contarini: A Bibliographic Essay." *Church History: Studies in Christianity and Culture* 41, no. 1 (1972) 22-45.
———. "Gasparo Contarini and His Friends." *Studies in the Renaissance* 17 (1970) 204-17.
Rowell, Geoffrey. *The Vision Glorious: Themes and Personalities of the Catholic Revival in Anglicanism.* Oxford: Oxford University Press, 1983.
Ruggles, Eleanor. *Journey into Faith: the Anglican life of John Henry Newman.* New York: Norton, 1948.
Russell, George William Erskine. *The Household of Faith: Portraits and Essays.* London: Hodder and Stoughton, 1902.
Ryle, J. C. *Knots Untied Being Plain Statements on Disputed Points in Religion from the Standpoint of an Evangelical Churchman.* London: National Protestant Church Union, 1898.
Ryle, J. C., and C. Sydney Carter. *Knots Untied : Being Plain Statements on Disputed Points in Religion from an Evangelical Standpoint.* 31st ed. London: James Clark, 1954.
Sambin, Paolo. "La formazione quattrocentesca della biblioteca di S. Giovanni di Verdara in Padova." *Atti dell'Istituto Veneto di Scienze Lettere ed Arti, Classe di scienze morali e lettere* 114 (1956) 263-80.
Santini, Luigi. "Appunti sulla ecclesiologia di P. M. Vermigli e la edificazione della Chiesa." *Bolletino della società di studi Valdési* 104 (1958) 69-75.
———. "La Tesi della fuga nella persecuzione nella teologia di P. M. Vermigli." *Bolletino della società di studi Valdési* 108 (1960) 37-49.
Schaff, Philip. "Periodization of Sixteenth-century Italian Religious History: The Post-Cantimori Paradigm Shift." *Journal of Modern History* 61 (1989) 269-84.
———. *The History of Creeds.* 4th ed. The Creeds of Christendom, with a History and Critical Notes, vol. 1. New York: Harper & Brothers, 1877.
Schenk, Wilhelm. *Reginald Pole, Cardinal of England.* London: Longmans, 1950.
Schlosser, Friedrich Christoph. *Leben des Theodor de Beza und des Peter Martyr Vermigli: Ein Beitrag zur Geschichte der Zeiten der Kirchen-Reformation.* Heidelberg: Mohr und Zimmer, 1809.
Schmidt, Charles. *Peter Martyr Vermigli: Leben und ausgewählte Schriften nach handschriftlichen und gleichzeitigen Quellen.* Elberfeld: Friderichs, 1858.
Schmitt, Charles B. "Towards a Reassessment of Renaissance Aristotelianism." *History of Science* 11 (1973) 159-93.
Schutte, Anne Jacobson. "The *Lettere Volgari* and the Crisis of Evangelism in Italy." *Renaissance Quarterly* 28 (1975) 639-88.

———. "Periodization of Sixteenth-century Italian Religious History: The Post-Cantimori Paradigm Shift." *Journal of Modern History* 61 (1989) 269–84.

Scott, Thomas. *Essays on the Most Important Subjects in Religion*. 4th ed. London: Jaques, 1800.

———. *Remarks on the Refutation of Calvinism*. 2nd ed. London: Macintosh, 1817.

———. *The Works of the Late Rev. Thomas Scott*. Edited by John Scott. London: Thames Ditton, 1823.

Seebaß, Gottfried. *Das reformatorische Werk des Andreas Osiander*. Vol. 44. Einzelarbeiten aus der Kirchengeschichte Bayerns. Nuremberg: Mohr, 1967.

Seeberg, Reinhold. *Textbook of the History of Doctrines*. Translated by Charles E. Hay. Grand Rapids: Baker, 1958.

Sheridan, Thomas L. "Justification." In *The Cambridge Companion to John Henry Newman*, edited by Ian Ker and Terrence Merrigan, 98–117. Cambridge: Cambridge University Press, 2009.

———. "Newman and Luther on Justification." *Journal of Ecumenical Studies* 38:2–3 (2001) 217–45.

———. *Newman on Justification: A Theological Biography*. New York: Alba House, 1967.

Short, Edward. *Newman and His Contemporaries*. London: T. & T. Clark, 2011.

Simler, Josiah, "Oration on the Life and Death of the Good Man and Outstanding Theologian, Doctor Peter Martyn Vermigli, Professor of Sacred Letters at the Surich Academy." In *Life, Letters, and Sermons*, by Peter Martyn Vermigli; translated and edited by John Patrick Donnelly, 9–62. The Peter Martyr Library, vol. 5 Kirksville, MO: Thomas Jefferson University Press, 1999.

Simler, Josias. *Oratio de vita et obitu clarissimi viri et præstantissimi theologi D. Petri Martyris Vermilii divinarum literarum professoris in schola Tigurina*. Zürich: Apud Christophorum Froschouerum iuniorem, 1563.

Simon Caroline J. "The Alchemy of Grace." In *The Gospel of Justification in Christ: Where Does the Church Stand Today?*, edited by Wayne C. Sturm, 160–65. Grand Rapids: Eerdmans, 2006.

Simoncelli, Paolo. *Evangelismo italiano del cinquecento: Questione religiosa e Nicodemismo politico. Italia e Europa*. Rome: Istituto storico italiano per l'età moderna e contemporanea, 1979.

———. "Nuove ipotesi e studi sul Beneficio di Cristo." *Critica storica* 12 (1975) 320–88.

Simuţ, Corneliu C. *The Doctrine of Salvation in the Sermons of Richard Hooker*. Arbeiten zur Kirchengeschichte, 94. Berlin: de Gruyter, 2005.

———. *Richard Hooker and His Early Doctrine of Justification: A Study of His Discourse of Justification*. Aldershot, UK: Ashgate, 2005.

Sleidan, John. *The General History of the Reformation of the Church, from the Errors and Corruptions of the Church of Rome: Begun in Germany by Martin Luther, with the Progress Thereof in All Parts of Christendom, from the year 1517, to the year 1556*. Translated by Edmund Bohun. London: Jones, Swall, and Bonwicke, 1689.

Smith, Richard. *De coelibatu sacerdotum liber vnus. Eiusdem de votis monasticis liber alter, nunc primum typis excusi*. Lovanii: Apud Ioannem Waen, 1550.

———. *Diatriba de hominis iustificatione . . . adversus P. M. Vermelinum*. Lovanii: Antonius Maria Bergaigne, 1550.

Smyth, Charles. *Simeon & Church Order: A Study of the Origins of the Evangelical Revival in Cambridge in the Eighteenth Century*. Cambridge: Cambridge University Press, 1940.

Steinmetz, David C. "The Intellectual Appeal of the Reformation," *Theology Today* 57 (2001) 459–72.

———. *Reformers in the Wings*. Philadelphia: Fortress, 1971.

Stephens, W. P. *The Holy Spirit in the Theology of Martin Bucer*. Cambridge: Cambridge University Press, 1970.

Storr, Vernon F. *The Development of English Theology in the Nineteenth Century, 1800–1860*. London: Longmans, 1913.

Strange, Roderick. *Newman and the Gospel of Christ*. Oxford Theological Monographs. Oxford: Oxford University Press, 1981.

Strype, John. *Annals of the Reformation and Establishment of Religion: And Other Various Occurrences in the Church of England during Queen Elizabeth's Happy Reign, Together with an Appendix of Original Papers of State, Records, and Letters*, vol. 1, pt. 1. London: John Wyat, 1709. Reprint, New York: Burt Franklin, 1966.

Stupperich, Martin. *Osiander in Preußen, 1549–1552*. Arbeiten zur Kirchengeschichte, Vol. 44. Berlin: De Graaf, 1973.

Sturm, Klaus. *Die Theologie Peter Martyr Vermiglis während seines ersten Aufenthalts in Strasbourg 1542–1547: Ein Reformkatholik unter den Vätern der reformierten Kirche. Beiträge zur Geschichte und Lehre der Reformierten Kirche*. Neukirchen-Vluyn: Neukirchener Verlag, 1971.

Sumner, John Bird. *Apostolical Preaching Considered, in an Examination of St. Paul's Epistles*. London: Hatchard and Son, 1815.

Tacchi Venturi, Pietro. *Storia della Compagnia di Gesù in Italia*. Vol. 1. Rome: La Civiltà cattolica, 1950.

Tailepied, Noël. *Histoire de vies, meurs, actes, doctrine et morts des quatre principaux Hérétiques de nostra temps*. Paris: Chez Jean Parent, 1580.

Tanner, N. P., ed. *Decrees of the Ecumenical Councils*. 2 vols. Washington, DC: Georgetown University Press, 1990.

Tappert, Theodore G., trans. and ed. *The Book of Concord: The Confession of the Evangelical Lutheran Church*. Philadelphia: Fortress, 1959.

Tedeschi, John. *The Italian Reformation of the Sixteenth Century and the Diffusion of Renaissance Culture: A Bibliography of the Secondary Literature (ca. 1750–1997)*. Modena, Italy: Panini, 2000.

Testa, Michael. "The Theological Anthropology of John Henry Newman." PhD diss., St. Louis University, 1993.

Thomas, Stephen. *Newman and Heresy: The Anglican Years*. Cambridge: Cambridge University Press, 1991.

Toon, Peter. "A Critical Review of John Henry Newman's Doctrine of Justification." *Churchman* 94, no. 4 (1980) 335–44.

———. *Evangelical Theology, 1833–1856: A Response to Tractarianism*. London: Marshall, Morgan and Scott, 1979.

Townsend, Ralph. "The Catholic Revival in the Church of England." In *The Study of Spirituality*, edited by Cheslyn Jones, 463–68. Oxford: Oxford University Press, 1986.

Trevor, Meriol. *Newman: Vol. 1. The Pillar of the Cloud*. London: Macmillan, 1962.

———. *Newman: Vol. 2. Light in Winter*. London: Macmillan, 1962.

Tristram, Henry. *Newman and His Friends*. London: Lane, 1933.

Turner, Frank M. *John Henry Newman: The Challenge to Evangelical Religion*. New Haven: Yale University Press, 2002.

Valdés, Juan de. *La epístola de San Pablo a los Romanos*. Reformistas antiguos españoles, vols. 10–11. Edited by Luis de Usoz i Rios. 1856. Reprint. Barcelona: Librería de Diego Gómez Flores, 1982.

———. *Valdés' Two Catechisms: The Dialogue on Christian Doctrine and the Christian Instruction for Children*. Edited by José C. Nieto. Translated by William B. Jones and Carol D. Jones. Lawrence, KS: Coronado, 1981.

Valdés, Juan de, and Don Benedetto. *The Benefit of Christ: Living Justified Because of Christ's Death*. Edited by James M. Houston. Vancouver, BC: Regent College, 2003.

Vasoli, Cesare. "*Loci Communes* and the Rhetorical and Dialetical Traditions." In *Peter Martyr Vermigli and Italian Reform*, edited by Joseph C. McLelland, 17–28. Waterloo, Ontario: Wilfred Laurier University Press, 1980.

Vermigli, Peter Martyr. *Commentary on Aristotle's Nicomachean Ethics*. Translated and edited by Emidio Campi and Joseph C. McLelland. The Peter Martyr Library, vol. 9. Kirksville, KS: Truman State University Press, 2006.

———. *Commentary on Lamentations of the Prophet Jeremiah*. Translated and edited by Daniel John Shute. The Peter Martyr Library, vol. 6. Kirksville, KS: Truman State University Press, 2002.

———. *Dialogue on the Two Natures in Christ*. Translated and edited by John Patrick Donnelly. The Peter Martyr Library, vol. 2. Kirksville, KS: Thomas Jefferson University Press, 1995.

———. *Early Writings: Creed, Scripture, Church*. Translated and edited by Mariano Di Gangi and Joseph C. McLelland. The Peter Martyr Library, vol. 1. Kirksville, KS: Thomas Jefferson University Press, 1994.

———. "Letter CCXXXII, Peter Martyr to Henry Bullinger." In *Original Letters Relative to the English Reformation, 1531–1558*, vol. 2, edited by Hastings Robinson, 493–95. Cambridge: Cambridge University Press, 1846–47.

———. *Life, Letters, and Sermons*. Translated and edited by John Patrick Donnelly. The Peter Martyr Library, vol. 5. Kirksville, KS: Thomas Jefferson University Press, 1999.

———. *Philosophical Works: On the Relation of Philosophy to Theology*. Translated and edited by Joseph C. McLelland. The Peter Martyr Library, vol. 4. Kirksville, KS: Truman State University Press, 1996.

———. *Predestination and Justification: Two Theological Loci*. Translated and edited by Frank A. James III. The Peter Martyr Library, vol. 8. Kirksville, KS: Truman State University Press, 2003.

———. *Sacred Prayers Drawn from the Psalms of David*. Translated and edited by John Patrick Donnelly. The Peter Martyr Library, vol. 3. Kirksville, KS: Thomas Jefferson University Press, 1996.

———. *The Oxford Treatise and Disputation on the Eucharist, 1549*. Translated and edited by Joseph C. McLelland. The Peter Martyr Library, vol. 7. Kirksville, KS: Truman State University Press, 2000.

———. *The Peter Martyr Reader*. Edited by John Patrick Donnelly, Frank A. James III, and Joseph C. McLelland. Kirksville, KS: Truman State University Press, 1999.

Vermigli, Pietro Martire. *In epistolam S. Pauli apostoli ad Romanos D. Petri Martyris Vermilii Florentini, professoris divinarum literarum in schola Tigurina, commentarii doctissimi, cum tractatione perutili rerum & locorum, qui ad eam epistolam pertinent*. Basel: Apud Petrum Perna, 1560.

———. *In primum librum Mosis, qui vulgo Genesis dicitur, commentarii doctissimi D. Petri Martyris Vermilii Florentini, professoris divinarum literarum in schola Tigurina, nunc denuo in lucem editi*. Zürich: Christophorus Froschouerus, 1579.

———. *In Selectissimam D. Pauli Apostoli Priorem ad Corinthios Epistolam Commentarii*. Zürich: Christophorum Froschouerus, 1579.

———. *Una Semplice Dichiaratione sopra gli XII Articola della Fede Christiana*. Basel: John Hervagrius, 1544.

Vermigli, Pietro Martire, Josias Simmler, Anthony Marten, Henry Denham, Henry Middleton, Thomas Chard, William Broome, and Andrew Maunsell. *The Common Places of the Most Famous and Renowmed Diuine Doctor Peter Martyr: Diuided into Foure Principall Parts: with a Large Addition of Manie Theologicall and Necessarie Discourses, Some Neuer Extant Before*. Translated by Anthonie Marten. London: Henry Denham and Henry Middleton, 1583.

Vinay, Valdo. "Die Schrift 'Il Beneficio di Giesu Cristo' und ihre Verbreitung in Europa nach der neueren Forschung." *Archiv für Reformationsgeschichte* 58 (1967) 29–72.

Walgrave, Jan Hendrik. *Newman the Theologian: The Nature of Belief and Doctrine as Exemplified in His Life and Works*. Translated by A. V. Littledale. London: Chapman, 1960.

Ward, Maisie. *Young Mr. Newman*. London: Sheed & Ward, 1948.

Ward, Wilfrid. *The Life of John Henry Cardinal Newman: Based on His Private Journals and Correspondence*. 2 vols. London: Longmans, 1912.

Wiffen, Benjamin B., and Juan de Valdés. *Life and Writings of Juán de Valdés, Otherwise Valdesso, Spanish Reformer in the Sixteenth Century*. Translated by John T. Betts. London: Trubner and Co., 1882.

Williams, Rowan. *Arius: Heresy and Tradition*. London: Darton, Longman and Todd, 1987.

Wood, Anthony à. *Athenae Oxonienses: An Exact History of All the Writers and Bishops Who Have Had Their Education in the University of Oxford: to Which are Added the Fasti, or Annals of the Said University*. 2nd ed. Vol. 1. London: F. C. and J. Rivington, et al., 1813.

Wright, T. R. *John Henry Newman: A Man for Our Time?* Newcastle upon Tyne, UK: Grevatt & Grevatt, 1983.

Yarnold, Edward. "*Duplex iustitia*: The Sixteenth Century and the Twentieth." In *Christian Authority: Essays in Honour of Henry Chadwick*, edited by G. R. Evans, 204–23. Oxford: Clarendon, 1988.

Young, Marianne. *The Life and Times of Aonio Paleario, or A history of the Italian Reformers in the Sixteenth Century*. 2 vols. London: Bell and Daldy, 1860.

Zanchi, Girolamo. *De religione christiana fides – Confession of Christian Religion*. Edited by Luca Baschera and Christian Moser. Leiden: Brill, 2007.

Zuidema, Jason. *Peter Martyr Vermigli (1499–1562) and the Outward Instruments of Divine Grace*. Göttingen: Vandenhoeck & Ruprecht, 2008.

———. "Flight from Persecution and the Honour of God in the Theology of Peter Martyr Vermigli." *Reformation and Renaissance Review* 15, no. 1 (2013) 112–16.

www.ingramcontent.com/pod-product-compliance
Lightning Source LLC
Chambersburg PA
CBHW062022220426
43662CB00010B/1439